GLEANINGS

FROM

THE POETS,

FOR

HOME AND SCHOOL.

SELECTED BY THE AUTHOR OF

"THEORY OF TEACHING," "ELEMENTS OF ASTRONOMY, OR THE WORLD AS IT IS, AND AS IT APPEARS," ETC., ETC.

A NEW EDITION, ENLARGED.

W. I. POOLEY,
HARPER & BROTHERS' BUILDING,
NEW-YORK.

PREFACE.

WHILE school education especially aims to develop the understanding and form good mental habits, it must not neglect to interest the imagination and refine the taste. There is a delicacy of taste and of sentiment, and an intellectual richness, which can be perfected only by an intimate acquaintance with nature and art and the human soul; and the foundation of these may be most successfully laid in childhood by the study of poetry, — of the finest thoughts clothed in the most attractive garb.

It is with this design of presenting beauty, both moral and natural, in its manifold shapes, as it is shown to us in the universe, that the present collection has been made. The pieces chosen are, with very few exceptions, entire, because passages are always injured by being taken from their connection, and because young persons like to know the whole of a thing. They are short, and selected from the whole range of English and American standard authors; it being thought better to offer sentiments as they arise in a great variety of minds, and "mould themselves into gentle verse." They are not exclusively of one school or time, — for beauty is not to be prisoned. The artist finds it not complete in one model, but studies it in all its appearances, and then, though he paint but one face or one landscape, he gives us the wealth of a world.

In matters of taste and genius we should not limit our children; we should rather rejoice that their larger souls perceive a beauty where ours find none. We must not say, "The trees of the forest may be beautiful, but I first learned beauty from my stately poplars, and they must satisfy my children." Nor should we reject the flora of a new world, because rumor says that Eden also has its weeds.

It is not necessary to make known to teachers the want of a collection like the one now offered. The best book of the sort has been for some time out of print, and was intended exclusively for older pupils. While this collection has many pieces which must delight persons of any age, it has some for the youngest readers, and is as well adapted to the family circle as to the school. It gives to children all they could cull from many volumes, and, if inwoven with their earliest recollections, will be remembered with delight in future years.

NOTE TO THE SECOND EDITION.

A new edition of the Poetry for Home and School being called for, it was desirable to reduce its contents sufficiently to form with the Second Part a volume of convenient size. For this reason, the Robin Hood Ballads, and some other pieces of limited interest, have been omitted.

The Second Part, being designed for pupils and readers of more mature minds, contains poems of a more imaginative cast than those in the former collection.

CONTENTS.

CONTENTS.

POETRY
FOR
HOME AND SCHOOL.

PART I.

THE BEGGAR MAN.—*Miss Lamb.*

Abject, stooping, old, and wan,
See yon wretched beggar man;
Once a father's hopeful heir,
Once a mother's tender care,
When too young to understand,
He but scorched his little hand,
By the candle's flaming light
Attracted, dancing, spiral, bright;
Clasping fond her darling round,
A thousand kisses healed the wound.
Now, abject, stooping, old, and wan,
No mother tends the beggar man.

Then nought too good for him to wear,
With cherub face and flaxen hair,
In fancy's choicest gauds arrayed,
Cap of lace, with rose to aid,
Milk-white hat with feather blue,
Shoes of red, and coral too,
With silver bells to please his ear,
And charm the frequent, ready tear.
Now, abject, stooping, old, and wan,
Neglected is the beggar man.

See the boy advance in age,
And learning spreads her useful page;
In vain! for giddy pleasure calls,
And shows the marbles, tops, and balls.
What 's learning to the charms of play?
The indulgent tutor must give way.
A heedless, wilful dunce, and wild,
The parents' fondness spoiled the child.
The youth in vagrant courses ran.
Now, abject, stooping, old, and wan,
Their fondling is the beggar man.

LULLABY ON AN INFANT CHIEF. — *W. Scott.*

O, HUSH thee, my baby, thy sire was a knight,
Thy mother a lady, both lovely and bright;
The woods and the glens, from the towers which we see,
They all are belonging, dear baby, to thee.

O, fear not the bugle, though loudly it blows,
It calls but the warders that guard thy repose;
Their bows would be bended, their blades would be red,
Ere the step of a foeman draws near to thy bed.

O, hush thee, my baby, the time will soon come
When thy sleep shall be broken by trumpet and drum;
Then hush thee, my darling, take rest while you may,
For strife comes with manhood, and waking with day.

THE REAPER'S CHILD. — *Miss Lamb.*

If you go to the field where the reapers now bind
The sheaves of ripe corn, there a fine little lass
Only three months of age, by the hedge-row you 'll find
Left alone by its mother upon the low grass.

While the mother is reaping, the infant is sleeping;
Not the basket that holds the provision is less,
By the hard-working reaper, than this little sleeper,
Regarded, till hunger does on the babe press.

Then it opens its eyes, and it utters loud cries,
Which its hard-working mother afar off will hear;
She comes at its calling, she quiets its squalling,
And feeds it, and leaves it again without fear.

When you were as young as this field-nursed daughter,
You were fed in the house and brought up on the knee;
So tenderly watched, thy fond mother thought her
Whole time well bestowed in nursing of thee.

FEIGNED COURAGE. — *Miss Lamb.*

Horatio, of ideal courage vain,
Was flourishing in air his father's cane,
And, as the fumes of valor swelled his pate,
Now thought himself this hero, and now that;
"And now," he cried, "I will Achilles be;
My sword I brandish; see the Trojans flee!

Now I'll be Hector, when his angry blade
A lane through heaps of slaughtered Grecians made
And now, by deeds still braver, I 'll evince
I am no less than Edward the Black Prince.
Give way, ye coward French!" As thus he spoke,
And aimed in fancy a sufficient stroke
To fix the fate of Cressy or Poictiers,
(The Muse relates the hero's fate with tears,)
He struck his milk-white hand against a nail,
Sees his own blood, and feels his courage fail.
Ah! where is now that boasted valor flown,
That in the tented field so late was shown?
Achilles weeps, great Hector hangs the head,
And the Black Prince goes whimpering to bed.

THE THIRSTY FLY

Busy, curious, thirsty fly,
Drink with me, and drink as I;
Freely welcome to my cup,
Couldst thou sip and sip it up;
Make the most of life you may,
Life is short and wears away,
Both alike are mine and thine,
Hastening quick to thy decline,
Thine 's a summer, mine no more,
Though repeated to threescore;
Threescore summers, when they 're gone,
Will appear as short as one.

GOING INTO BREECHES. — *Miss Lamb.*

Joy to Philip, he this day
Has his long coats cast away,
And (the childish season gone)
Puts the manly breeches on.
Officer on gay parade,
Red coat in his first cockade,
Bridegroom in his wedding trim,
Birth-day beau surpassing him,
Never did with conscious gait
Strut about in half the state,
Or the pride, (yet free from sin,)
Of my little manikin;
Never was there pride or bliss
Half so rational as his.
Sashes, frocks, to those that need 'em, —
Philip's limbs have got their freedom, —
He can run, or he can ride,
And do twenty things beside,
Which his petticoats forbade,
Is he not a happy lad?
Now he 's under other banners,
He must leave his former manners;
Bid adieu to female games,
And forget their very names.
Puss in corners, hide and seek,
Sports for girls and punies weak!
Baste the bear he now may play at,
Leap-frog, football, sport away at,
Show his skill and strength at cricket,
Mark his distance, pitch his wicket,
Run about in winter's snow
Till his cheeks and fingers glow,

Climb a tree, or scale a wall,
Without any fear to fall.
If he get a hurt or bruise,
To complain he must refuse.
Though the anguish and the smart
Go unto his little heart,
He must have his courage ready,
Keep his voice and visage steady,
Brace his eyeballs stiff as drum,
That a tear may never come,
And his grief must only speak
From the color in his cheek.
This and more he must endure,
Hero he in miniature!
This and more must now be done,
Now the breeches are put on.

LADY MOON. — *Milnes.*

Lady Moon, Lady Moon, where are you roving?
Over the sea.
Lady Moon, Lady Moon, whom are you loving?
All who love me.
Are you not tired with rolling, and never
Resting to sleep?
Why look so pale, and so sad, as forever
Wishing to weep?
Ask me not this, little child, if you love me;
You are too bold;
I must obey my dear Father above me,
And do as I 'm told.
Lady Moon, Lady Moon, where are you roving?
Over the sea.
Lady Moon, Lady Moon, whom are you loving?
All who love me.

THE ORPHAN BROTHER. — *Miss Lamb.*

O, HUSH, my little baby brother;
Sleep, my love, upon my knee;
What though, dear child, we 've lost our mother,
That can never trouble thee.

You are but ten weeks old to-morrow;
What can you know of our loss?
The house is full enough of sorrow, —
Little baby, don't be cross.

Peace, cry not so, my dearest love,
Hush, my baby bird, lie still; —
He 's quiet now, he does not move;
Fast asleep is little Will.

My only solace, only joy,
Since the sad day I lost my mother,
Is nursing her own Willy boy,
My little orphan brother.

ULYSSES' DOG. — *Pope.*

WHEN wise Ulysses, from his native coast
Long kept by wars, and long by tempests tost,
Arrived at last, poor, old, disguised, alone,
To all his friends, and e'en his queen, unknown;
Changed as he was with age, and toils, and cares,
Furrowed his reverend face, and white his hairs;
In his own palace forced to ask his bread,
Scorned by those slaves his former bounty fed,

Forgot of all his own domestic crew;
The faithful dog alone his master knew;
Unfed, unhoused, neglected, on the clay,
Like an old servant, now cashiered, he lay
And, though e'en then expiring on the plain,
Touched with resentment of ungrateful man,
And longing to behold his ancient lord again.
Him when he saw, he rose, and crawled to meet, —
'T was all he could, — and fawned, and kissed his feet
Seized with dumb joy; then, falling by his side,
Owned his returning lord, looked up, and died.

THE COMPLAINTS OF THE POOR. — *Southey*

"And wherefore do the poor complain?"
  The rich man asked of me.
"Come, walk abroad with me," I said,
  "And I will answer thee."

'T was evening, and the frozen streets
  Were cheerless to behold,
And we were wrapt and coated well,
  And yet we were a-cold.

We met an old bareheaded man,
  His locks were few and white;
I asked him what he did abroad
  In that cold winter's night.

'T was bitter keen, indeed, he said,
  But at home no fire had he,
And therefore he had come abroad,
  To ask for charity.

We met a young, barefooted child,
  And she begged loud and bold;
I asked her what she did abroad
  When the wind it blew so cold.

She said her father was at home,
  And he lay sick abed;
And therefore was it she was sent
  Abroad to beg for bread.

We saw a woman sitting down
  Upon a stone to rest;
She had a baby at her back,
  And another at her breast.

I asked her why she loitered there,
  When the night-wind was so chill;
She turned her head and bade the child,
  That screamed behind, be still.

She told us that her husband served,
  A soldier, far away,
And therefore to her parish she
  Was begging back her way.

I turned me to the rich man then,
  For silently stood he;—
"You asked me why the poor complain,
  And these have answered thee."

CLEANLINESS.—*Miss Lamb.*

Come, my little Robert, near,—
Fie! what filthy hands are here!—
Who that e'er could understand
The rare structure of a hand,
With its branching fingers fine,
Work itself of hands divine,
Strong yet delicately knit,
For ten thousand uses fit,
Overlaid with so clear skin
You may see the blood within,
And the curious palm disposed
In such lines some have supposed
You may read the fortunes there
By the figures that appear,—
Who this hand would choose to cover
With a crust of dirt all over,
Till it looked in hue and shape
Like the forefoot of an ape?
Man or boy, that works or plays
In the fields or the highways,
May, without offence or hurt,
From the soil contract a dirt,
Which the next clear spring or river
Washes out and out forever;
But to cherish stains impure,
Soil deliberate to endure,
On the skin to fix a stain
Till it works into the grain,
Argues a degenerate mind,
Sordid, slothful, ill-inclined,
Wanting in that self-respect
Which does virtue best protect.

All-endearing cleanliness,
Virtue next to godliness,
Easiest, cheapest, needfullest duty,
To the body health and beauty,
Who that's human would refuse it,
When a little water does it?

THE BLIND BOY. — *Colley Cibber.*

O SAY what is that thing called light,
Which I must ne'er enjoy?
What are the blessings of thy sight?
O, tell your poor blind boy!

You talk of wondrous things you see,
You say the sun shines bright;
I feel him warm, but how can he
Or make it day or night?

My day or night myself I make,
Whene'er I sleep or play;
And could I ever keep awake,
With me 't were always day.

With heavy sighs I often hear
You mourn my hapless woe;
But sure with patience I can bear
A loss I ne'er can know.

Then let not what I cannot have
My cheer of mind destroy;
Whilst thus I sing, I am a king,
Although a poor blind boy.

THE LAME BROTHER. — *Miss Lamb.*

My parents sleep both in one grave;
My only friend 's a brother,
The dearest things upon the earth
We are to one another.

A fine, stout boy I knew him once,
With active form and limb;
Whene'er he leaped, or jumped, or ran,
O, I was proud of him!

He leaped too far, he got a hurt,
He now does limping go;
When I think on his active days,
My heart is full of woe.

He leans on me, when we to school
Do every morning walk;
I cheer him on his weary way, —
He loves to hear my talk,

The theme of which is mostly this,
What things he once could do;
He listens pleased, — then sadly says,
"Sister, I lean on you!"

Then I reply, "Indeed you 're not
Scarce any weight at all, —
And let us now still younger years
To memory recall.

Led by your little elder hand,
  I learned to walk alone;
Careful you used to be of me,
  My little brother John.

"How often, when my young feet tired,
  You've carried me a mile,—
And still together we can sit,
  And rest a little while.

"For our kind master never minds,
  If we're the very last;
He bids us never tire ourselves
  With walking on too fast."

A BALLAD.

TRANSLATED FROM HERDER, BY MARY HOWITT.

Among green, pleasant meadows,
  All in a grove so wild,
Was set a marble image
  Of the Virgin and the child.

Here, oft, on summer evenings,
  A lovely boy would rove,
To play beside the image
  That sanctified the grove.

Oft sat his mother by him,
  Among the shadows dim,
And told how the Lord Jesus
  Was once a child like him.

"And now from highest heaven
  He doth look down each day,
And sees whate'er thou doest,
  And hears what thou dost say!"

Thus spoke his tender mother;
  And on an evening bright,
When the red, round sun descended
  'Mid clouds of crimson light,

Again the boy was playing,
  And earnestly said he,
"O beautiful child Jesus,
  Come down and play with me!

"I will find thee flowers the fairest,
  And weave for thee a crown;
I will get thee ripe, red strawberries,
  If thou wilt but come down!

"O holy, holy Mother,
  Put him down from off thy knee;
For in these silent meadows
  There are none to play with me!"

Thus spoke the boy so lovely,
  The while his mother heard,
And on his prayer she pondered,
  But spoke to him no word.

That self-same night she dreamed
  A lovely dream of joy;
She thought she saw young Jesus
  There, playing with the boy.

'And for the fruits and flowers
Which thou hast brought to me,
Rich blessing shall be given
A thousand-fold to thee!

"For in the fields of heaven
Thou shalt roam with me at will,
And of bright fruits celestial
Thou shalt have, dear child, thy fill!"

Thus tenderly and kindly
The fair child Jesus spoke;
And, full of careful musings,
The anxious mother woke.

And thus it was accomplished:—
In a short month and a day,
That lovely boy, so gentle,
Upon his deathbed lay.

And thus he spoke in dying:—
"O mother dear, I see
The beautiful child Jesus
A coming down to me!

"And in his hand he beareth
Bright flowers as white as snow,
And red and juicy strawberries,—
Dear mother, let me go!"

He died—but that fond mother
Her sorrow did restrain,
For she knew he was with Jesus,
And she asked him not again!

THE BROKEN DOLL.—*Miss Lamb.*

An infant is a selfish sprite;
But what of that? the sweet delight
Which from participation springs
Is quite unknown to these young things.
We elder children, then, will smile
At our dear little John a while,
And bear with him, until he see
There is a sweet felicity
In pleasing more than only one,
Dear little, craving, selfish John.

He laughs, and thinks it a fine joke,
That he our new wax-doll has broke.
Anger will never teach him better;
We will the spirit and the letter
Of courtesy to him display,
By taking in a friendly way
These baby frolics, till he learn
True sport from mischief to discern.

Reproof a parent's province is;
A sister's discipline is this,—
By studied kindness to effect
A little brother's young respect.
What is a doll? a fragile toy;
What is its loss? if the dear boy,
Who half perceives he has done amiss,
Retain impression of the kiss
That followed instant on his cheek,—
If the kind, loving words we speak
Of "Never mind it," "We forgive,"—
If these in his short memory live,

Only perchance for half a day, —
Who minds a doll, if that should lay
The first impression in his mind,
That sisters are to brothers kind?
For thus the broken doll may prove
Foundation to fraternal love.

BLINDNESS. — *Miss Lamb.*

In a stage-coach, where late I chanced to be,
A little, quiet girl my notice caught;
I saw she looked at nothing by the way,
Her mind seemed busy on some childish thought.

I, with an old man's courtesy, addressed
The child, and called her pretty, dark-eyed maid,
And bid her turn those pretty eyes, and see
The wide-extended prospect. — "Sir," she said,

"I cannot see the prospect, — I am blind."
Never did tongue of child utter a sound
So mournful as her words fell on my ear.
Her mother then related how she found

Her child was sightless. On a fine, bright day,
She saw her lay her needlework aside,
And, as on such occasions mothers will,
For leaving off her work began to chide.

"I'll do it when 't is day-light, if you please;
I cannot work, mamma, now it is night."
The sun shone bright upon her when she spoke,
And yet her eyes received no ray of light.

A NEGRO'S SONG.

FROM PARK'S TRAVELS IN AFRICA. VERSIFIED BY THE DUCHESS OF DEVONSHIRE.

The loud wind roared, the rain fell fast,
The white man yielded to the blast;
He sat him down beneath the tree,
For weary, faint, and sad was he;
And, ah! no wife, or mother's care,
For him the milk or corn prepare.

CHORUS.

The white man shall our pity share;
Alas! no wife, or mother's care,
For him the milk or corn prepare.

The storm is o'er, the tempest past,
And mercy's voice has hushed the blast.
The wind is heard in whispers low;
The white man far away must go;
But ever in his heart will bear
Remembrance of the negro's care.

CHORUS.

Go, white man, go; but with thee bear
The negro's wish, the negro's prayer,
Remembrance of the negro's care.

MABEL ON MIDSUMMER DAY.—*Mary Howitt.*

A STORY OF THE OLDEN TIME.

"Arise, my maiden, Mabel,"
The mother said; "arise,
For the golden sun of midsummer
Is shining in the skies.

"Arise, my little maiden,
For thou must speed away,
To wait upon thy grandmother
This livelong summer day.

"And thou must carry with thee
This wheaten cake so fine,
This new-made pat of butter,
This little flask of wine.

"And tell the dear old body,
This day I cannot come,
For the good man went out yester-morn,
And he is not come home.

"And more than this, poor Amy
Upon my knee doth lie;
I fear me, with this fever-pain
The little child will die!

"And thou canst help thy grandmother;
The table thou canst spread;
Canst feed the little dog and bird;
And thou canst make her bed.

"And thou canst fetch the water
  From the lady-well hard by;
And thou canst gather from the wood
  The fagots brown and dry;

"Canst go down to the lonesome glen,
  To milk the mother-ewe;
This is the work, my Mabel,
  That thou wilt have to do.

"But listen now, my Mabel,
  This is midsummer day,
When all the fairy people
  From elf-land come away.

"And when thou 'rt in the lonesome glen,
  Keep by the running burn,
And do not pluck the strawberry-flower,
  Nor break the lady-fern.

"But think not of the fairy folk,
  Lest mischief should befall;
Think only of poor Amy,
  And how thou lov'st us all.

"Yet keep good heart, my Mabel,
  If thou the fairies see,
And give them kindly answer
  If they should speak to thee.

"And when into the fir-wood
  Thou goest for fagots brown,
Do not, like idle children,
  Go wandering up and down.

"But fill thy little apron,
My child, with earnest speed;
And that thou break no living bough
Within the wood, take heed.

"For they are spiteful brownies
Who in the wood abide,
So be thou careful of this thing,
Lest evil should betide.

"But think not, little Mabel,
Whilst thou art in the wood,
Of dwarfish, wilful brownies,
But of the Father good.

"And when thou goest to the spring
To fetch the water thence,
Do not disturb the little stream,
Lest this should give offence.

"For the queen of all the fairies,
She loves that water bright;
I've seen her drinking there myself
On many a summer night.

"But she's a gracious lady,
And her thou need'st not fear;
Only disturb thou not the stream,
Nor spill the water clear."

"Now all this I will heed, mother,
Will no word disobey,
And wait upon the grandmother
This livelong summer day."

PART II.

Away tripped little Mabel,
  With the wheaten cake so fine,
With the new-made pat of butter,
  And the little flask of wine.

And long before the sun was hot,
  And summer mist had cleared,
Beside the good old grandmother
  The willing child appeared.

And all her mother's message
  She told with right good-will,
How that the father was away,
  And the little child was ill.

And then she swept the hearth up clean,
  And then the table spread;
And next she fed the dog and bird;
  And then she made the bed.

"And go now," said the grandmother,
  "Ten paces down the dell,
And bring in water for the day,—
  Thou know'st the lady-well."

The first time that good Mabel went,
  Nothing at all saw she,
Except a bird, a sky-blue bird,
  That sat upon a tree.

The next time that good Mabel went,
  There sat a lady bright
Beside the well,—a lady small,
  All clothed in green and white.

A courtesy low made Mabel,
  And then she stooped to fill
Her pitcher at the sparkling spring,
  But no drop did she spill.

"Thou art a handy maiden,"
  The fairy lady said;
"Thou hast not spilt a drop, nor yet
  The fairy spring troubled!

"And for this thing which thou hast done,
  Yet mayst not understand,
I give to thee a better gift
  Than houses or than land.

"Thou shalt do well whate'er thou dost,
  As thou hast done this day;
Shalt have the will and power to please,
  And shalt be loved alway."

Thus having said, she passed from sight,
  And nought could Mabel see,
But the little bird, the sky-blue bird,
  Upon the leafy tree.

"And now go," said the grandmother,
  "And fetch in fagots dry;
All in the neighboring fir-wood
  Beneath the trees they lie."

Away went kind, good Mabel,
  Into the fir-wood near,
Where all the ground was dry and brown,
  And the grass grew thin and sere.

She did not wander up and down,
  Nor yet a live branch pull,
But steadily of the fallen boughs
  She picked her apron full.

And when the wild-wood brownies
  Came sliding to her mind,
She drove them thence, as she was told,
  With home-thoughts sweet and kind.

But all that while the brownies
  Within the fir-wood still,
They watched her how she picked the wood,
  And strove to do no ill.

"And, O, but she is small and neat,"
  Said one; "'t were shame to spite
A creature so demure and meek,
  A creature harmless quite!"

"Look only," said another,
  "At her little gown of blue;
At her kerchief pinned about her head,
  And at her little shoe!"

"O, but she is a comely child,"
  Said a third; "and we will lay
A good-luck penny in her path,
  A boon for her this day,—
Seeing she broke no living wood;
  No live thing did affray!"

With that the smallest penny,
  Of the finest silver ore,
Upon the dry and slippery path,
  Lay Mabel's feet before.

With joy she picked the penny up,
  The fairy penny good;
And with her fagots dry and brown
  Went wandering from the wood.

"Now she has that," said the brownies,
  "Let flax be ever so dear,
'T will buy her clothes of the very best,
  For many and many a year!"

"And go now," said the grandmother,
  "Since falling is the dew,
Go down unto the lonesome glen,
  And milk the mother-ewe!"

All down into the lonesome glen,
  Through copses thick and wild,
Through moist rank grass, by trickling streams,
  Went on the willing child.

And when she came to the lonesome glen,
  She kept beside the burn,
And neither plucked the strawberry-flower
  Nor broke the lady-fern.

And while she milked the mother-ewe
  Within this lonesome glen,
She wished that little Amy
  Were strong and well again.

And soon as she had thought this thought,
  She heard a coming sound,
As if a thousand fairy-folk
  Were gathering all around.

And then she heard a little voice,
Shrill as the midge's wing,
That spake aloud, — "A human child
Is here; yet mark this thing, —

"The lady-fern is all unbroke,
The strawberry-flower unta'en!
What shall be done for her who still
From mischief can refrain?"

"Give her a fairy cake!" said one;
"Grant her a wish!" said three;
"The latest wish that she hath wished,"
Said all, "whate'er it be!"

Kind Mabel heard the words they spake,
And from the lonesome glen
Unto the good old grandmother
Went gladly back again.

Thus happened it to Mabel
On that midsummer day,
And these three fairy-blessings
She took with her away.

'T is good to make all duty sweet,
To be alert and kind;
'T is good, like little Mabel,
To have a willing mind.

THE ATHEIST AND THE ACORN.

"Methinks this world seems oddly made,
And everything amiss,"
A dull, complaining atheist said,
As stretched he lay beneath the shade,
And instanced it in this:

"Behold," quoth he, "that mighty thing,
A pumpkin large and round,
Is held but by a little string,
Which upward cannot make it spring,
Nor bear it from the ground,

"While on this oak an acorn small,
So disproportioned, grows,
That whosoe'er surveys this all,
This universal casual ball,
Its ill contrivance knows.

"My better judgment would have hung
The pumpkin on the tree,
And left the acorn slightly strung,
'Mong things that on the surface sprung,
And weak and feeble be."

No more the caviller could say,
No further faults descry;
For, upwards gazing as he lay,
An acorn, loosened from its spray,
Fell down upon his eye.

The wounded part with tears ran o'er,
As punished for the sin;
Fool! had that bough a pumpkin bore,
Thy whimsies would have worked no more,
Nor skull have kept them in.

THE PIN, NEEDLE, AND SCISSORS.—*Mrs. Follen.*

T 'IS true, although 't is sad to say,
Disputes are rising every day.
You 'd think, if no one did deny it,
A little work-box might be quiet;
But 't is not so, for I did hear—
Or else I dreamed it, 't is so queer—
A Pin and Needle in the cushion
Maintain the following discussion.
The Needle, "extra-fine, gold-eyed,"
Was very sharp and full of pride.
And thus, methought, she did begin:—
"You clumsy, thick, short, ugly Pin,
I wish you were not quite so near;
How could my mistress stick me here?
She should have put me in my place,
With my bright sisters in the case."
"Would you were there!" the Pin replied;
"I do not want you by my side.
I 'm rather short and thick, 't is true;
Who 'd be so long and thin as you?
I 've got a head, though, of my own,
That you had better let alone."
"You make me laugh," the Needle cried;
"That you 've a head can't be denied;
For *you* a very proper head,
Without an eye and full of lead.'

"You are so cross, and sharp, and thin,"
Replied the poor, insulted Pin,
"I hardly dare a word to say,
And wish, indeed, you were away.
That golden eye in your poor head
Was only made to hold a thread;
All your fine airs are foolish fudge,
For you are nothing but a drudge;
But I, in spite of your abuse,
Am made for pleasure and for use.
I fasten the bouquet and sash,
And help the ladies make a dash;
I go abroad and gaily roam,
While you are rusting here at home."
"Stop!" cried the Needle, "you 're too much;
You 've brass enough to beat the Dutch:
Do I not make the ladies' clothes,
Ere I retire to my repose?
Then who, forsooth, the glory wins?
Alas! 't is finery and pins.
This is the world's unjust decree,
But what is this vain world to me?
I 'd rather live with my own kin,
Than dance about like you, vain Pin.
I 'm taken care of every day;
You 're used a while, then thrown away;
Or else you get all bent up double,
And a snug crack for all your trouble."
"True," said the Pin, "I am abused,
And sometimes very roughly used;
I often get an ugly crook,
Or fall into a dirty nook;
But there I lie, and never mind it;
Who wants a pin is sure to find it.
In time I am picked up, and then
I lead a merry life again.

You fuss so at a fall or hurt,
And if you touch a little dirt
You keep up such an odious creaking,
That where you are there is no speaking;
And then your lackey Emery 's called,
And he, poor thing, is pricked and mauled
Until your daintiness — O, shocking! —
Is fit for what? — To mend a stocking!"
The Needle now began to speak, —
They might have quarrelled for a week, —
But here the Scissors interposed,
And thus the warm debate was closed.
"You angry Needle! foolish Pin!
How did this nonsense first begin?
You should have both been better taught,
But I will cut the matter short.
You both are wrong and both are right,
And both are very impolite.
E'en in a work-box, 't will not do
To talk of everything that 's true.
All personal remarks avoid,
For every one will be annoyed
At hearing disagreeable truth;
Besides, it shows you quite uncouth,
And sadly wanting in good taste.
But what advantages you waste!
Think, Pins and Needles, while you may,
How much you hear in one short day;
No servants wait on lordly man
Can hear one half of what you can.
'T is not worth while to mince the matter;
Nor men nor boys like girls can chatter.
All now are learning, forward moving,
E'en Pins and Needles are improving;
And in this glorious, busy day,
All have some useful part to play.

Go forth, ye Pins, and bring home news
Ye Needles, in your cases muse!
And take me for your kind adviser,
And only think of growing wiser;
Then, when you meet again, no doubt,
Something you 'll have to talk about,
And need not get into a passion,
And quarrel in this vulgar fashion.
Less of yourselves you 'll think, and more
Of others, than you did before.
You 'll learn that, in their own right sphere,
All things with dignity appear,
And have, when in their proper place,
Peculiar use, intrinsic grace."
Methought the polished Scissors blushed
To have said so much, — and all was hushed.

WE ARE SEVEN.

—— A SIMPLE child,
That lightly draws its breath,
And feels its life in every limb,
What should it know of death?

I met a little cottage girl;
She was eight years old, she said;
Her hair was thick with many a curl,
That clustered round her head.

She had a rustic, woodland air,
And she was wildly clad;
Her eyes were fair and very fair,
Her beauty made me glad.

"Sisters and brothers, little maid,
How many may you be?"
"How many? Seven in all," she said,
And wondering looked at me.

"And where are they, I pray you tell?"
She answered, "Seven are we;
And two of us at Conway dwell,
And two are gone to sea.

"Two of us in the churchyard lie,
My sister and my brother;
And, in the churchyard cottage, I
Dwell near them, with my mother."

"You say that two at Conway dwell,
And two are gone to sea,
Yet ye are seven;—I pray you tell,
Sweet maid, how this may be."

Then did the little maid reply,—
"Seven boys and girls are we·
Two of us in the churchyard lie,
Beneath the churchyard tree.'

"You run about, my little maid,
Your limbs they are alive;
If two are in the churchyard laid,
Then ye are only five."

"Their graves are green, they may be seen,"
The little maid replied,
"Twelve steps or more from my mother's door,
And they are side by side.

"My stockings there I often knit,
  My kerchief there I hem;
And there upon the ground I sit,
  I sit and sing to them.

"And often, after sunset, sir,
  When it is light and fair,
I take my little porringer,
  And eat my supper there.

"The first that died was little Jane;
  In bed she moaning lay
Till God released her from her pain,
  And then she went away.

"So in the churchyard she was laid;
  And when the grass was dry,
Together round the grave we played,
  My brother John and I.

"And when the ground was white with snow,
  And I could run and slide,
My brother John was forced to go,
  And he lies by her side."

"How many are you, then," said I,
  "If they two are in heaven?"
The little maiden did reply,
  "O master, we are seven."

"But they are dead, those two are dead!
  Their spirits are in heaven."
'T was throwing words away; for still
The little maid would have her will,
  And said, "Nay, we are seven."

JOHN BARLEYCORN.—*Burns.*

There were three kings into the East,
  Three kings, both great and high,
An' they hae sworn a solemn oath
  John Barleycorn should die.

They took a plough and ploughed him down
  Put clods upon his head,
An' they hae sworn a solemn oath
  John Barleycorn was dead.

But the cheerful spring came kindly on,
  And showers began to fall,
And Barleycorn got up again,
  And sore surprised them all.

The sultry suns of summer came,
  And he grew thick and strong,
His head well armed with pointed spears,
  That no one should him wrong.

The sober autumn entered mild,
  When he grew wan and pale,
His bending joints and drooping head
  Showed he began to fail.

His color sickened more and more,
  He faded into age;
And then his enemies began
  To show their deadly rage.

They 've ta'en a weapon long and sharp,
And cut him by the knee;
Then tied him fast upon a cart,
Like a rogue for forgery.

They laid him down upon his back,
And cudgelled him full sore;
They hung him up before the storm,
And turned him o'er and o'er.

They filled up a darksome pit
With water to the brim,
They heaved in John Barleycorn,
There let him sink or swim.

They laid him out upon the floor,
To work him further woe,
And still, as signs of life appeared,
They tossed him to and fro.

They wasted o'er a scorching flame
The marrow of his bones;
But a miller used him worst of all,
For he crushed him 'tween two stones.

And they have ta'en his very heart's blood,
And drunk it round and round;
And still the more and more they drank,
Their joy did more abound

THE GREAT-GRANDFATHER. — *Miss Lamb.*

MOTHER'S grandfather lives still,
  His age is fourscore years and ten;
He looks a monument of time,
  The agedest of aged men.

Though years lie on him like a load,
  A happier man you will not see
Than he, whenever he can get
  His great-grandchildren on his knee.

When we our parents have displeased,
  He stands between us as a screen;
By him our good deeds in the sun,
  Our bad ones in the shade, are seen.

His love 's a line that 's long drawn out,
  Yet lasteth firm unto the end;
His heart is oak, yet unto us
  It like the gentlest reed can bend.

A fighting soldier he has been, —
  Yet by his manners you would guess
That he his whole long life had spent
  In scenes of country quietness.

His talk is all of things long past,
  For modern facts no pleasure yield, —
Of the famed year of forty-five,
  Of William, and Culloden's field.

The deeds of this eventful age,
  Which princes from their thrones have hurled,
Can no more interest wake in him
  Than stories of another world.

When I his length of days revolve,
  How like a strong tree he hath stood,
It brings into my mind almost
  Those patriarchs old before the flood.

THE WIND IN A FROLIC. — *William Howitt.*

The wind one morning sprang up from sleep,
Saying, "Now for a frolic! now for a leap!
Now for a madcap galloping chase!
I 'll make a commotion in every place!"
So it swept with a bustle right through a great town.
Creaking the signs, and scattering down
Shutters, and whisking, with merciless squalls,
Old women's bonnets and gingerbread stalls.
There never was heard a much lustier shout,
As the apples and oranges tumbled about;
And the urchins, that stand with their thievish eyes
Forever on watch, ran off each with a prize.
  Then away to the fields it went blustering and humming,
And the cattle all wondered whatever was coming.
It plucked by their tails the grave, matronly cows,
And tossed the colts' manes all about their brows,
Till, offended at such a familiar salute,
They all turned their backs and stood silently mute.
So on it went, capering and playing its pranks;
Whistling with reeds on the broad river banks:

Puffing the birds, as they sat on the spray,
Or the traveller grave on the king's highway.
It was not too nice to bustle the bags
Of the beggar, and flutter his dirty rags.
'T was so bold that it feared not to play its joke
With the doctor's wig, and the gentleman's cloak.
Through the forest it roared, and cried gayly, "Now
You sturdy old oaks, I 'll make you bow!"
And it made them bow without more ado,
Or it cracked their great branches through and through.
Then it rushed like a monster o'er cottage and farm,
Striking their inmates with sudden alarm;
And they ran out like bees in a midsummer swarm.
There were dames with their kerchiefs tied over their caps,
To see if their poultry were free from mishaps;
The turkeys they gobbled, the geese screamed aloud,
And the hens crept to roost in a terrified crowd;
There was rearing of ladders, and logs laying on,
Where the thatch from the roof threatened soon to be gone.
But the wind had passed on, and had met in a lane
With a schoolboy, who panted and struggled in vain,
For it tossed him, and twirled him, then passed, and he stood
With his hat in a pool, and his shoe in the mud.

THE NORTHERN SEAS.—*William Howitt.*

UP! up! let us a voyage take;
Why sit we here at ease?
Find us a vessel tight and snug,
Bound for the Northern Seas.

I long to see the Northern Lights,
  With their rushing splendors, fly,
Like living things, with flaming wings,
  Wide o'er the wondrous sky.

I long to see those icebergs vast,
  With heads all crowned with snow;
Whose green roots sleep in the awful deep,
  Two hundred fathoms low.

I long to hear the thundering crash
  Of their terrific fall;
And the echoes from a thousand cliffs,
  Like lonely voices call.

There shall we see the fierce white bear,
  The sleepy seals aground,
And the spouting whales that to and fro
  Sail with a dreary sound.

There may we tread on depths of ice,
  That the hairy mammoth hide;
Perfect as when, in times of old,
  The mighty creature died.

And while the unsetting sun shines on
  Through the still heaven's deep blue,
We 'll traverse the azure waves, the herds
  Of the dread sea-horse to view.

We 'll pass the shores of solemn pine,
  Where wolves and black bears prowl,
And away to the rocky isles of mist,
  To rouse the northern fowl.

Up there shall start ten thousand wings,
With a rushing, whistling din;
Up shall the auk and fulmar start, —
All but the fat penguin.

And there, in the wastes of the silent sky,
With the silent earth below,
We shall see far off to his lonely rock
The lonely eagle go.

Then softly, softly will we tread
By inland streams, to see
Where the pelican of the silent North
Sits there all silently.

THE CHILDREN IN THE WOOD.

Now ponder well, you parents dear,
The words which I shall write;
A doleful story you shall hear,
In time brought forth to light: —
A gentleman of good account
In Norfolk lived of late,
Whose wealth and riches did surmount
Most men of his estate.

Sore sick he was, and like to die,
No help that he could have;
His wife by him as sick did lie,
And both possessed one grave.
No love between these two was lost,
Each was to other kind;
In love they lived, in love they died,
And left two babes behind;

The one a fine and pretty boy,
  Not passing three years old;
The other a girl, more young than he,
  And made in beauty's mould.
The father left his little son,
  As plainly doth appear,
When he to perfect age should come,
  Three hundred pounds a year;

And to his little daughter Jane
  Five hundred pounds in gold,
To be paid down on marriage-day,
  Which might not be controlled;
But if the children chance to die
  Ere they to age should come,
Their uncle should possess their wealth,
  For so the will did run.

"Now, brother," said the dying man,
  "Look to my children dear;
Be good unto my boy and girl,
  No friends else have I here.
To God and you I do commend
  My children night and day;
But little while, be sure, we have
  Within this world to stay.

"You must be father and mother both,
  And uncle, all in one;
God knows what will become of them
  When I am dead and gone."
With that bespake their mother dear:
  "O brother kind," quoth she,
"You are the man must bring our babes
  To wealth or misery.

"And if you keep them carefully,
  Then God will you reward;
If otherwise you seem to deal,
  God will your deeds regard."
With lips as cold as any stone,
  She kissed her children small:
"God bless you both, my children dear!"
  With that the tears did fall.

These speeches then their brother spoke
  To this sick couple there:
"The keeping of your children dear,
  Sweet sister, do not fear;
God never prosper me nor mine,
  Nor aught else that I have,
If I do wrong your children dear,
  When you are laid in grave."

Their parents being dead and gone,
  The children home he takes,
And brings them home unto his house,
  And much of them he makes.
He had not kept these pretty babes
  A twelvemonth and a day,
When for their wealth he did devise
  To make them both away.

He bargained with two ruffians rude,
  Which were of furious mood,
That they should take the children young,
  And slay them in the wood.
He told his wife, and all he had,
  He did the children send
To be brought up in fair London,
  With one that was his friend.

Away then went these pretty babes,
  Rejoicing at that tide,
Rejoicing with a merry mind,
  They should on cock-horse ride.
They prate and prattle pleasantly,
  As they rode on their way,
To those that should their butchers be,
  And work their lives' decay.

So that the pretty speech they had
  Made murderous hearts relent;
And they that undertook the deed,
  Full sore they did repent.
Yet one of them, more hard of heart,
  Did vow to do his charge,
Because the wretch that hired him
  Had paid him very large.

The other would not agree thereto,
  So here they fell at strife;
With one another they did fight
  About the children's life;
And he that was of mildest mood
  Did slay the other there,
Within an unfrequented wood,
  While babes did quake for fear.

He took the children by the hand,
  When tears stood in their eye;
And bade them come and go with him,
  And look they did not cry.
And two long miles he led them on,
  While they for food complain:
"Stay here," quoth he, "I 'll bring you bread,
  When I do come again."

These pretty babes, with hand in hand,
  Went wandering up and down;
But never more they saw the man
  Approaching from the town.
Their pretty lips with blackberries
  Were all besmeared and dyed,
And when they saw the darksome night,
  They sat them down and cried.

Thus wandered these two pretty babes,
  Till death did end their grief;
In one another's arms they died,
  As babes wanting relief;
No burial these pretty babes
  Of any man receives,
Till Robin-redbreast painfully
  Did cover them with leaves.

And now the heavy wrath of God
  Upon their uncle fell;
Yes, fearful fiends did haunt his house,
  His conscience felt a hell;
His barns were fired, his goods consumed,
  His lands were barren made;
His cattle died within the field,
  And nothing with him stayed.

And in the voyage of Portugal,
  Two of his sons did die;
And, to conclude, himself was brought
  To extreme misery.
He pawned and mortgaged all his land
  Ere seven years came about,
And now at length this wicked act
  Did by this means come out.

The fellow that did take in hand
  These children for to kill
Was for a robbery judged to die,
  As was God's blessed will;
Who did confess the very truth,
  The which is here expressed;
Their uncle died while he for debt
  In prison long did rest.

All you that be executors made,
  And overseers eke,
Of children that be fatherless,
  And infants mild and meek,
Take your example by this thing,
  And yield to each his right;
Lest God, with such like misery,
  Your wicked minds requite.

THE USE OF FLOWERS.—*Mary Howitt.*

God might have bade the earth bring forth
  Enough for great and small,
The oak-tree and the cedar-tree,
  Without a flower at all.

We might have had enough, enough
  For every want of ours,
For luxury, medicine, and toil,
  And yet have had no flowers.

The ore within the mountain mine
  Requireth none to grow;
Nor doth it need the lotus-flower
  To make the river flow.

The clouds might give abundant rain,
  The nightly dews might fall,
And the herb that keepeth life in man
  Might yet have drunk them all.

Then wherefore, wherefore were they made,
  All dyed with rainbow light,
All fashioned with supremest grace,
  Upspringing day and night,—

Springing in valleys green and low,
  And on the mountains high,
And in the silent wilderness,
  Where no man passes by?

Our outward life requires them not,—
  Then wherefore had they birth?
To minister delight to man,
  To beautify the earth;

To comfort man, to whisper hope
  Whene'er his faith is dim;
For whoso careth for the flowers
  Will much more care for him.

TO MY LITTLE COUSIN WITH HER FIRST BONNET.—*Mrs. Southey.*

Fairies! guard the baby's bonnet,—
Set a special watch upon it;
Elfin people! to your care
I commit it, fresh and fair;
Neat as neatness, white as snow,—
See ye make it ever so.

Watch and ward set all about,
Some within and some without;
Over it, with dainty hand,
One her kirtle green expand;
One take post at every ring;
One at each unwrinkled string;
Two or three about the bow
Vigilant concern bestow;
A score, at least, on either side,
'Gainst evil accident provide,
(Jolt or jar or overlay;)
And so the precious charge convey
Through all the dangers of the way.
But when those are battled through,
Fairies! more remains to do;
Ye must gift, before ye go,
The bonnet, and the babe also,—
Gift it to protect her well,
Fays! from all malignant spell.
Charms and seasons to defy,
Blighting winds and evil eye;
And the bonny babe! on her
All your choicest gifts confer;—
Just as much of wit and sense
As may be hers without pretence,—
Just as much of grace and beauty
As shall not interfere with duty,—
Just as much of sprightliness
As may companion gentleness,—
Just as much of firmness, too,
As with self-will hath naught to do,—
Just as much light-hearted cheer
As may be melted to a tear,
By a word, a tone, a look,
Pity's touch, or Love's rebuke,—
As much of frankness, sweetly free,

As may consort with modesty,—
As much of feeling as will bear
Of after life the wear and tear,—
As much of life—But, fairies, there
Ye vanish into thinnest air;
And with ye parts the playful vein
That loved a light and trivial strain.
Befits me better, babe, for thee
T' invoke Almighty agency,
Almighty love, Almighty power,
To nurture up the human flower;
To cherish it with heavenly dew,
Sustain with earthly blessings too;
And when the ripe, full time shall be,
Engraft it on eternity!

THE YOUNG LETTER-WRITER.—*Miss Lamb.*

Dear Sir, Dear Madam, or Dear Friend,
  With ease are written at the top;
When those two happy words are penned
  A youthful writer oft will stop,

And bite his pen, and lift his eyes,
  As if he thinks to find in air
The wished-for following words, or tries
  To fix his thoughts by fixéd stare.

But haply all in vain,—the next
  Two words may be so long before
They 'll come, the writer, sore perplext,
  Gives in despair the matter o'er;

And when maturer age he sees
  With ready pen so swift inditing,
With envy he beholds the ease
  Of long-accustomed letter-writing.

Courage, young friend; the time may be,
  When you attain maturer age,
Some, young as you are now, may see
  You with like ease glide down a page.

Even then, when you, to years a debtor,
  In varied phrase your meaning wrap,
The welcom'st words in all your letter
  May be those two kind ones at the top.

ON ANOTHER'S SORROW.—*Blake.*

Can I see another's woe,
And not be in sorrow too?
Can I see another's grief,
And not seek for kind relief?

Can I see a falling tear,
And not feel my sorrow's share?
Can a father see his child
Weep, nor be with sorrow filled?

Can a mother sit and hear
An infant groan, an infant fear?
No! no! never can it be!
Never, never can it be!

And can He who smiles on all
Hear the wren with sorrows small,

Hear the small bird's grief and care,
Hear the woes that infants bear,—

And not sit beside the nest,
Pouring pity in their breast?
And not sit the table near,
Weeping tear on infant's tear?

And not sit, both night and day,
Weeping all our tears away?
O, no! never can it be!
Never, never can it be!

He doth give his joy to all;
He becomes an infant small;
He becomes a man of woe;
He doth feel the sorrow too.

Think not thou canst sigh a sigh,
And thy Maker is not nigh;
Think not thou canst weep a tear,
And thy Maker is not near.

O, he gives to us his joy,
That our griefs he may destroy;
Till our grief is fled and gone,
He doth sit by us and moan.

THE PEBBLE AND THE ACORN.—*H. F. Gould.*

"I AM a Pebble! and yield to none!"
Were the swelling words of a tiny stone;
"Nor time nor seasons can alter me;
I am abiding, while ages flee.

The pelting hail and the drizzling rain
Have tried to soften me, long, in vain;
And the tender dew has sought to melt
Or touch my heart; but it was not felt.
There 's none that can tell about my birth,
For I 'm as old as the big, round earth.
The children of men arise and pass
Out of the world, like the blades of grass;
And many a foot on me has trod
That 's gone from sight, and under the sod!
I am a Pebble! but who art thou,
Rattling along from the restless bough?"

The Acorn was shocked at this rude salute,
And lay for a moment abashed and mute;
She never before had been so near
This gravelly ball, and mundane sphere;
And she felt for a time at a loss to know
How to answer a thing so coarse and low.
But to give reproof of a nobler sort
Than the angry look or the keen retort,
At length she said, in a gentle tone: —
"Since it has happened that I am thrown
From the lighter element, where I grew,
Down to another, so hard and new,
And beside a personage so august,
Abased I will cover my head with dust,
And quickly retire from the sight of one
Whom time, nor season, nor storm, nor sun,
Nor the gentle dew, nor the grinding heel,
Has ever subdued or made to feel!"
And soon in the earth she sunk away
From the comfortless spot where the Pebble lay,

But it was not long ere the soil was broke
By the peering head of an infant oak!

And as it arose and its branches spread,
The Pebble looked up, and wondering said: —
"A modest Acorn! never to tell
What was enclosed in its simple shell;
That the pride of the forest was folded up
In the narrow space of its little cup!
And meekly to sink in the darksome earth,
Which proves that nothing could hide her worth
And, O, how many will tread on me,
To come and admire the beautiful tree,
Whose head is towering toward the sky,
Above such a worthless thing as I!
Useless and vain, a cumberer here,
I have been idling from year to year.
But never from this shall a vaunting word
From the humbled Pebble again be heard,
Till something without me or within
Shall show the purpose for which I 've been!"
The Pebble its vow could not forget,
And it lies there wrapt in silence yet.

NIGHT. — *Blake.*

THE sun descending in the west,
  The evening star doth shine;
The birds are silent in their nest,
  And I must seek for mine.
    The moon, like a flower
    In heaven's high bower,
    With silent delight
    Sits and smiles on the night.

Farewell, green fields and happy grove,
Where flocks have ta'en delight;
Where lambs have nibbled, silent move
The feet of angels bright;
Unseen, they pour blessing,
And joy without ceasing,
On each bud and blossom,
On each sleeping bosom.

They look in every thoughtless nest,
Where birds are covered warm;
They visit caves of every beast,
To keep them from all harm;
If they see any weeping
That should have been sleeping,
They pour sleep on their head,
And sit down on their bed.

When wolves and tigers howl for prey,
They pitying stand and weep,
Seeking to drive their thirst away,
And keep them from the sheep;
But if they rush dreadful,
The angels most heedful,
Receive each mild spirit,
New worlds to inherit.

CHILDHOOD. — *Scott.*

Childhood! happiest stage of life!
Free from care, and free from strife,
Free from memory's ruthless reign,
Fraught with scenes of former pain;

Free from fancy's cruel skill,
Fabricating future ill;
Time when all that meets the view,
All can charm, for all is new;
How thy long-lost hours I mourn,
Never, never to return!

Then to toss the circling ball,
Caught rebounding from the wall;
Then the mimic ship to guide
Down the kennel's dirty tide;
Then the hoop's revolving pace
Through the dirty street to chase;
O what joy! it once was mine;
Childhood! matchless boon of thine!
How thy long-lost hours I mourn,
Never, never to return!

RANGER'S GRAVE.—*Mrs. Southey.*

He 's dead and gone! he 's dead and gone!
And the lime-tree branches wave,
And the daisy blows,
And the green grass grows,
Upon his grave.

He 's dead and gone! he 's dead and gone!
And he sleeps by the flowering lime,
Where he loved to lie,
When the sun was high,
In summer time.

We 've laid him there, where the blessed air
  Disports with the lovely light,
    And raineth showers
    Of those sweet flowers,
      So silver white;

Where the blackbird sings, and the wild bee's wings
  Make music all day long,
    And the cricket at night
    (A dusky sprite!)
      Takes up the song.

He loved to lie where his wakeful eye
  Could keep me still in sight,
    Whence a word or a sign,
    Or a look of mine,
      Brought him like light.

Nor word, nor sign, nor look of mine,
  From under the lime-tree bough,
    With bark and bound,
    And frolic round,
      Shall bring him now.

But he taketh his rest, where he loved best
  In the days of his life to be,
    And that place will not
    Be a common spot
      Of earth to me.

CHRISTMAS TIMES. — *Howard.*

'TWAS the night before Christmas, and all thro
the house
Not a creature was stirring, not even a mouse;
The stockings were hung by the chimney with ca
In the hope that St. Nicholas soon would be there
The children were nestled all snug in their beds,
While visions of sugar-plums danced in their heads,
And mamma in her kerchief, and I in my cap,
Had just settled our brains for a long winter's nap;
When out on the lawn there arose such a clatter,
I sprang from the bed to see what was the matter.
Away to the window I flew like a flash,
Tore open the shutters and threw up the sash, —
The moon on the breast of the new-fallen snow
Gave the lustre of mid-day to objects below, —
When what to my wondering eyes should appear
But a miniature sleigh, and eight tiny reindeer,
With a little old driver so lively and quick
I knew in a moment it must be St. Nick.
More rapid than eagles his coursers they came,
And he whistled, and shouted, and called them by
name: —
"Now, Dasher! now, Dancer! now, Prancer! now,
Vixen!
On, Comet! on, Cupid! on, Dunder and Blixen!
To the top of the porch, to the top of the wall,
Now, dash away! dash away! dash away, all!"
As dry leaves before the wild hurricane fly,
When they meet with an obstacle mount to the sky
So up to the house-top the coursers they flew,
With the sleigh full of toys, and St. Nicholas too.

And then, in a twinkling, I heard on the roof
The prancing and pawing of each tiny hoof;
As I drew in my head, and was turning around,
Down the chimney St. Nicholas came with a bound.
He was dressed all in fur, from his head to his foot,
And his clothes were all tarnished with ashes and
soot;
A bundle of toys was flung on his back,
And he looked like a pedler just opening his pack.
His eyes — how they twinkled! his dimples how
merry!
His cheeks were like roses, his nose like a cherry;
His droll little mouth was drawn up like a bow,
And the beard of his chin was as white as the snow;
The stump of a pipe he held tight in his teeth,
And the smoke it encircled his head like a wreath.
He was chubby and plump, a right jolly old elf,
And I laughed when I saw him, in spite of myself.
A wink of his eye, and a twist of his head,
Soon gave me to know I had nothing to dread.
He spoke not a word, but went straight to his work,
And filled all his stockings, — then turned with a jerk,
And laying his finger aside of his nose,
And giving a nod, up the chimney he rose.
He sprang to his sleigh, to his team gave a whistle,
And away they all flew, like the down of a thistle;
But I heard him exclaim, ere he drove out of sight,
"Merry Christmas to all, and to all a good night!"

THE PET LAMB. — *Wordsworth.*

The dew was falling fast, the stars began to blink;
I heard a voice; it said, "Drink, pretty creature,
drink."

And, looking o'er the hedge, before me I espied
A snow-white mountain lamb, with a maiden at its side.

No other sheep were near, the lamb was all alone,
And by a slender cord was tethered to a stone;
With one knee on the grass did the little maiden kneel,
While to that mountain lamb she gave its evening meal.

The lamb, while from her hand he thus his supper took,
Seemed to feast with head and ears, and his tail with pleasure shook;
"Drink, pretty creature, drink," she said, in such a tone,
That I almost received her heart into my own.

'T was little Barbara Lethwaite, a child of beauty rare!
I watched them with delight, they were a lovely pair.
Now with her empty can the maiden turned away;
But ere ten yards were gone, her footsteps she did stay.

Towards the lamb she looked; and from that shady place
I unobserved could see the workings of her face;
If nature to her tongue could measured numbers bring,
Thus, thought I, to her lamb that little maid might sing:—

"What ails thee, young one? what? why pull so at
thy cord?
Is it not well with thee? well both for bed and
board?
Thy plot of grass is soft, and green as grass can be;
Rest, little, young one, rest; what is 't that aileth
thee?

"What is it thou wouldst seek? what is wanting to
thy heart?
Thy limbs are they not strong? and beautiful thou
art.
This grass is tender grass; these flowers they have no
peers,
And that green corn all day long is rustling in thy
ears!

"If the sun be shining hot, do but stretch thy woollen
chain,
This birch is standing by, its covert thou canst gain;
For rain and mountain storms — the like thou need'st
not fear —
The rain and storm are things that scarcely can come
here.

"Rest, little, young one, rest; thou hast forgot the
day
When my father found thee first, in places far away;
Many flocks were on the hills, but thou wert owned
by none,
And thy mother from thy side forevermore was
gone.

"He took thee in his arms, and in pity brought thee
home;
O blessed day for thee! then whither wouldst thou
roam?

A faithful nurse thou hast, the dam that did thee yean
Upon the mountain-tops no kinder could have been.

"Thou knowest that twice a day I have brought thee in this can
Fresh water from the brook, as clear as ever ran;
And twice in the day, when the ground is wet with dew,
I bring thee draughts of milk, warm milk it is, and new.

"Thy limbs will shortly be twice as stout as they are now;
Then I'll yoke thee to my cart, like a pony in the plough;
My playmate thou shalt be; and when the wind is cold
Our hearth shall be thy bed, our house shall be thy fold.

"Alas! the mountain-tops that look so green and fair,
I've heard of fearful winds and darkness that come there;
The little brooks that seem all pastime and all play,
When they are angry roar like lions for their prey.

"Here thou need'st not dread the raven in the sky;
Night and day thou art safe — our cottage is hard by.
Why bleat so after me? why pull so at thy chain?
Sleep — and at break of day I will come to thee again."

As homeward through the lane I went, with lazy feet,
This song to myself did I oftentimes repeat;

And it seemed, as I retraced the ballad line by line,
That but half of it was hers, and one half of it was mine.

Again, and once again, did I repeat the song:
"Nay," said I, "more than half to the damsel must belong,
For she looked with such a look, and she spoke with such a tone,
That I almost received her heart into my own."

THE LITTLE BLACK BOY.—*Blake.*

My mother bore me in the southern wild,
And I am black, but, O, my soul is white!
White as an angel is the English child,
But I am black, as if bereaved of light.

My mother taught me underneath a tree,
And, sitting down before the heat of day,
She took me on her lap and kissèd me,
And, pointing to the east, began to say:—

"Look on the rising sun,—there God does live,
And gives his light, and gives his heat away;
And flowers, and trees, and beasts, and men, receive
Comfort in morning, joy in the noonday.

"And we are put on earth a little space,
That we may learn to bear the beams of love;
And these black bodies and this sunburnt face
Are but a cloud, and like a shady grove.

"For when our souls have learnt the heat to bear,
The clouds will vanish, we shall hear his voice,
Saying, 'Come from the grove, my love and care,
And round my golden tent like lambs rejoice.'"

Thus did my mother say, and kissèd me;
And thus say I to little English boy—
When I from black and he from white cloud free,
And round the tent of God like lambs we joy;

I'll shade him from the heat till he can bear
To lean with joy upon our Father's knee;
And then I'll stand and stroke his silver hair,
And be like him, and he will then love me.

THE SPARTAN BOY.—*Miss Lamb.*

When I the memory repeat
Of the heroic actions great,
Which, in contempt of pain and death,
Were done by men who drew their breath
In ages past, I find no deed
That can in fortitude exceed
The noble boy, in Sparta bred,
Who in the temple ministered.
By the sacrifice he stands,
The lighted incense in his hands;
Through the smoking censer's lid
Dropped a burning coal, which slid
Into his sleeve, and passed in
Between the folds, e'en to the skin.
Dire was the pain which then he proved,
But not for this his sleeve he moved.

Or would the scorching ember shake
Out from the folds, lest it should make
Any confusion, or excite
Disturbance at the sacred rite,
But close he kept the burning coal,
Till it eat itself a hole
In his flesh. The standers-by
Saw no sign, and heard no cry.
All this he did in noble scorn,
And for he was a Spartan born.
Young student who this story readest,
And with the same thy thoughts now feedest,
Thy weaker nerves might thee forbid
To do the thing the Spartan did;
Thy feebler heart could not sustain
Such dire extremity of pain.
But in this story thou mayst see
That may useful prove to thee.
By this example thou wilt find,
That to the ingenuous mind
Shame can greater anguish bring
Than the body's suffering;
That pain is not the worst of ills, —
Not when it the body kills;
That in fair religion's cause
For thy country, or the laws,
When occasion dire shall offer,
'T is reproachful not to suffer.

MY BIRTHDAY. — *Miss Lamb.*

A DOZEN years since, in this house what commotion,
What bustle, what stir, and what joyful ado!
Every soul in the family at my devotion,
When into the world I came, twelve years ago.

I 've been told by my friends (if they do not belie me)
My promise was such as no parent would scorn;
The wise and the aged who prophesied by me
Augured nothing but good of me when I was born.

But vain are the hopes which are formed by a parent,
Fallacious the marks which in infancy shine;
My frail constitution soon made it apparent
I nourished within me the seeds of decline.

On a sick-bed I lay, through the flesh my bones started,
My grief-wasted frame to a skeleton fell;
My physicians, foreboding, took leave and departed,
And they wished me dead now who wished me well.

Life and soul were kept in by a mother's assistance,
Who struggled with faith, and prevailed 'gainst despair;
Like an angel she watched o'er the lamp of existence,
And never would leave while a glimmer was there.

By her care I 'm alive now; — but what retribution
Can I for a life twice bestowed thus confer?
Were I to be silent, each year's revolution
Proclaims each new birthday is owing to her.

The chance-rooted tree that by way-sides is planted,
Where no friendly hand will watch o'er its young shoots,
Has less blame if, in autumn, when produce is wanted,
Enriched by small culture, it put forth small fruits.

But that which with labor in hotbeds is reared,
Secured by nice art from the dews and the rains,
Unsound at the root may with justice be feared,
If it pay not with interest the tiller his pains.

THE RIDE. — *Miss Lamb.*

Lately an equipage I overtook,
And helped to lift it o'er a narrow brook.
No horse it had, except one boy, who drew
His sister out in it the fields to view.
O happy town-bred girl, in fine chaise going,
For the first time, to see the green grass growing!
This was the end and purport of the ride,
I learned, as, walking slowly by their side,
I heard their conversation. Often she, —
" Brother, is this the country that I see?"
The bricks were smoking, and the ground was broke,
There were no signs of verdure when she spoke.
He, as the well-informed delight in chiding
The ignorant, her questions still deriding,
To his good judgment modestly she yields,
Till, brick-kilns past, they reached the open fields.
Then, as with rapturous wonder round she gazes
On the green grass, the buttercups, and daisies,
" This is the country sure enough!" she cries;
'Is 't not a charming place?" The boy replies,
" We 'll go no further." " No," she says, " no need,
No finer place than this can be indeed."
I left them gathering flowers, the happiest pair
That ever London sent to breathe the fine fresh air.

GENTLE RIVER. — *Percy's Reliques.*

Gentle river, gentle river,
  Lo! thy streams are stained with gore;
Many a brave and noble captain
  Floats along thy willowed shore.

All beside thy impid waters,
  All beside thy sands so bright,
Moorish chiefs and Christian warriors
  Joined in fierce and mortal fight.

Lords, and dukes, and noble princes,
  On thy fatal banks were slain;
Fatal banks, that gave to slaughter
  All the pride and flower of Spain!

There the hero, brave Alonzo,
  Full of wounds and glory, died;
There the fearless Urdiales
  Fell a victim, by his side.

Lo! where yonder Don Saavedra
  Through their squadrons slow retires;
Proud Seville, his native city,
  Proud Seville his worth admires.

Close behind, a renegado
  Loudly shouts, with taunting cry,
"Yield thee, yield thee, Don Saavedra
  Dost thou from the battle fly?

"Well I know thee, haughty Christian,
  Long I lived beneath thy roof;
Oft I 've in the lists of glory
  Seen thee win the prize of proof.

"Well I know thy aged parents,
  Well thy blooming bride I know;
Seven years I was thy captive,
  Seven years of pain and woe.

"May our prophet grant my wishes,
Haughty chief, thou shalt be mine;
Thou shalt drink that cup of sorrow
Which I drank when I was thine."

Like a lion turns the warrior,
Back he sends an angry glare;
Whizzing came the Moorish javelin,
Vainly whizzing, through the air.

Back the hero, full of fury,
Sent a deep and mortal wound;
Instant sunk the renegado,
Mute and lifeless, on the ground.

With a thousand Moors surrounded,
Brave Saavedra stands at bay;
Wearied out, but never daunted,
Cold at length the warrior lay.

Near him fighting, great Alonzo
Stout resists the Paynim bands;
From his slaughtered steed dismounted,
Firm intrenched behind him stands.

Furious press the hostile squadron,
Furious he repels their rage;
Loss of blood at length enfeebles;
Who can war with thousands wage?

Where yon rock the plain o'ershadows,
Close beneath its foot retired,
Fainting sunk the bleeding hero,
And without a groan expired.

NOSE AND EYES.—*Cowper.*

BETWEEN Nose and Eyes a strange contest arose;
The spectacles set them unhappily wrong;
The point in dispute was, as all the world knows,
To which the said spectacles ought to belong.

So the Tongue was the lawyer, and argued the cause
With a great deal of skill, and a wig full of learning
While Chief-justice Ear sat to balance the laws,
So famed for his talent in nicely discerning.

"In behalf of the Nose, it will quickly appear,
And your lordship," he said, "will undoubtedly find,
That the Nose has had spectacles always in wear,—
Which amounts to possession time out of mind."

Then holding the spectacles up to the court,—
"Your lordship observes they are made with a straddle
As wide as the ridge of the Nose is; in short,
Designed to sit close to it, just like a saddle.

"Again, would your lordship a moment suppose
('T is a case that has happened, and may be again)
That the visage or countenance had not a Nose,
Pray who would or who could wear spectacles then

"On the whole it appears, and my argument shows,
With a reasoning the court will never condemn,
That the spectacles plainly were made for the Nose,
And the Nose was as plainly intended for them."

Then, shifting his side, as a lawyer knows how,
He pleaded again in behalf of the Eyes;
But what were his arguments few people know,
For the Court did not think they were equally wise.

So his lordship decreed, with a grave solemn tone,—
Decisive and clear, without one *if* or *but*,—
That whenever the Nose put his spectacles on,
By daylight or candle-light, Eyes should be shut.

TRADITIONARY BALLAD—*Mary Howitt.*

THE FAIRIES OF THE CALDON-LOW. A MIDSUMMER LEGEND.

"AND where have you been, my Mary,
And where have you been from me?"
"I've been at the top of the Caldon-Low,
The midsummer night to see!"

"And what did you see, my Mary,
All up on the Caldon-Low?"
"I saw the blithe sunshine come down,
And I saw the merry winds blow."

"And what did you hear, my Mary,
All up on the Caldon-Hill?"
"I heard the drops of water made,
And the green corn-ears to fill."

"O, tell me all, my Mary,—
All, all that ever you know;
For you must have seen the fairies,
Last night, on Caldon-Low."

"'Then take me on your knee, mother,
And listen, mother of mine;—
A hundred fairies danced last night,
And the harpers they were nine.

"And merry was the glee of the harp-strings,
And their dancing feet so small;
But, O, the sound of the talking
Was merrier far than all!"

"And what were the words, my Mary,
That you did hear them say?"
"I 'll tell you all, my mother,—
But let me have my way!

"And some, they played with the water,
And rolled it down the hill:—
'And this,' they said, 'shall speedily turn
The poor old miller's mill;

"'For there has been no water
Ever since the first of May;
And a busy man shall the miller be
By the dawning of the day!

"'O, the miller, how he will laugh
When he sees the mill-dam rise!
The jolly old miller, how he will laugh,
Till the tears fill both his eyes!'

"And some, they seized the little winds
That sounded over the hill,
And each put a horn into his mouth,
And blew so sharp and shrill:—

"'And there,' said they, 'the merry winds go,
Away from every horn;
And those shall clear the mildew dank
From the blind old widow's corn!

"'O, the poor, blind old widow,—
Though she has been blind so long,
She'll be merry enough when the mildew's gone.
And the corn stands stiff and strong!'

"And some they brought the brown lint-seed,
And flung it down from the Low:—
'And this,' said they, 'by the sunrise,
In the weaver's croft shall grow!

"'O the poor, lame weaver,
How he will laugh outright
When he sees his dwindling flax-field
All full of flowers by night!'

"And then upspoke a brownie,
With a long beard on his chin:—
'I have spun up all the tow,' said he,
'And I want some more to spin.

"'I've spun a piece of hempen cloth,
And I want to spin another,—
A little sheet for Mary's bed,
And an apron for her mother!'

"And with that I could not help but laugh,
And I laughed out loud and free;
And then on the top of the Caldon-Low
There was no one left but me.

"And all on the top of the Caldon-Low
  The mists were cold and gray,
And nothing I saw but the mossy stones
  That round about me lay.

"But as I came down from the hill-top,
  I heard a jar below;
How busy the jolly miller was,
  And how merry the wheel did go!

"And I peeped into the widow's field,
  And, sure enough, were seen
The yellow ears of the mildewed corn
  All standing stiff and green.

"And down by the weaver's croft I stole,
  To see if the flax were high;
But I saw the weaver at his gate,
  With the good news in his eye!

"Now, this is all I heard, mother,
  And all that I did see;
So, prythee, make my bed, mother,
  For I'm tired as I can be!"

TO THE LADY-BIRD. — *Mrs. Southey.*

LADY-BIRD! lady-bird! fly away home, —
  The field-mouse is gone to her nest,
The daisies have shut up their sleepy red ey
  And the bees and the birds are at rest.

Lady-bird! lady-bird! fly away home,—
  The glow-worm is lighting her lamp,
The dew 's falling fast, and your fine speckled wings
  Will flag with the close-clinging damp.

Lady-bird! lady-bird! fly away home,—
  Good luck if you reach it at last!
The owl 's come abroad, and the bat 's on the roam,
  Sharp set from their Ramazan fast.

Lady-bird! lady-bird! fly away home,—
  The fairy bells tinkle afar!
Make haste, or they 'll catch ye, and harness ye fast
  With a cobweb to Oberon's car.

Lady-bird! lady-bird! fly away home,—
  To your house in the old willow-tree,
Where your children, so dear, have invited the ant
  And a few cosey neighbors to tea.

Lady-bird! lady-bird! fly away home,—
  And, if not gobbled up by the way,
Nor yoked by the fairies to Oberon's car,
  You 're in luck,—and that 's all I 've to say.

THE ROOK AND THE SPARROW.—*Miss Lamb*

A LITTLE boy with crumbs of bread
Many a hungry sparrow fed.
It was a child of little sense
Who this kind bounty did dispense;
For suddenly it was withdrawn,
And all the birds were left forlorn,

In a hard time of frost and snow,
Not knowing where for food to go.
He would no longer give them bread,
Because he had observed (he said)
That sometimes to the window came
A great black bird, a rook by name,
And took away a small bird's share :
So foolish Henry did not care
What became of the great rook
That from the little sparrows took,
Now and then, as 't were by stealth,
A part of their abundant wealth,
Nor evermore would feed his sparrows.
Thus ignorance a kind heart narrows.
I wish I had been there; I would
Have told the child rooks live by food
In the same way that sparrows do.
I also would have told him, too,
Birds act by instinct, and ne'er can
Attain the rectitude of man.
Nay, that even when distress
Does on poor human nature press,
We need not be too strict in seeing
The failings of a fellow-being.

TO A REDBREAST.—*Langhorne.*

Little bird with bosom red,
Welcome to my humble shed!
Courtly domes of high degree
Have no room for thee or me;
Pride and pleasure's fickle throng
Nothing mind an idle song.

Daily near my table steal,
While I pick my scanty meal
Doubt not, little though there be,
But I 'll cast a crumb to thee,
Well rewarded if I spy
Pleasure in thy glancing eye;
See thee, when thou 'st eat thy fill,
Plume thy breast, and wipe thy bill.
Come, my feathered friend, again,
Well thou know'st the broken pane.

MARINER'S HYMN. — *Mrs. Southey.*

Launch thy bark, mariner!
  Christian, God speed thee;
Let loose the rudder bands,
  Good angels lead thee!
Set thy sails warily,
  Tempests will come;
Steer thy course steadily,
  Christian, steer home!

Look to the weather bow,
  Breakers are round thee;
Let fall the plummet now,
  Shallows may ground thee.
Reef in the foresail, there!
  Hold the helm fast!
So, — let the vessel wear, —
  There swept the blast.

What of the night, watchman?
  What of the night?
"Cloudy, all quiet, —
  No land yet, — all 's right."

Be wakeful, be vigilant, —
   Danger may be
At an hour when all seemeth
   Securest to thee.

How! gains the leak so fast?
   Clear out the hold, —
Hoist up thy merchandise,
   Heave out thy gold; —
There, let the ingots go; —
   Now the ship rights;
Hurra! the harbor 's near, —
   Lo! the red lights.

Slacken not sail yet
   At inlet or island;
Straight for the beacon steer,
   Straight for the high land;
Crowd all thy canvass on,
   Cut through the foam; —
Christian! cast anchor now, —
   Heaven is thy home!

THE TWO ESTATES. — *Mary Howitt.*

The children of the rich man, no carking care they know;
Like lilies in the sunshine, how beautiful they grow!
And well may they be beautiful; in raiment of the best,
In velvet, gold, and ermine, their little forms are drest.
With a hat and jaunty feather set lightly on their head,
And golden hair, like angels' locks, over their shoulders spread.

And well may they be beautiful; they toil not, neither spin,
Nor dig, nor delve, nor do they aught their daily bread to win.
They eat from gold and silver all luxuries wealth can buy;
They sleep on beds of softest down, in chambers rich and high.
They dwell in lordly houses, with gardens round about,
And servants do attend them if they go in or out.

They have music for the hearing, and pictures for the eye,
And exquisite and costly things each sense to gratify.
No wonder they are beautiful! and if they chance to die,
Among dead lords and ladies, in the chancel-vault, they lie,
With marble tablets on the wall inscribed, that all may know
The children of the rich man are mouldering below.

The children of the poor man, around the humble doors
They throng of city alleys and solitary moors.
In hot and noisy factories they turn the ceaseless wheel,
And eat with feeble appetite their coarse and joyless meal.
They rise up in the morning, ne'er dreaming of delight,
And weary, spent, and heartsore, they go to bed at night.

They have no brave apparel, with golden clasp and gem;
So their clothes keep out the weather, they 're good enough for them.
Their hands are broad and horny; they hunger and are cold;
They learn what toil and sorrow mean ere they are five years old.
The poor man's child must step aside if the rich man's child go by;
And scarcely aught may minister to his little vanity.

And of what could he be vain? — his most beautiful array
Is what the rich man's children have worn and cast away.
The finely-spun, the many-hued, the *new*, are not for him,
He must clothe himself, with thankfulness, in garments soiled and dim.
He sees the children of the rich in chariots gay go by,
And, "What a heavenly life is theirs!" he sayeth with a sigh.

Then straightway to his work he goeth, for, feeble though he be,
His daily toil must still be done to help the family.
Thus live the poor man's children; and if they chance to die,
In plain, uncostly coffins, 'mong common graves, they lie;
Nor monument nor headstone their humble names declare; —
But thou, O God, wilt not forget the poor man's children there!

THE TOWN AND COUNTRY CHILD. — *Cunningham.*

Child of the country! free as air
Art thou, and as the sunshine fair;
Born, like the lily, where the dew
Lies odorous when the day is new;
Fed 'mid the May-flowers like the bee;
Nursed to sweet music on the knee;
Lulled in the breast to that glad tune
Which winds make 'mong the woods of June;
I sing of thee; — 't is sweet to sing
Of such a fair and gladsome thing.
Child of the town! for thee I sigh;
A gilded roof 's thy golden sky,
A carpet is thy daisied sod,
A narrow street thy boundless road,
Thy rushing deer 's the clattering tramp
Of watchmen, thy best light 's a lamp, —
Through smoke, and not through trellised vines
And blooming trees, thy sunbeam shines;
I sing of thee in sadness; where
Else is wreck wrought in aught so farr?
Child of the country! thy small feet
Tread on strawberries red and sweet;
With thee I wander forth to see
The flowers which most delight the bee;
The bush o'er which the throstle sung
In April, while she nursed her young;
The den beneath the sloe-thorn, where
She bred her twins, the timorous hare;
The knoll, wrought o'er with wild blue-bells,
Where brown bees build their balmy cells;
The greenwood stream, the shady pool,
Where trouts leap when the day is cool.

The shilfa's nest, that seems to be
A portion of the sheltering tree, —
And other marvels, which my verse
Can find no language to rehearse.
Child of the town! for thee, alas!
Glad nature spreads nor flowers nor grass.
Birds build no nests, nor in the sun
Glad streams come singing as they run;
A May-pole is thy blossomed tree,
A beetle is thy murmuring bee;
Thy bird is caged, thy dove is where
Thy poulterer dwells, beside thy hare;
Thy fruit is plucked, and by the pound
Hawked clamorous all the city round;
No roses, twin-born on the stalk,
Perfume thee in thy evening walk;
No voice of birds, — but to thee comes
The mingled din of cars and drums,
And startling cries, such as are rife
When wine and wassail waken strife.
Child of the country! on the lawn
I see thee like the bounding fawn,
Blithe as the bird which tries its wing
The first time on the winds of spring;
Bright as the sun when from the cloud
He comes as cocks are crowing loud;
Now running, shouting, 'mid sunbeams,
Now groping trouts in lucid streams,
Now spinning like a mill-wheel round,
Now hunting echo's empty sound,
Now climbing up some old, tall tree,
For climbing's sake. 'T is sweet to thee
To sit where birds can sit alone,
Or share with thee thy venturous throne.
Child of the town and bustling street,
What woes and snares await thy feet!

Thy paths are paved for five long miles,
Thy groves and hills are peaks and tiles;
Thy fragrant air is yon thick smoke,
Which shrouds thee like a mourning-cloak;
And thou art cabined and confined
At once from sun, and dew, and wind;
Or set thy tottering feet but on
Thy lengthened walks of slippery stone;
The coachman there careering reels,
With goaded steeds and maddening wheels:
And Commerce pours each poring son
In pelf's pursuit and hollos' run;
While, flushed with wine, and stung at play,
Men rush from darkness into day,
The stream 's too strong for thy small bark;
There nought can sail, save what is stark.
Fly from the town, sweet child! for health
Is happiness, and strength, and wealth.
There is a lesson in each flower,
A story in each stream and bower;
On every herb on which you tread
Are written words which, rightly read,
Will lead you from earth's fragrant sod
To hope, and holiness, and God.

THE TWO BOYS.—*Miss Lamb.*

I SAW a boy with eager eye
Open a book upon a stall,
And read as he 'd devour it all;
Which when the stall-man did espy,
Soon to the boy I heard him call:—
"You sir, you never buy a book,
Therefore in one you shall not look."

The boy passed slowly on, and, with a sigh,
He wished he never had been taught to read,
Then of the old churl's books he should have had no need.

Of sufferings the poor have many,
Which never can the rich annoy.
I soon perceived another boy,
Who looked as if he 'd not had any
Food for that day at least, enjoy
The sight of cold meat in a tavern larder.
This boy's case, thought I, is surely harder;
Thus hungry longing, thus without a penny,
Beholding choice of dainty-dressed meat;
No wonder if he wish he ne'er had learned to eat.

A SONG TO CREATING WISDOM.— *Watts.*

Eternal Wisdom, thee we praise,
Thee the creation sings;
With thy loud name, rocks, hills, and seas,
And heaven's high palace rings.

Place me on the bright wings of day,
To travel with the sun;
With what amaze shall I survey
The wonders thou hast done!

Thy hand, how wide it spread the sky,
How glorious to behold!
Tinged with a blue of heavenly dye,
And starred with sparkling gold

There thou hast bid the globes of light
  Their endless circles run;
There the pale planet rules the night,
  And day obeys the sun.

Downward I turn my wondering eyes
  On clouds and storms below,
Those under regions of the skies
  Thy numerous glories show.

The noisy winds stand ready there
  Thy orders to obey,
With sounding wings they sweep the air
  To make thy chariot way.

There, like a trumpet, loud and strong,
  Thy thunder shakes our coast;
While the red lightnings wave along
  The banners of thine host.

On the thin air, without a prop,
  Hang fruitful showers around;
At thy command they sink and drop
  Their fatness on the ground.

How did thy wondrous skill array
  The fields in charming green;
A thousand herbs thy art display,
  A thousand flowers between!

The rolling mountains of the deep
  Observe thy strong command;
Thy breath can raise the billows steep,
  Or sink them to the sand.

Amidst thy watery kingdoms, Lord,
 The finny nations play,
And scaly monsters, at thy word,
 Rush through the northern sea.

Thy glories blaze all nature round,
 And strike the gazing sight,
Through skies, and seas, and solid ground,
 With terror and delight.

Infinite strength, and equal skill,
 Shine through the worlds abroad,
Our souls with vast amazement fill,
 And speak the builder God.

But the sweet beauties of thy grace
 Our softer passions move;
Pity divine in Jesus' face
 We see, adore and love!

THE COFFEE SLIPS. — *Miss Lamb.*

Whene'er I fragrant coffee drink,
I on the generous Frenchman think,
Whose noble perseverance bore
The tree to Martinico's shore.
While yet her colony was new,
Her island products but a few,
Two shoots from off a coffee-tree
He carried with him o'er the sea.
Each little, tender coffee slip
He waters daily in the ship;
And, as he tends his embryo trees,
Feels he is raising 'midst the seas

Coffee groves, whose ample shade
Shall screen the dark Creolian maid.
But soon, alas! his darling pleasure
In watching this his precious treasure
Is like to fade, — for water fails
On board the ship in which he sails.
Now all the reservoirs are shut,
The crew on short allowance put.
So small a drop is each man's share,
Few leavings you may think there are
To water these poor coffee plants;
But he supplies their gasping wants;
E'en from his own dry, parchéd lips
He spares it for his coffee slips.
Water he gives his nurslings first,
Ere he allays his own deep thirst;
Lest, if he first the water sip,
He bear too far his eager lip.
He sees them droop for want of more,
Yet, when they reach the destined shore,
With pride the heroic gardener sees
A living sap still in the trees.
The islanders his praise resound;
Coffee plantations rise around;
And Martinico loads her ships
With produce from those dear-saved slips.

THE BATTLE OF BLENHEIM. — *Southey.*

It was a summer evening,
  Old Kaspar's work was done,
And he before his cottage-door
  Was sitting in the sun;
And by him sported on the green
His little grandchild, Wilhelmine.

She saw her brother Peterkin
   Roll something large and round,
Which he beside the rivulet,
   In playing there, had found;
He came to ask what he had found,
That was so large, and smooth, and round.

Old Kaspar took it from the boy,
   Who stood expectant by;
And then the old man shook his head,
   And, with a natural sigh, —
" 'T is some poor fellow's skull," said he,
" Who fell in the great victory.

"I find them in the garden,
   For there 's many here about;
And often, when I go to plough,
   The ploughshare turns them out.
For many thousand men," said he,
" Were slain in that great victory."

" Now tell us what 't was all about,"
   Young Peterkin he cries;
And little Wilhelmine looks up,
   With wonder-waiting eyes;
" Now tell us all about the war,
And what they killed each other for."

"It was the English," Kaspar cried,
   "Who put the French to rout;
But what they killed each other for,
   I could not well make out.
But everybody said," quoth he,
" That 't was a famous victory.

"My father lived at Blenheim then,
  Yon little stream hard by;
They burned his dwelling to the ground,
  And he was forced to fly;
So with his wife and child he fled,
Nor had he where to rest his head.

"With fire and sword the country round
  Was wasted far and wide;
And many a hapless mother then,
  And new-born baby, died.
But things like that, you know, must be
At every famous victory.

"Great praise the Duke of Marlborough won,
  And our good Prince Eugene!"
"Why, 't was a very wicked thing!"
  Said little Wilhelmine.
"Nay, nay, my little girl," quoth he,
"It was a famous victory,

"And every body praised the Duke,
  Who this great fight did win."
"But what good came of it at last?"
  Quoth little Peterkin.
"Why, that I cannot tell," said he,
"But 't was a famous victory."

THE INCHCAPE ROCK. — *Southey.*

No stir in the air, no stir in the sea,
The ship was still as she could be;
Her sails from heaven received no motion,
Her keel was steady in the ocean.

Without either sign or sound of their shock,
The waves flowed over the Inchcape rock;
So little they rose, so little they fell,
They did not move the Inchcape bell.

The abbot of Aberbrothok
Had placed that bell on the Inchcape rock;
On a buoy in the storm it floated and swung,
And over the waves its warning rung.

When the rocks were hid by the surge's swell
The mariners heard the warning bell;
And then they knew the perilous rock,
And blessed the abbot of Aberbrothok.

The sun in heaven was shining gay,
All things were joyful on that day;
The sea-birds screamed as they wheeled round,
And there was joyance in their sound.

The buoy of the Inchcape bell was seen,
A darker speck on the ocean green;
Sir Ralph the Rover walked his deck,
And he fixed his eye on the darker speck.

He felt the cheering power of spring,
It made him whistle, it made him sing;
His heart was mirthful to excess,
But the Rover's mirth was wickedness.

His eye was on the Inchcape float;
Quoth he, — "My men, put out the boat,
And row me to the Inchcape rock,
And I'll plague the abbot of Aberbrothok."

The boat is lowered, the boatmen row,
And to the Inchcape rock they go;
Sir Ralph bent over from the boat,
And he cut the bell from the Inchcape float.

Down sunk the bell with a gurgling sound,
The bubbles rose and burst around;
Quoth Sir Ralph, — "The next who comes to
the rock
Wont bless the abbot of Aberbrothok."

Sir Ralph the Rover sailed away;
He scoured the seas for many a day;
And now, grown rich with plundered store,
He steers his course for Scotland's shore.

So thick a haze o'erspreads the sky,
They cannot see the sun on high;
The wind hath blown a gale all day,
At evening it hath died away.

On the deck the Rover takes his stand;
So dark it is they see no land;
Quoth Sir Ralph, — "It will be lighter soon,
For there is the dawn of the rising moon."

"Can'st hear," said one, "the breakers roar,
For methinks we should be near the shore?"
"Now where we are I cannot tell,
But I wish we could hear the Inchcape bell."

They hear no sound; the swell is strong;
Though the wind hath fallen, they drift along;
Till the vessel strikes with a shivering shock;
O Death! it is the Inchcape rock.

Sir Ralph the Rover tore his hair,
He cursed himself in his despair;
The waves rush in on every side,
The ship is sinking beneath the tide.

TO MY BIRDIE. — *Mrs. Southey.*

HERE 's only you an' me, Birdie! here 's only you an' me!
An' there you sit, you humdrum fowl!
Sae mute an' mopish as an owl, —
Sour companie!

Sing me a little song, Birdie! lift up a little lay!
When folks are here, fu' fain are ye
To stun them with your minstrelsie,
The lee lang day;

An' now we 're only twa, Birdie! an' now we 're only twa;
'T were sure but kind and cozie, Birdie!
To charm wi' yere wee hurdie-gurdie
Dull care awa'.

Ye ken when folks are paired, Birdie! ye ken when folks are paired,
Life's fair, an' foul, and freakish weather,
An' light an' lumbring loads, thegither
Maun a' be shared;

An' shared wi' looin' hearts, Birdie! wi' looin hearts and free,
Fu' fashious loads may weel be borne;
An' roughest roads to velvet turn,
Trod cheerfully.

We 've all our cares and crosses, Birdie! we 've a our cares an' crosses;
But then to sulk an' sit so glum,
Hout! tout! what guid o' that can come
To mend one's losses?

Ye 're clipt in wiry fence, Birdie! ye 're clipt in wiry fence,
An' aiblins I, gin I mote gang
Upo' a wish, wad be or lang
Wi' friends far hence;

But what 's a wish, ye ken, Birdie! but what 's a wish, ye ken,
Nae cantrip nag, like hers of Fife,
Who darnit wi' the auld weird wife,
Flood, fell, an' fen.

T is true ye 're furnished fair, Birdie! 't is true ye 're furnished fair,
Wi' a braw pair of bonnie wings
Wad lift ye whar yon lav'rock sings
High up i' th' air;

But then that wire 's sae strang, Birdie! but then that wire 's sae strang!
An' I myself, sae seemin' free, —
Nae wings have I to waften me
Whar fain I 'd gang.

An' sae we 'd baith our wills, Birdie! we 'd each our wilfu' way;
Whar lav'rocks hover, falcons fly;
An' snares an' pitfa's often lie
Whar wishes stray.

An' ae thing weel I wot, Birdie! an' ae thing weel I wot,
There 's ane abune the highest sphere
Wha cares for a' his creatures here,
Marks every lot;

Wha guards the crownéd king, Birdie! wha guards the crownéd king,
An' taketh heed for sic as me, —
Sae little worth, — an' e'en for thee,
Puir witless thing!

Sae now, let 's baith cheer up, Birdie! an' sin' we 're only twa
Aff han'— let 's ilk ane do our best,
To ding that crabbit, cankered pest,
Dull care awa'!

THE GRASSHOPPER. — *Cowley.*

HAPPY insect! what can be
In happiness compared to thee?
Fed with nourishment divine,
The dewy morning's gentle wine!
Nature waits upon thee still,
And thy verdant cup doth fill;

'T is filled wherever thou dost tread,
Nature's self 's thy Ganymede.
Thou dost drink, and dance, and sing;
Happier than the happiest king!
All the fields which thou dost see,
All the plants, belong to thee;
All that summer-hours produce,
Fertile made with early juice.
Man for thee does sow and plough:
Farmer he, and landlord thou!
Thou dost innocently joy,
Nor does thy luxury destroy;
The shepherd gladly heareth thee,
More harmonious than he.
Thee country hinds with gladness hear,
Prophet of the ripened year!
Thee Phœbus loves, and does inspire;
Phœbus is himself thy sire.
To thee, of all things upon earth,
Life is no longer than thy mirth.
Happy insect! happy thou
Dost neither age nor winter know;
But, when thou 'st drunk, and danced, and sung
Thy fill, the flowery leaves among,
Sated with thy summer feast,
Thou retir'st to endless rest.

THE CASTLE BY THE SEA.

FROM THE GERMAN OF UHLAND. TRANSLATED BY LONGFELLOW.

"Hast thou seen that lordly castle,
  That castle by the sea?
Golden and red above it
  The clouds float gorgeously.

"And fain it would stoop downward
  To the mirrored wave below;
And fain it would soar upward
  In the evening's crimson glow."

"Well have I seen that castle,
  That castle by the sea,
And the moon above it standing,
  And the mist rise solemnly."

"The winds and the waves of ocean,
  Had they a merry chime?
Didst thou hear, from those lofty chambers,
  The harp and the minstrel's rhyme?"

"The winds and the waves of ocean,
  They rested quietly;
But I heard on the gale a sound of wail,
  And tears came to mine eye."

"And sawest thou on the turrets
  The king and his royal bride?
And the wave of their crimson mantles?
  And the golden crown of pride?

"Led they not forth, in rapture,
  A beauteous maiden there,
Resplendent as the morning sun,
  Beaming with golden hair?"

"Well saw I the ancient parents,
  Without the crown of pride;
They were moving slow, in weeds of woe;
  No maiden was by their side!"

CASABIANCA. — *Mrs. Hemans.*

THE boy stood on the burning deck,
Whence all but him had fled;
The flame that lit the battle's wreck
Shone round him o'er the dead.

Yet beautiful and bright he stood,
As born to rule the storm;
A creature of heroic blood,
A proud, though childlike, form.

The flames rolled on, — he would not go,
Without his father's word;
That father, faint in death below,
His voice no longer heard.

He called aloud, — "Say, father, say
If yet my task is done!"
He knew not that the chieftain lay
Unconscious of his son.

"Speak, father!" once again he cried,
"If I may yet be gone,"—
And but the booming shots replied,
And fast the flames rolled on.

Upon his brow he felt their breath,
And in his waving hair,
And looked from that lone post of death
In still, yet brave despair.

And shouted but once more aloud,
"My father! must I stay?"
While o'er him fast, through sail and shroud,
The wreathing fires made way.

They wrapt the ship in splendor wild,
They caught the flag on high,
And streamed above the gallant child,
Like banners in the sky.

There came a burst of thunder sound;
The boy, — O, where was he?
Ask of the winds, that far around
With fragments strewed the sea!

With mast, and helm, and pennon fair,
That well had borne their part;
But the noblest thing that perished there
Was that young, faithful heart.

LAMENTATION FOR THE DEATH OF CELIN. — *Lockhart.*

At the gate of old Grenada, when all its bolts are barred,
At twilight, at the Vega-gate, there is a trampling heard;
There is a trampling heard, as of horses treading slow,
And a weeping voice of women, and a heavy sound of woe.
"What tower is fallen? what star is set? what chief come these bewailing?"
"A tower is fallen! A star is set! — Alas! alas for Celin!"

Three times they knock, three times they cry, the doors wide open throw;
Dejectedly they enter, and mournfully they go!
In gloomy lines they mustering stand beneath the hollow porch,
Each horseman holding in his hand a black and flaming torch.
Wet is each eye as they go by, and all around is wailing,
For all have heard the misery,—"Alas! alas for Celin!"

Him yesterday a Moor did slay, of Bencerrage's blood;
'T was at the solemn jousting; around the nobles stood;
The nobles of the land were there, and the ladies bright and fair
Looked from their latticed windows, the haughty sight to share;
But now the nobles all lament, the ladies are bewailing,
For he was Grenada's darling knight,—"Alas! alas for Celin!"

Before him ride his vassals, in order two by two,
With ashes on their turbans spread, most pitiful to view;
Behind him his four sisters, each wrapped in sable veil,
Between the tambour's dismal strokes take up their doleful tale;
When stops the muffled drum, ye hear their brotherless wailing,
And all the people, far and near, cry,—"Alas! alas for Celin!"

The Moorish maid at her lattice stands, the Moor stands at his door;
One maid is wringing of her hands, and one is weeping sore;

Down to the dust men bow their heads and ashes black they strew
Upon their broidered garments, of crimson, green, and blue;
Before each gate the bier stands still, then bursts the loud bewailing,
From door and lattice, high and low,—"Alas! alas for Celin!"

An old, old woman cometh forth, when she hears the people cry,
Her hair is white as silver, like horn her glazéd eye;
It's she who nursed him at her breast, who nursed him long ago;
She knows not whom they all lament, but ah! she soon shall know.
With one loud shriek, she forward breaks, when her ears receive their wailing,—
"Let me kiss my Celin ere I die!—Alas! alas for Celin!"

FLOWERS.—*Leigh Hunt.*

We are the sweet flowers,
Born of sunny showers,
(Think, whene'er you see us, what our beauty saith;)
Utterance mute and bright,
Of some unknown delight,
We fill the air with pleasure by our simple breath;
All who see us love us,—
We befit all places;
Unto sorrow we give smiles, and unto graces, graces.

Mark our ways, how noiseless
All, and sweetly voiceless,
Though the March-winds pipe, to make our passage clear;
Not a whisper tells
Where our small seed dwells,
Nor is known the moment green when our tips appear.
We thread the earth in silence,
In silence build our bowers, —
And leaf by leaf in silence show, till we laugh a-top, sweet flowers.

GLENARA.— *Campbell.*

O, HEARD ye yon pibroch sound sad in the gale,
Where a band cometh slowly with weeping and wail?
'T is the chief of Glenara laments for his dear;
And her sire and her people are called to the bier.

Glenara came first, with the mourners and shroud;
Her kinsmen they followed, but mourned not aloud;
Their plaids all their bosoms were folded around;
They marched all in silence, — they looked on the ground.

In silence they reached, over mountain and moor,
To a heath where the oak-tree grew lonely and hoar;
"Now here let us place the gray stone of her cairn; —
Why speak ye no word?" said Glenara the stern.

"And tell me, I charge ye, ye clan of my spouse,
Why fold ye your mantles, why cloud ye your brows?"
So spake the rude chieftain; no answer is made,
But each mantle, unfolding, a dagger displayed.

"I dreamt of my lady, I dreamt of her shroud,"
Cried a voice from the kinsmen, all wrathful and loud
"And empty that shroud and that coffin did seem;
Glenara! Glenara! now read me my dream!"

O, pale grew the cheek of that chieftain, I ween,
When the shroud was unclosed and no lady was seen;
When a voice from the kinsmen spoke louder in scorn,—
'Twas the youth who had loved the fair Ellen of Lorn,—

"I dreamt of my lady, I dreamt of her grief,
I dreamt that her lord was a barbarous chief;
On a rock of the ocean fair Ellen did seem;
Glenara! Glenara! now read me my dream!"

In dust low the traitor has knelt to the ground,
And the desert revealed where his lady was found;
From a rock of the ocean that lady is borne;
Now joy to the house of fair Ellen of Lorn.

TO THE GRASSHOPPER AND CRICKET.—*Hunt.*

GREEN little vaulter in the sunny grass,
Catching your heart up at the feel of June,
Sole voice that's heard amidst the lazy noon,
When even the bees lag at the summoning brass;
And you, warm little housekeeper, who class
With those who think the candles come too soon,
Loving the fire, and with your tricksome tune
Nick the glad silent moments as they pass.

O sweet and tiny cousins, that belong,
One to the fields, the other to the hearth,
Both have your sunshine, both, though small, are strong
At your clear hearts; and both seem given to earth
To sing in thoughtful ears this natural song, —
In doors and out, summer and winter — mirth.

LORD ULLEN'S DAUGHTER. — *Campbell.*

A CHIEFTAIN to the Highlands bound
Cries, "Boatman, do not tarry,
And I'll give thee a silver pound
To row us o'er the ferry."

"Now who be ye would cross Lochgyle,
This dark and stormy water?"
"O, I'm the chief of Ulva's Isle,
And this Lord Ullen's daughter.

"And fast before her father's men
Three days we've fled together;
For should he find us in the glen,
My blood would stain the heather.

"His horsemen fast behind us ride, —
Should they our steps discover,
Then who will cheer my bonny bride
When they have slain her lover?"

Outspoke the hardy Highland wight,
"I'll go, my chief, — I'm ready, —
It is not for your silver bright,
But for your winsome lady!

"And, by my word, the bonny bird
 In danger shall not tarry;
So, though the waves are raging white,
 I 'll row you o'er the ferry."

By this the storm grew loud apace,
 The water-wraith was shrieking;
And in the scowl of heaven each face
 Grew dark as they were speaking.

But still, as wilder blew the wind,
 And as the night grew drearer,
Adown the glen rode armèd men, —
 Their trampling sounded nearer.

"O, haste thee, haste," the lady cries,
 "Though tempests round us gather;
I 'll meet the raging of the skies,
 But not an angry father."

The boat has left a stormy land,
 A stormy sea before her, —
When, O, too strong for human hand,
 The tempest gathered o'er her!

And still they rowed, amidst the roar
 Of waters fast prevailing;
Lord Ullen reached that fatal shore,
 His wrath was changed to wailing.

For, sore dismayed, through storm and sh
 His child he did discover;
One lovely hand she stretched for aid,
 And one was round her lover.

"Come back! come back!" he cried in grief,
"Across this stormy water;
And I'll forgive your Highland chief,—
My daughter! O my daughter!"

'T was vain; the loud waves lashed the shore,
Return or aid preventing;
The waters wild went o'er his child,—
And he was left lamenting.

TO THE FRINGED GENTIAN.—*Bryant.*

Thou blossom bright with autumn dew,
And colored with the heavens' own blue,
That openest when the quiet light
Succeeds the keen and frosty night.

Thou comest not when violets lean
O'er wandering brooks and springs unseen,
Or columbines, in purple dressed,
Nod o'er the ground-bird's hidden nest.

Thou waitest late, and com'st alone,
When woods are bare and birds are flown,
And frosts and shortening days portend
The aged year is near his end.

Then doth thy sweet and quiet eye
Look through its fringes to the sky,
Blue,—blue,—as if that sky let fall
A flower from its cerulean wall.

I would that thus, when I shall see
The hour of death draw near to me,
Hope, blossoming within my heart,
May look to heaven as I depart.

MY DOVES.—*Miss Barrett.*

My little doves have left a nest
  Upon an Indian tree,
Whose leaves fantastic take their rest
  Or motion from the sea;
Forever there the sea winds go,
With sunlit faces, to and fro.

The tropic flowers looked up to it,
  The tropic stars looked down;
And there my little doves did sit,
  With feathers softly brown;
And glittering eyes, that showed their right
To general nature's deep delight.

And God them taught, at every close
  Of water far, and wind,
And lifted leaf, to interpose
  Their chanting voices kind;
Interpreting that love must be
The meaning of the earth and sea.

Fit ministers! of living loves
  Theirs hath the calmest sound,—
Their living voice the likest moves
  To lifeless noises round,—
In such sweet monotone as clings
To music of insensate things!

My little doves were taken away
  From that glad nest of theirs;
Across an ocean foaming aye,
  And tempest-clouded airs.
My little doves! who lately knew
The sky and wave by warmth and blue

And now, within the city prison
  In mist and chillness pent,
With sudden upward look they listen
  For sounds of past content,—
Nor lapse of water, swell of breeze,
Or nut-fruit falling from the trees!

The stir without, the glow of passion,—
  The triumph of the mart,—
The gold and silver's dreary clashing
  With man's metallic heart,—
The wheeléd pomp, the pauper tread,—
These only sounds are heard instead.

Yet still, as on my human hand
  Their fearless heads they lean,
And almost seem to understand
  What human musings mean,—
With such a plaintive gaze their eyne
Are fastened upwardly to mine!

Their chant is soft as on the nest
  Beneath the sunny sky;
For love, that stirred it in their breast,
  Remains undyingly,
And, 'neath the city's shade, can keep
The well of music clear and deep.

And love, that keeps the music, fills
  With pastoral memories!
All echoings from out the hills,
  All droppings from the skies,
All flowings from the wave and wind,
Remembered in their chant I find.

So teach ye me the wisest part,
  My little doves! to move
Along the city ways, with heart
  Assured by holy love,
And vocal with such songs as own
A fountain to the world unknown.

To me fair memories belong
  Of scenes that erst did bless;
For no regret, — but present song,
  And lasting thankfulness, —
And very soon to break away,
Like types, in purer things than they

I will have hopes that cannot fade,
  For flowers the valley yields, —
I will have humble thoughts, instead
  Of silent, dewy fields!
My spirit and my God shall be
My seaward hill, my boundless sea.

TROUBADOUR SONG. — *Mrs. Hemans.*

The warrior crossed the ocean's foam
  For the stormy fields of war, —
The maid was left in a smiling home,
  And a sunny land, afar.

His voice was heard where javelin-showers
Poured on the steel-clad line;
Her step was 'midst the summer-flowers,
Her seat beneath the vine.

His shield was cleft, his lance was riven,
And the red blood stained his crest;
While she — the gentlest wind of heaven
Might scarcely fan her breast.

Yet a thousand arrows passed him by,
And again he crossed the seas;
But she had died, as roses die,
That perish with a breeze.

As roses die, when the blast is come
For all things bright and fair, —
There was death within the smiling home,
How had death found her there?

HUMAN FRAILTY. — *Cowper.*

Weak and irresolute is man,
The purpose of to-day,
Woven with pains into his plan,
To-morrow rends away.

The bow well bent and smart the spring,
Vice seems already slain;
But passion rudely snaps the string,
And it revives again.

Some foe to his upright intent
   Finds out his weaker part;
Virtue engages his assent,
   But pleasure wins his heart.

'T is here the folly of the wise,
   Through all his art, we view;
And while his tongue the charge denies,
   His conscience owns it true.

Bound on a voyage of awful length,
   And dangers little known,
A stranger to superior strength,
   Man vainly trusts his own.

But oars alone can ne'er prevail
   To reach the distant coast;
The breath of heaven must swell the sail,
   Or all the toil is lost.

THE UNIVERSAL PRAYER.—*Pope.*

Father of all! in every age,
   In every clime, adored,
By saint, by savage, and by sage,
   Jehovah, Jove, or Lord!

Thou great First Cause, least understood,
   Who all my sense confined
To know but this, that thou art good,
   And that myself am blind;

Yet gave me, in this dark estate,
   To see the good from ill;
And, binding nature fast in fate,
   Left free the human will.

What conscience dictates to be done,
Or warns me not to do,
This teach me more than hell to shun,
That, more than heaven pursue.

What blessings thy free bounty gives,
Let me not cast away;
For God is paid when man receives, —
To enjoy is to obey.

Yet not to earth's contracted span
Thy goodness let me bound;
Or think thee Lord alone of man,
When thousand worlds are round.

Let not this weak, unknowing hand
Presume thy bolts to throw,
And deal damnation round the land
On each I judge thy foe.

If I am right, thy grace impart
Still in the right to stay;
If I am wrong, O, teach my heart
To find that better way.

Save me alike from foolish pride,
Or impious discontent
At aught thy wisdom has denied,
Or aught thy goodness lent.

Teach me to feel another's woe;
To hide the fault I see;
That mercy I to others show,
That mercy show to me.

Mean though I am, not wholly so,
   Since quickened by thy breath;
O, lead me, wheresoe'er I go,—
   Through this day's life or death.

This day be bread and peace my lot;
   All else beneath the sun
Thou know'st if best bestowed or not,
   And let thy will be done.

To Thee, whose temple is all space,
   Whose altar, earth, sea, skies!
One chorus let all being raise!
   All nature's incense rise!

SIR PATRICK SPENCE.

The king sits in Dunfermline town,
   Drinking the blude-red wine:
"O, where shall I get a skeely skipper
   To sail this ship of mine?"

O, up and spake an eldern knight,—
   Sat at the king's right knee,—
"Sir Patrick Spence is the best sailor
   That sails upon the sea."

The king has written a braid letter,
   And sealed it with his hand;
And sent it to Sir Patrick Spence,
   Was walking on the strand.

"To Noroway, to Noroway,
   To Noroway o'er the faem;
The king's daughter of Noroway,
   'T is thou maun bring her hame."

The first line that Sir Patrick read,
  Sae loud, loud, laughed he;
The next line that Sir Patrick read,
  The tear blinded his e'e.

"O, wha is this has done this deed,
  This ill deed done to me;
To send me out, this time o' the year,
  To sail upon the sea?

"Be it wind, be it weet, be it hail, be it sleet,
  Our ship must sail the faem;
The king's daughter of Noroway,
  'T is we must fetch her hame.

"Make ready, make ready, my merry men all!
  Our gude ship sails the morn."
"Now, ever alake, my master dear,
  I fear a deadly storm.

"Late, late yestreen, I saw the new moon
  Wi' the old moon in her arm;
And I fear, I fear, my dear master,
  That we will come to harm."

They hadna sailed a league, a league,
  A league but barely three,
When the lift grew dark, and the wind blew loud,
  And gurly grew the sea.

The anchors brak, and the topmasts lap,
  It was sik a deadly storm;
And the waves came o'er the broken ship,
  Till all her sides were torn.

"O, where will I get a gude sailor
To take my helm in hand,
Till I get up to the tall top-mast;
To see if I can spy land?"

"O, here am I, a sailor gude,
To take the helm in hand,
Till you go up to the tall top-mast;
But I fear you 'll ne'er spy land."

He hadna gone a step, a step,
A step but barely ane,
When a bout flew out of our goodly ship,
And the salt sea it came in.

"Gae, fetch a web o' the silken claith,
Another o' the twine,
And wap them into our ship's side,
And let nae the sea come in."

They fetched a web o' the silken claith,
Another o' the twine,
And they wapped them round that gude ship's side
And still the sea came in.

O, laith, laith, were our gude Scots lords
To weet their cork-heeled shoon!
But lang or a' the play was played,
They wat their hats aboon.

And mony was the feather-bed
That flattered on the faem;
And mony was the gude lord's son,
That never mair came hame.

The ladies wrang their fingers white,
  The maidens tore their hair,
A' for the sake of their true loves,
  For them they 'll see nae mair.

O, lang, lang, may the ladies sit,
  Wi' their fans into their hand,
Before they see Sir Patrick Spence
  Come sailing to the land.

And lang, lang, may the maidens sit,
  Wi' their gold kaims in their hair,
A' waiting for their ain dear loves!
  For they 'll see them nae mair.

O, forty miles off Aberdeen,
  'T is fifty fathoms deep,
And there lies gude Sir Patrick Spence,
  Wi' the Scots lords at his feet.

LUCY. — *Wordsworth.*

She dwelt among the untrodden ways
  Beside the springs of Dove,
A maid whom there were none to praise
  And very few to love, —

A violet by a mossy stone
  Half hidden from the eye!
Fair as a star, when only one
  Is shining in the sky.

She lived unknown, — and few could know
When Lucy ceased to be;
But she is in her grave, and, O,
The difference to me!

I travelled among unknown men,
In lands beyond the sea;
Nor, England! did I know till then
What love I bore to thee.

'T is past, that melancholy dream!
Nor will I quit thy shore
A second time; for still I seem
To love thee more and more.

Among thy mountains did I feel
The joy of my desire;
And she I cherished turned her wheel
Beside an English fire.

Thy morning showed, thy nights concealed,
The bowers where Lucy played;
And thine, too, is the last green field
That Lucy's eyes surveyed.

TO A MOUSE,

ON HER NEST BEING TURNED UP BY A PLOUGH. — *Burns*

Wee, sleekit, cow'rin, timorous beastie,
O, what a panic 's in thy breastie!
Thou need na start awa sae hastie,
Wi' bickering brattle!
I wad be laith to rin and chase thee,
Wi' murdering pattle!

I 'm truly sorry man's dominion
Has broken nature's social union,
An' justifies that ill opinion
Which makes thee startle
At me, thy poor earth-born companion
An' fellow-mortal!

I doubt na, whyles, but thou may thieve;
What then? poor beastie, thou maun live;
A daimen-icker[1] in a thrave
'S a sma' request;
I 'll get a blessing wi' the lave,[2]
An' never miss 't!

Thy wee-bit housie, too, in ruin,
Its silly wa's the wins are strewin;
An' naething, now, to big[3] a new ane,
O' foggage green!
An' bleak December's wind ensuin',
Baith snell[4] and keen!

Thou saw the fields laid bare an' waste,
An' weary winter comin' fast,
An' cozie here, beneath the blast,
Thou thought to dwell
Till, crash! the cruel coulter past
Out thro' thy cell.

That wee-bit heap o' leaves an' stibble
Has cost thee mony a weary nibble!
Now thou 's turned out, for a' thy trouble
But[5] house or hald,
To thole[6] the winter's sleety dribble,
An' cranreuch[7] cauld:

---

[1] ..n ear of corn, now and then. [2] Rest. [3] Build. [4] ..iting. [5] Without. [6] Endure. [7] Hoar-frost

But, mousie, thou art no thy lane,[1]
In proving foresight may be vain;
The best laid schemes o' mice an' men
Gang aft a-gley,[2]
An' leave us naught but grief an' pain
For promised joy.

Still thou art blessed, compared with me!
The present only toucheth thee;
But, Och! I backward cast my e'e
On prospects drear,—
An' forward, tho' I canna see,
I guess an' fear.

TO A MOUNTAIN DAISY,

TURNED DOWN BY A PLOUGH.—*Burns.*

Wee, modest, crimson-tippéd flower,
Thou 's met me in an evil hour;
For I maun crush amang the stoure[3]
Thy slender stem:
To spare thee now is past my power,
Thou bonnie gem!

Alas, it 's not thy neebor sweet,
The bonnie lark, companion meet!
Bending thee 'mang the dewy weet!
Wi' speckled breast,
When upward springing, blythe, to greet
The purpling east.

---

1 Alone. 2 Wrong. 3 Dust.

Cauld blew the bitter, biting north
Upon thy early humble birth;
Yet cheerfully thou glinted[1] forth,
Amid the storm!
Scarce reared above the parent earth
Thy tender form.

The flaunting flowers our gardens yield,
High sheltering woods and wa's maun shield;
But thou, beneath the random bield[2]
O' clod or stane,
Adorns the histie[3] stibble-field,
Unseen, alane.

There, in thy scanty mantle clad,
Thy snawie bosom sunward spread,
Thou lifts thy unassuming head
In humble guise;
But now the share uptears thy bed,
And low thou lies!

Such is the fate of simple bard,
On life's rough ocean luckless starred!
Unskilful he to note the card
Of prudent lore,
Till billows rage, and gales blow hard,
And whelm him o'er.

Such fate to suffering worth is given,
Who long with wants and woes has striven;
By human pride or cunning driven
To mis'ry's brink;
Till, wrenched of every stay but Heaven,
He, ruined, sink.

---

[1] Peeped. [2] Shelter. [3] Barren.

E'en thou who mourn'st the daisy's fate,
That fate is thine, — no distant date;
Stern ruin's ploughshare drives, elate,
Full on thy bloom;
Till crushed beneath the furrow's weight
Shall be thy doom!

THE GRAVES OF A HOUSEHOLD. — *Mrs. Hemans*

They grew in beauty, side by side,
They filled one home with glee, —
Their graves are severed far and wide,
By mount, and stream, and sea.

The same fond mother bent at night
O'er each fair sleeping brow;
She had each folded flower in sight, —
Where are those dreamers now?

One, 'midst the forests of the west,
By a dark stream, is laid, —
The Indian knows his place of rest,
Far in the cedar shade.

The sea, the blue, lone sea, hath one,
He lies where pearls lie deep, —
He was the loved of all, yet none
O'er his low bed may weep.

One sleeps where southern vines are drest,
Above the noble slain;
He wrapped his colors round his breast,
On a blood-red field of Spain.

And one, — o'er *her* the myrtle showers
  Its leaves, by soft winds fanned;
She faded 'midst Italian flowers,
  The last of that bright band.

And parted thus they rest, who played
  Beneath the same green tree;
Whose voices mingled as they prayed
  About one parent knee!

They that with smiles lit up the hall,
  And cheered with song the hearth, —
Alas for love, if *thou* wert all,
  And naught beyond, O Earth!

THE SOLITARY REAPER. — *Wordsworth.*

BEHOLD her, single in the field,
Yon solitary Highland lass!
Reaping and singing by herself;
Stop here, or gently pass!
Alone she cuts and binds the grain,
And sings a melancholy strain;
O, listen! for the vale profound
Is overflowing with the sound.

No nightingale did ever chant
More welcome notes to weary bands
Of travellers, in some shady haunt
Among Arabian sands;
Such thrilling voice was never heard
In spring-time from the cuckoo bird,

Breaking the silence of the seas
Among the farthest Hebrides.

Will no one tell me what she sings?
Perhaps the plaintive numbers flow
For old, unhappy, far-off things,
And battles long ago,—
Or is it some more humble lay,
Familiar matter of to-day?
Some natural sorrow, loss, or pain,
That has been, and may be again!

Whate'er the theme, the maiden sang
As if her song could have no ending;
I saw her singing at her work,
And o'er the sickle bending;—
I listened,—motionless and still;
And when I mounted up the hill,
The music in my heart I bore,
Long after it was heard no more.

THE ADOPTED CHILD.—*Mrs. Hemans.*

'Why wouldst thou leave me, O gentle child?
Thy home on the mountains is bleak and wild,
A straw-roofed cabin with lowly wall;—
Mine is a fair and a pillared hall,
Where many an image of marble gleams,
And the sunshine of picture forever streams."

"O, green is the turf where my brothers play,
Through the long bright hours of the summer day;
They find the red cup-moss where they climb,
And they chase the bee o'er the scented thyme;

And the rocks where the heathflower blooms they know, —
Lady, kind lady! O, let me go!"

"Content thee, boy! in my bower to dwell;
Here are sweet sounds which thou lovest well;
Flutes on the air in the stilly noon,
Harps which the wandering breezes tune;
And the silvery wood-note of many a bird,
Whose voice was ne'er in thy mountains heard."

"My mother sings, at the twilight's fall,
A song of the hills, far more sweet than all;
She sings it under our own green tree,
To the babe half slumbering on her knee;
I dreamt last night of that music low, —
Lady, kind lady! O, let me go!"

"Thy mother is gone from her cares to rest,
She hath taken the babe on her quiet breast;
Thou wouldst meet her footstep, my boy, no more,
Nor hear her song at the cabin-door.
Come thou with me to the vineyards nigh,
And we 'll pluck the grapes of the richest dye."

"Is my mother gone from her home away? —
But I know that my brothers are there at play,
I know they are gathering the foxglove's bell,
Or the long fern leaves by the sparkling well,
Or they launch their boats where the bright streams flow, —
Lady, kind lady! O, let me go!"

"Fair child! thy brothers are wanderers now,
They sport no more on the mountain's brow;

They have left the fern by the spring's green side,
And the streams where the fairy barks were tried.
Be thou at peace in thy brighter lot,
For thy cabin home is a lonely spot."

"Are they gone, all gone from the sunny hill?—
But the bird and the blue fly rove o'er it still,
And the red deer bound in their gladness free,
And the turf is bent by the singing bee,
And the waters leap, and the fresh winds blow,—
Lady, kind lady! O, let me go!"

PSALM CXLVIII.

VERSIFIED BY SANDYS, BORN IN 1577.

You who dwell above the skies,
Free from human miseries;
You whom highest heaven embowers,
Praise the Lord with all your powers!
Angels, your clear voices raise!
Him you heavenly armies praise!
Sun, and moon with borrowed light,
All you sparkling eyes of night,
Waters hanging in the air,
Heaven of heavens, his praise declare!
His deservéd praise record,
His, who made you by his word,—
Made you evermore to last,
Set your bounds not to be past.
Let the earth his praise resound!
Monstrous whales, and seas profound,
Vapors, lightning, hail and snow,
Storms, which, when he bids them, blow;

Flowery hills, and mountains high,
Cedars, neighbors to the sky,
Trees, that fruit in season yield,
All the cattle of the field,
Savage beasts, all creeping things,
All that cut the air with wings;
You who awful sceptres sway,
You, inured to obey,
Princes, judges of the earth,
All, of high and humble birth;
Youth, and virgins, flourishing
In the beauty of your spring;
You who bow with age's weight,
You who were but born of late;
Praise his name with one consent!
O, how great! how excellent!

PEACE OF MIND. — *From Old English Poetry.*

My mind to me a kingdom is;
  Such perfect joy therein I find
As far exceeds all earthly bliss
  That God or nature hath assigned:
Though much I want that most would have,
Yet still my mind forbids to crave.

Content I live, this is my stay;
  I seek no more than may suffice;
I press to bear no haughty sway;
  Look what I lack my mind supplies
Lo! thus I triumph like a king,
Content with that my mind doth bring.

I see how plenty surfeits oft,
  And hasty climbers soonest fall;
I see that such as sit aloft
  Mishap doth threaten most of all;
These get with toil, and keep with fear;
Such cares my mind could never bear.

No princely pomp, nor wealthy store,
  No force to win a victory,
No wily wit to salve a sore,
  No shape to win a lover's eye;
To none of these I yield as thrall,
For why? my mind despiseth all.

Some have too much, yet still they crave;
  I little have, yet seek no more;
They are but poor, though much they have;
  And I am rich with little store;
They poor, I rich; they beg, I give;
They lack, I lend; they pine, I live.

I laugh not at another's loss,
  I grudge not at another's gain;
No worldly wave my mind can toss;
  I brook that is another's bane.
I fear no foe, nor fawn no friend;
I loathe not life, nor dread mine end.

My wealth is health and perfect ease;
  My conscience clear my chief defence;
I never seek by bribes to please,
  Nor by desert to give offence;
Thus do I live, thus will I die;
Would all did so as well as I!

I take no joy in earthly bliss;
  I weigh not Crœsus' wealth a straw;

For care, I care not what it is;
  I fear not Fortune's fatal law.
My mind is such as may not move
For beauty bright, or force of love.

I wish but what I have at will;
  I wander not to seek for more;
I like the plain, I climb no hill;
  In greatest storms I sit on shore,
And laugh at them that toil in vain
To get what must be lost again.

I kiss not where I wish to kill;
  I feign not love where most I hate;
I break no sleep to win my will;
  I wait not at the mighty's gate;
I scorn no poor, I fear no rich;
I feel no want, nor have too much.

The court, ne cart, I like ne loathe;
  Extremes are counted worst of all;
The golden mean betwixt them both
  Doth surest sit, and fears no fall;
This is my choice; for why? I find
No wealth is like a quiet mind.

AN ELEGY WRITTEN IN A COUNTRY CHURCHYARD. — *Gray.*

The curfew tolls the knell of parting day,
  The lowing herd winds slowly o'er the lea,
The ploughman homeward plods his weary way,
  And leaves the world to darkness and to me.

Now fades the glimmering landscape on the sight,
  And all the air a solemn stillness holds,
Save where the beetle wheels his drony flight,
  And drowsy tinklings lull the distant folds;

Save that, from yonder ivy-mantled tower,
  The moping owl does to the moon complain
Of such as, wandering near her secret bower,
  Molest her ancient, solitary reign.

Beneath those rugged elms, that yew-tree's shade,
  Where heaves the turf in many a mouldering heap,
Each in his narrow cell forever laid,
  The rude forefathers of the hamlet sleep.

The breezy call of incense-breathing morn,
  The swallow, twittering from the straw-built shed,
The cock's shrill clarion, or the echoing horn,
  No more shall rouse them from their lowly bed.

For them no more the blazing hearth shall burn,
  Nor busy housewife ply her evening care;
No children run to lisp their sire's return,
  Or climb his knees the envied kiss to share.

Oft did the harvest to their sickle yield;
  Their furrow oft the stubborn glebe has broke;
How jocund did they drive their teams afield!
  How bowed the woods beneath their sturdy stroke!

Let not Ambition mock their useful toil,
  Their homely joys, and destiny obscure;
Nor Grandeur hear with a disdainful smile
  The short and simple annals of the poor.

The boast of heraldry, the pomp of power,
  And all that beauty, all that wealth, e'er gave,
Await alike the inevitable hour;
  The paths of glory lead but to the grave,

Nor you, ye proud, impute to these the fault,
  If memory o'er their tomb no trophies raise,
Where, through the long-drawn aisle and fretted vault,
  The pealing anthem swells the note of praise.

Can storied urn, or animated bust,
  Back to its mansion call the fleeting breath?
Can honor's voice provoke the silent dust,
  Or flattery soothe the dull, cold ear of death?

Perhaps in this neglected spot is laid
  Some heart once pregnant with celestial fire;
Hands that the rod of empire might have swayed,
  Or waked to ecstasy the living lyre.

But Knowledge to their eyes her ample page,
  Rich with the spoils of time, did ne'er unroll;
Chill Penury repressed their noble rage,
  And froze the genial current of the soul,

Full many a gem, of purest ray serene,
  The dark, unfathomed caves of ocean bear;
Full many a flower is born to blush unseen,
  And waste its fragrance on the desert air.

Some village Hampden,* that with dauntless breast
  The little tyrant of his fields withstood;
Some mute, inglorious Milton here may rest;
  Some Cromwell, guiltless of his country's blood.

---

*An English patriot, who resisted King Charles the First's usurpation of power.

The applause of listening senates to command,
  The threats of pain and ruin to despise,
To scatter plenty o'er a smiling land,
  And read their history in a nation's eyes,

Their lot forbade; nor circumscribed alone
  Their growing virtues, but their crimes confined;
Forbade to wade through slaughter to a throne,
  And shut the gates of mercy on mankind;

The struggling pangs of conscious Truth to hide,
  To quench the blushes of ingenuous Shame,
Or heap the shrine of Luxury and Pride
  With incense kindled at the Muses' flame.

Far from the madding crowd's ignoble strife,
  Their sober wishes never learned to stray;
Along the cool, sequestered vale of life
  They kept the noiseless tenor of their way.

Yet e'en these bones from insult to protect,
  Some frail memorial still erected nigh,
With uncouth rhymes and shapeless sculpture decked,
  Implores the passing tribute of a sigh.

Their name, their years, spelt by the unlettered Muse
  The place of fame and elegy supply;
And many a holy text around she strews,
  That teach the rustic moralist to die.

For who, to dumb forgetfulness a prey,
  This pleasing, anxious being e'er resigned,
Left the warm precincts of the cheerful day,
  Nor cast one longing, lingering look behind?

On some fond breast the parting soul relies,
  Some pious drops the closing eye requires;
E'en from the tomb the voice of Nature cries,
  E'en in our ashes live their wonted fires.

For thee, who, mindful of the unhonored dead,
  Dost in these lines their artless tale relate,
If, chance, by lonely contemplation led,
  Some kindred spirit should inquire thy fate,

Haply some hoary-headed swain may say, —
  "Oft have we seen him, at the peep of dawn,
Brushing with hasty steps the dews away,
  To meet the sun upon the upland lawn.

"There, at the foot of yonder nodding beech,
  That wreathes its old, fantastic roots so high,
His listless length at noontide would he stretch,
  And pore upon the brook that babbles by.

"Hard by yon wood, now smiling, as in scorn,
  Muttering his wayward fancies, he would rove;
Now drooping, woful-wan, like one forlorn,
  Or crazed with care, or crossed in hopeless love.

"One morn I missed him on the 'customed hill,
  Along the heath, and near his favorite tree;
Another came; nor yet beside the rill,
  Nor up the lawn, nor at the wood, was he.

"The next, with dirges due, in sad array,
  Slow through the church-way path we saw him borne;
Approach and read (for thou canst read) the lay,
  Graved on the stone beneath yon aged thorn.

"There scattered oft, the earliest of the year,
By hands unseen, are showers of violets found;
The redbreast loves to build and warble there,
And little footsteps lightly print the ground."

THE EPITAPH.

Here rests his head upon the lap of earth,
A youth, to fortune and to fame unknown;
Fair Science frowned not on his humble birth,
And Melancholy marked him for her own.

Large was his bounty, and his soul sincere;
Heaven did a recompense as largely send;—
He gave to misery all he had,—a tear;
He gained from Heaven ('t was all he wished) a friend.

No further seek his merits to disclose,
Or draw his frailties from their dread abode,
(There they alike in trembling hope repose,)
The bosom of his Father and his God.

YE MARINERS OF ENGLAND.—*Campbell.*

Ye Mariners of England!
That guard our native seas;
Whose flag has braved, a thousand years,
The battle and the breeze:
Your glorious standard launch again,
To match another foe!
And sweep through the deep,
While the stormy tempests blow;

While the battle rages loud and long,
And the stormy tempests blow.

The spirit of your fathers
Shall start from every wave:
For the deck it was their field of fame,
And ocean was their grave;
Where Blake and mighty Nelson fell
Your manly hearts shall glow,—
As ye sweep through the deep,
While the stormy tempests blow;
While the battle rages loud and long,
And the stormy tempests blow.

Britannia needs no bulwark,—
No towers along the steep;
Her march is o'er the mountain-waves,
Her home is on the deep.
With thunders from her native oak
She quells the floods below,—
As they roar on the shore,
When the stormy tempests blow;
When the battle rages loud and long,
And the stormy tempests blow.

The meteor flag of England
Shall yet terrific burn,
Till danger's troubled night depart,
And the star of peace return.
Then, then, ye ocean warriors,
Our song and feast shall flow
To the fame of your name,
When the storm has ceased to blow,
When the fiery fight is heard no more,
And the storm has ceased to blow.

ON MUNGO PARK'S FINDING A TUFT OF GREEN MOSS IN THE AFRICAN DESERT.—*Edinburgh Christian Herald.*

THE sun had reached its midday height,
And poured down floods of burning light
On Afric's burning land;
No cloudy veil obscured the sky,
And the hot breeze that struggled by
Was filled with glowing sand.

No mighty rock upreared its head
To bless the wanderer with its shade,
In all the weary plain;
No palm-trees, with refreshing green,
To glad the dazzled eyes, were seen,—
But one wide, sandy main.

Dauntless and daring was the mind
That left all home-born joys behind
Those deserts to explore;
To trace the mighty Niger's course,
And find it bubbling from its source
In wilds untrod before.

And, ah! shall we less daring show,
Who nobler ends and motives know
Than ever heroes dream;
Who seek to lead the savage mind
The precious fountain-head to find
Whence flows salvation's stream?

Let peril, nakedness, and sword,
Hot, barren lands, and despot's word,
Our burning zeal oppose;

Yet, martyr-like, we 'll lift the voice,
Bidding the wilderness rejoice,
And blossom as the rose.

Sad, faint, and weary, on the sand
Our traveller sat him down; his hand
Covered his burning head;
Above, beneath, behind, around,
No resting for the eye he found;
All nature seemed as dead.

One tiny tuft of moss alone,
Mantling with freshest green a stone,
Fixed his delighted gaze;
Through bursting tears of joy he smiled,
And, while he raised the tendril wild,
His lips o'erflowed with praise.

O, shall not He who keeps thee green,
Here in the waste, unknown, unseen,
Thy fellow-exile save?
He who commands the dew to feed
Thy gentle flower can surely lead
Me from a scorching grave.

The heaven-sent plant new hope inspired,
New courage all his bosom fired,
And bore him safe along,—
Till, with the evening's cooling shade,
He slept within the verdant glade,
Lulled by the negro's song.

Thus we, in this world's wilderness,
Where sin and sorrow, — guilt, — distress,
Seem undisturbed to reign,

May faint because we feel alone,
With none to strike our favorite tone,
And join our homeward strain.

Yet often, in the bleakest wild
Of this dark world, some heaven-born child,
Expectant of the skies,
Amid the low and vicious crowd,
Or in the dwellings of the proud,
Meets our admiring eyes.

From gazing on the tender flower,
We lift our eye to Him whose power
Hath all its beauty given;
Who in this atmosphere of death
Hath given it life, and form, and breath,
And brilliant hues of heaven.

Our drooping faith, revived by sight,
Anew her pinions plumes for flight,
New hope distends the breast;
With joy we mount on eagle wing,
With bolder tone our anthem sing,
And seek the pilgrim's rest.

LANDING OF THE PILGRIM FATHERS. — *Mrs. Hemans.*

The breaking waves dashed high
On a stern and rock-bound coast,
And the woods against a stormy sky
Their giant branches tost;

And the heavy night hung dark
  The hills and waters o'er,
When a band of exiles moored their bark
  On the wild New England shore.

Not as the conqueror comes,
  They, the true-hearted, came;
Not with the roll of stirring drums,
  And the trumpet that sings of fame;

Not as the flying come,
  In silence and in fear, —
They shook the depths of the desert's gloom
  With their hymns of lofty cheer.

Amidst the storm they sang,
  And the stars heard and the sea!
And the sounding aisles of the dim wood rang
  To the anthems of the free!

The ocean-eagle soared
  From his nest by the white wave's foam,
And the rocking pines of the forest roared, —
  This was their welcome home!

There were men with hoary hair
  Amidst that pilgrim-band; —
Why had they come to wither there,
  Away from their childhood's land?

There was woman's fearless eye,
  Lit by her deep love's truth;
There was manhood's brow serenely high,
  And the fiery heart of youth.

What sought they thus afar?
   Bright jewels of the mine?
The wealth of seas, the spoils of war?—
   They sought a faith's pure shrine!

Ay, call it holy ground,
   The soil where first they trod!
They have left unstained what there they found,—
   Freedom to worship God!

A CHILD'S FIRST IMPRESSION OF A STAR.—*Willis*

SHE had been told that God made all the stars
That twinkled up in heaven, and now she stood
Watching the coming of the twilight on,
As if it were a new and perfect world,
And this were its first eve. How beautiful
Must be the work of nature to a child
In its first fresh impression! Laura stood
By the low window, with the silken lash
Of her soft eye upraised, and her sweet mouth
Half parted with the new and strange delight
Of beauty that she could not comprehend,
And had not seen before. The purple folds
Of the low sunset clouds, and the blue sky
That looked so still and delicate above,
Filled her young heart with gladness, and the eve
Stole on with its deep shadows, and she still
Stood looking at the west with that half smile,
As if a pleasant thought were at her heart.
Presently, in the edge of the last tint
Of sunset, where the blue was melted in

To the first golden mellowness, a star
Stood suddenly. A laugh of wild delight
Burst from her lips, and, putting up her hands,
Her simple thought broke forth expressively,—
"Father, dear father, God has made a star."

TO A CHILD DURING SICKNESS.—*Leigh Hunt.*

Sleep breathes at last from out thee,
My little, patient boy!
And balmy rest about thee
Smooths off the day's annoy.
I sit me down, and think
Of all thy winning ways;
Yet almost wish, with sudden shrink,
That I had less to praise.

Thy sidelong, pillowed meekness,
Thy thanks to all that aid,
Thy heart, in pain and weakness,
Of fancied faults afraid,
The little trembling hand
That wipes thy quiet tears,—
These, these are things that may demand
Dread memories for years.

Sorrows I've had, severe ones
I will not think of now;
And calmly, midst my dear ones,
Have wasted with dry brow;
But when thy fingers press,
And pat my stooping head,
I cannot bear the gentleness,—
The tears are in their bed.

Ah! first-born of thy mother,
When life and hope were new!
Kind playmate of thy brother,
Thy sister, father, too!
My light where'er I go,
My bird when prison-bound,—
My hand-in-hand companion,—no,
My prayers shall hold thee round,

To say, "He has departed,"—
"His voice,"—"his face,"—"is gone,'
To feel impatient-hearted,
Yet feel we must bear on;
Ah! I could not endure
To whisper of such woe,
Unless I felt this sleep insure
That it will not be so.

Yes, still he 's fixed and sleeping!
This silence too the while,—
Its very hush and creeping
Seem whispering us a smile;—
Something divine and dim
Seems going by one's ear,
Like parting wings of cherubim,
Who say,—"We 've finished here."

THE DIRGE IN CYMBELINE.—*Collins.*

To fair Fidele's grassy tomb
Soft maids and village hinds shall bring
Each opening sweet, of earliest bloom,
And rifle all the breathing spring.

No wailing ghost shall dare appear
  To vex with shrieks this quiet grove;
But shepherd lads assemble here,
  And youthful virgins own their love.

No withered witch shall here be seen,
  No goblins lead their nightly crew;
The female fays shall haunt the green,
  And dress thy grave with pearly dew.

The redbreast oft at evening's hours
  Shall kindly lend his little aid,
With hoary moss, and gathered flowers,
  To deck the ground where thou art laid.

When howling winds, and beating rain,
  In tempests shake thy sylvan cell;
Or 'midst the chase on every plain,
  The tender thought on thee shall dwell;

Each lonely scene shall thee restore,
  For thee the tear be duly shed;
Beloved, till life can charm no more;
  And mourned, till Pity's self be dead.

THE PASSAGE.

FROM THE GERMAN OF UHLAND.

Many a year is in its grave,
Since I crossed this restless wave:
And the evening, fair as ever,
Shines on ruin, rock, and river.

Then, in this same boat, beside,
Sat two comrades, old and tried;
One with all a father's truth,
One with all the fire of youth.

One on earth in silence wrought,
And his grave in silence sought;
But the younger, brighter form
Passed in battle and in storm!

So, whene'er I turn my eye
Back upon the days gone by,
Saddening thoughts of friends come o'er me
Friends who closed their course before me.

Yet what binds us, friend to friend,
But that soul with soul can blend?
Soul-like were those hours of yore;
Let us walk in soul once more!

Take, O boatman, thrice thy fee;
Take, — I give it willingly;
For, invisible to thee,
Spirits twain have crossed with me!

THAT EACH THING IS HURT OF ITSELF. — *Old English Poetry.*

Why fearest thou the outward foe,
  When thou thyself thy harm doth feed?
Of grief or hurt, of pain or woe,
  Within each thing is sown the seed.

So fine was never yet the cloth,
  No smith so hard his iron did beat,
But the one consuméd was by moth,
  T' other with canker all to fret.

The knotty oak, and wainscoat old,
  Within doth eat the silly worm;
Even so a mind in envy rolled
  Always within itself doth burn.

Thus everything that nature wrought
  Within itself his hurt doth bear;
No outward harm need to be sought,
  Where enemies be within so near.

THE KING OF THE CROCODILES.—*Southey.*

"Now, woman, why without your veil?
And wherefore do you look so pale?
And, woman, why do you groan so sadly,
And wherefore beat your bosom madly?"

"O, I have lost my darling boy,
In whom my soul had all its joy;
And I for sorrow have torn my veil;
And sorrow hath made my very heart pale.

"O, I have lost my darling child,
And that's the loss that makes me wild;
He stooped to the river down to drink,
And there was a crocodile by the brink.

"He did not venture in to swim,
He only stooped to drink at the brim;
But under the reeds the crocodile lay,
And struck with his tail and swept him away.

"Now take me in your boat, I pray,
For down the river lies my way,
And me to the Reed Island bring,
For I will go to the Crocodile King.

"The King of the Crocodiles never does wrong,
He has no tail so stiff and strong,
He has no tail to strike and slay,
But he has ears to hear what I say.

"And to the King I will complain,
How my poor child was wickedly slain;
The King of the Crocodiles he is good,
And I shall have the murderer's blood."

The man replied,—"No, woman, no,
To the Island of Reeds I will not go;
I would not for any worldly thing
See the face of the Crocodile King."

"Then lend me now your little boat,
And I will down the river float.
I tell thee that no earthly thing
Shall keep me from the Crocodile King."

The woman she leapt into the boat,
And down the river alone did she float;
And fast with the stream the boat proceeds,
And now she is come to the Island of Reeds.

The King of the Crocodiles there was seen,—
He sat upon the eggs of the Queen,—
And all around, a numerous rout,
The young Prince Crocodiles crawled about.

The woman shook every limb with fear,
As she to the Crocodile King came near,
For never man without fear and awe
The face of his Crocodile Majesty saw.

She fell upon her bended knee,
And said,—"O King, have pity on me,
For I have lost my darling child,
And that 's the loss that makes me wild

"A crocodile ate him for his food;
Now let me have the murderer's blood,
Let me have vengeance for my boy,
The only thing that can give me joy.

"I know that you, sire! never do wrong,
You have no tail so stiff and strong,
You have no tail to strike and slay,
But you have ears to hear what I say."

"You have done well," the King replies,
And fixed on her his little eyes;
"Good woman, yes, you have done right,
But you have not described me quite.

"I have no tail to strike and slay,
And I have ears to hear what you say;
I have teeth, moreover, as you may see,
And I will make a meal of thee."

BURIAL OF SIR JOHN MOORE. — *Wolfe.*

Not a drum was heard, nor a funeral note,
  As his corse to the rampart we hurried;
Not a soldier discharged his farewell shot
  O'er the grave where our hero was buried.

We buried him darkly at dead of night,
  The sods with our bayonets turning, —
By the struggling moonbeam's misty light,
  And the lantern dimly burning.

No useless coffin enclosed his breast,
  Nor in sheet, nor in shroud, we bound him;
But he lay like a warrior taking his rest,
  With his martial cloak around him.

Few and short were the prayers we said,
  And we spoke not a word of sorrow;
But we steadfastly gazed on the face of the dead,
  And we bitterly thought of the morrow.

We thought as we hollowed his narrow bed,
  And smoothed down his lonely pillow,
That the foe and the stranger would tread o'er his head,
  And we far away on the billow!

Lightly they 'll talk of the spirit that 's gone,
  And o'er his cold ashes upbraid him;
But nothing he 'll reck, if they 'll let him sleep on
  In the grave where a Briton has laid him.

But half of our heavy task was done,
   When the clock told the hour for retiring;
And we heard the distant and random gun
   That the foe was suddenly firing.

Slowly and sadly we laid him down,
   From the field of his fame fresh and gory;
We carved not a line, and we raised not a stone,
   But we left him alone in his glory.

THE TRAVELLER'S RETURN. — *Southey.*

Sweet to the morning traveller
   The song amid the sky,
Where, twinkling in the dewy light,
   The skylark soars on high.

And cheering to the traveller
   The gales that round him play,
When faint and heavily he drags
   Along his noontide way.

And when beneath the unclouded sun
   Full wearily toils he,
The flowing water makes to him
   A soothing melody.

And when the evening light decays,
   And all is calm around,
There is sweet music to his ear
   In the distant sheep-bell's sound.

But, O, of all delightful sounds,
  Of evening or of morn,
The sweetest is the voice of love
  That welcomes his return.

ADORATION OF THE DEITY IN THE MIDST OF HIS WORKS. — *T. Moore.*

THE turf shall be my fragrant shrine,
My temple, Lord! that arch of thine;
My censer's breath the mountain airs,
And silent thoughts my only prayers.

My choir shall be the moonlit waves,
When murmuring homeward to their caves,
Or when the stillness of the sea,
Even more than music, breathes of Thee.

I 'll seek by day some glade unknown,
All light and silence, like thy throne!
And the pale stars shall be, at night,
The only eyes that watch my rite.

Thy heaven, on which 't is bliss to look,
Shall be my pure and shining book,
Where I shall read, in words of flame,
The glories of thy wondrous name.

I 'll read thy anger in the rock
That clouds a while the day-beam's track,
Thy mercy in the azure hue
Of sunny brightness breaking through!

There 's nothing bright, above, below,
From flowers that bloom to stars that glow
But in its light my soul can see
Some feature of the Deity.

There 's nothing dark, below, above,
But in its gloom I trace thy love,
And meekly wait that moment when
Thy touch shall turn all bright again.

CHARADE. — *By Praed.*

Come from my First, ay, come!
For the battle-hour is nigh:
And the screaming trump and thundering drum
Are calling thee to die!
Fight, as thy father fought!
Fall, as thy father fell!
Thy task is taught, thy shroud is wrought;—
So — onward — and farewell.

Toll ye my Second, toll!
Fling wide the flambeau's light,
And sing the hymn for a parted soul
Beneath the silent night.
With the wreath upon his head,
And the cross upon his breast,
Let the prayer be said, and the tear be shed;—
So — take him to his rest!

Call ye my Whole, — ay, — call
The lord of lute and lay!
And let him greet the sable pall
With a noble song to-day!

Ay, call him by his name!
Nor fitter hand may crave
To light the flame of a soldier's fame
On the turf of a soldier's grave!

ANSWER. — *Campbell.*

WINTER. — *Burns.*

THE wintry west extends his blast,
  And hail and rain do blow;
Or the stormy north sends driving forth
  The blinding sleet and snow;
While tumbling brown, the burn comes down,
  And roars from bank to brae;
And bird and beast in covert rest,
  And pass the heartless day.

The sweeping blast, the sky o'ercast,
  The joyless winter day,
Let others fear, — to me more dear
  Than all the pride of May;
The tempest's howl, it soothes my soul,
  My griefs it seems to join;
The leafless trees my fancy please,
  Their fate resembles mine.

Thou Power Supreme, whose mighty scheme
  These woes of mine fulfil;
Here, firm, I rest, — they must be best,
  Because they are *Thy* will!
Then all I want, (O, do Thou grant
  This one request of mine!)
Since to enjoy Thou dost deny,
  Assist me to resign.

LAUNCHING INTO ETERNITY.—*Watts.*

It was a brave attempt! adventurous he
Who in the first ship broke the unknown sea,
And, leaving his dear native shores behind,
Trusted his life to the licentious wind.
I see the surging brine; the tempest raves;
He on the pine-plank rides across the waves,
Exulting on the edge of thousand gaping graves;
He steers the wingéd boat, and shifts the sails,
Conquers the flood, and manages the gales.
  Such is the soul that leaves this mortal land,
Fearless, when the great Master gives command.
Death is the storm; she smiles to hear it roar,
And bids the tempest waft her from the shore;
Then with a skilful helm she sweeps the seas,
And manages the raging storm with ease;
(Her faith can govern death;) she spreads her wings
Wide to the wind, and as she sails she sings,
And loses by degrees the sight of mortal things.
As the shores lessen, so her joys arise,
The waves roll gentler, and the tempest dies;
Now vast eternity fills all her sight,
She floats on the broad deep with infinite delight,
The seas forever calm, the skies forever bright.

ON A LEAF FROM THE TOMB OF VIRGIL.—*Mrs Hemans.*

And was thy home, pale, withered thing,
  Beneath the rich blue southern sky?
Wert thou a nursling of the spring,
  The winds and suns of glorious Italy?

Those suns, in golden light, e'en now
  Look o'er the poet's lovely grave;
Those winds are breathing soft, but thou,
  Answering their whisper, there no more shalt wave

The flowers o'er Posilippo's* brow
  May cluster in their purple bloom,
But on the o'ershadowing ilex-bough
  Thy breezy place is void, by Virgil's tomb.

Thy place is void, — O, none on earth,
  This crowded earth, may so remain,
Save that which souls of loftiest birth
  Leave when they part, their brighter home to gain!

Another leaf ere now hath sprung
  On the green stem which once was thine; —
When shall another strain be sung
  Like his whose dust hath made that spot a shrine?

THE MAY QUEEN. — *Tennyson.*

You must wake and call me early, call me early, mother dear,
To-morrow 'll be the happiest time of all the blithe New Year;

---

* A mountain skirting the shores of the Bay of Naples, on one of the most beautiful heights of which stands the tomb of Virgil.

Of all the glad New Year, mother, the maddest, merriest day,
For I 'm to be Queen o' the May, mother, I 'm to be Queen o' the May.

There 's many a black, black eye, they say, but none so bright as mine;
There 's Margaret and Mary, there 's Kate and Caroline;
But none so fair as little Alice, in all the land, they say,
So I 'm to be Queen o' the May, mother, I 'm to be Queen o' the May.

I sleep so sound all night, mother, that I shall never wake,
If ye do not call me loud when the day begins to break;
For I must gather knots of flowers and buds, and garlands gay;
For I 'm to be Queen o' the May, mother, I 'm to be Queen o' the May.

As I came up the valley, whom think ye I should see
But Robin, leaning on the bridge, beneath the hazle-tree?
He thought of that sharp look, mother, I gave him yesterday,—
But I 'm to be Queen o' the May, mother, I 'm to be Queen o' the May.

He thought I was a ghost, mother, for I was all in white,
And I ran by him without speaking, like a flash o' light.

They call me cruel-hearted, but I care not what they say,
For I 'm to be Queen o' the May, mother, I 'm to be Queen o' the May.

They say he 's dying all for love, — but that can never be;
They say his heart is breaking, mother, — but what is that to me?
There 's many a bolder lad 'll woo me any summer day, —
And I 'm to be Queen o' the May, mother, I 'm to be Queen o' the May.

Little Effie shall go with me to-morrow to the green,
And you 'll be there too, mother, to see me made the Queen;
For the shepherd lads on every side 'll come from far away,
And I 'm to be Queen o' the May, mother, I 'm to be Queen o' the May.

The honeysuckle round the porch has woven its wavy bowers,
And by the meadow-trenches blow the faint, sweet cuckoo-flowers,
And the wild marsh-marigold shines like fire in swamps and hollows gray,
And I 'm to be Queen o' the May, mother, I 'm to be Queen o' the May.

The night-winds come and go, mother, upon the meadow-grass,
And the happy stars above them seem to brighten as they pass;

There will not be a drop o' rain the whole of the live-
long day,
And I 'm to be Queen o' the May, mother, I 'm to be
Queen o' the May.

All the valley, mother, 'll be fresh and green and
still,
And the cowslip and the crowfoot are over all the
hill,
And the rivulet in the flowery dale 'll merrily glance
and play,
For I 'm to be Queen o' the May, mother, I 'm to be
Queen o' the May.

So you must wake and call me early, call me early,
mother dear,
To-morrow 'll be the happiest time of all the blithe
New Year;
To-morrow 'll be of all the year the maddest, mer-
riest day,
For I 'm to be Queen o' the May, mother, I 'm to be
Queen o' the May.

NEW YEAR'S EVE. — *Tennyson.*

If you 're waking, call me early, call me early, mother
dear,
For I would see the sun rise upon the glad New Year;
It is the last New Year that I shall ever see,
Then ye may lay me low in the mould, and think no
more o' me

To-night I saw the sun set; he set and left behind
The good old year, the dear old time, and all my peace
of mind;

And the New Year 's coming up, mother, but I shall never see
The May upon the blackthorn, the leaf upon the tree

Last May we made a crown of flowers; we had a merry day!
Beneath the hawthorn on the green they made me Queen o' May;
And we danced about the May-pole, and in the hazle-copse,
Till Charles's-wain* came out above the tall, white chimney-tops.

There 's not a flower on all the hills; the frost is on the pane;
I only wish to live till the snowdrops come again;
I wish the snow would melt, and the sun come out on high;
I long to see a flower so, before the day I die.

The building rook 'll caw from the windy, tall elm-tree,
And the tufted plover pipe along the fallow lea;
And the swallow 'll come back again with summe o'er the wave,
But I shall lie alone, mother, within the mouldering grave.

Upon the chancel-casement and upon that grave o' mine,
In the early, early morning, the summer sun 'll shine,
Before the red cock crows from the farm upon the hill,
When you are warm-asleep, mother, and all the world is still.

---

* A constellation in the heavens.

When the flowers come again, mother, beneath the waving light,
Ye 'll never see me more in the long, gray fields at night;
When from the dry dark wold the summer airs blow cool
On the oat-grass and the sword-grass and the bulrush in the pool.

Ye 'll bury me, my mother, just beneath the hawthorn-shade,
And ye 'll come sometimes and see me where I am lowly laid;
I shall not forget you, mother, I shall hear you when you pass,
With your feet above my head, in the long and pleasant grass.

I have been wild and wayward, but ye 'll forgive me now;
Ye 'll kiss me, my own mother, upon my cheek and brow;
Nay,—nay,—ye must not weep, nor let your grief be wild,
Ye shall not fret for me, mother, ye have another child.

If I can I 'll come again, mother, from out my resting-place;
Though ye 'll not see me, mother, I shall look upon your face;
Though I cannot speak a word, I shall hearken what ye say,
And be often and often with you, when ye think I 'm far away.

Good-night, good-night, when I have said good-night
for evermore,
And ye see me carried out from the threshold of the
door,
Don't let Effie come to see me till my grave be grow-
ing green;
She 'll be a better child to you than I have ever been.

She 'll find my garden-tools upon the granary-floor;
Let her take 'em; they are hers; I shall never gar
den more;
But tell her, when I 'm gone, to train the rosebush
that I set
About the parlor-window, and the box of mignonette.

Good-night, sweet mother! call me when it begins to
dawn;
All night I lie awake, but I fall asleep at morn;
But I would see the sun rise upon the glad New Year,
So, if you 're waking, call me, call me early, mother
dear.

SHE WAS A PHANTOM OF DELIGHT. — *Wordsworth.*

SHE was a phantom of delight
When first she gleamed upon my sight;
A lovely apparition, sent
To be a moment's ornament;
Her eyes as stars of twilight fair;
Like twilight 's, too, her dusky hair;
But all things else about her drawn
From May-time and the cheerful dawn;
A dancing shape, an image gay,
To haunt, to startle, and waylay.

I saw her upon nearer view,
A spirit, yet a woman too!
Her household motions light and free,
And steps of virgin liberty;
A countenance in which did meet
Sweet records, promises as sweet;
A creature not too bright or good
For human nature's daily food;
For transient sorrows, simple wiles,
Praise, blame, love, kisses, tears, and smiles.

And now I see, with eye serene,
The very pulse of the machine;
A being breathing thoughtful breath,
A traveller between life and death;
The reason firm, the temperate will,
Endurance, foresight, strength, and skill;
A perfect woman, nobly planned
To warn, to comfort, and command;
And yet a spirit still, and bright
With something of an angel light.

THE LOST PLEIAD. — *Mrs. Hemans.*

AND is there glory from the heavens departed?—
O void unmarked!—thy sisters of the sky
Still hold their place on high,
Though from its rank thine orb so long hath started,
Thou, that no more art seen of mortal eye.

Hath the night lost a gem, the regal night?
She wears her crown of old magnificence,
Though thou art exiled thence;
No desert seems to part those urns of light,
'Midst the far depths of purple gloom intense,

They rise in joy, the starry myriads burning,—
The shepherd greets them on his mountains free;
And from the silvery sea
To them the sailor's wakeful eye is turning,—
Unchanged they rise, they have not mourned for thee.

Couldst thou be shaken from thy radiant place,
E'en as a dew-drop from the myrtle spray
Swept by the wind away?
Wert thou not peopled by some glorious race,
And was there power to smite them with decay?

Why, who shall talk of thrones, of sceptres riven?
Bowed be our hearts to think of what *we* are,
When, from its height afar,
A world sinks thus,—and yon majestic heaven
Shines not the less for that one vanished star!

CORONACH.*—*Sir W. Scott.*

He is gone on the mountain,
He is lost to the forest,
Like a summer-dried fountain,
When our need was the sorest.
The fount, reäppearing,
From the rain-drops shall borrow,
But to us comes no cheering,
To Duncan no morrow!

The hand of the reaper
Takes the ears that are hoary,
But the voice of the weeper
Wails manhood in glory;

* Funeral song.

The autumn winds, rushing,
  Waft the leaves that are serest,
But our flower was in flushing
  When blighting was nearest.

Fleet foot on the corei,*
  Sage counsel in cumber,
Red hand in the foray,
  How sound is thy slumber!
Like the dew on the mountain,
  Like the foam on the river,
Like the bubble on the fountain,
  Thou art gone, and forever!

THE PAUPER'S DEATHBED. — *Mrs. Southey.*

TREAD softly, — bow the head, —
  In reverent silence bow, —
No passing bell doth toll, —
Yet an immortal soul
    Is passing now.

Stranger! however great,
  With lowly reverence bow;
There 's one in that poor shed,
One by that paltry bed,
    Greater than thou.

Beneath that beggar's roof,
  Lo! Death doth keep his state;
Enter! no crowds attend;
Enter! no guards defend
    This palace-gate.

---

* The hollow side of the hill, where game usually lies.

That pavement damp and cold
  No smiling courtiers tread;
One silent woman stands,
Lifting with meagre hands
    A dying head.

No mingling voices sound, —
  An infant wail alone; —
A sob suppressed, — again
That short, deep gasp, and then
    The parting groan.

O change! — O wondrous change! —
  Burst are the prison-bars; —
This moment *there*, so low,
So agonized, and now
    Beyond the stars!

O change, stupendous change!
  There lies the soulless clod;
The sun eternal breaks, —
The new immortal wakes, —
    Wakes with his God.

AN INVITATION TO PRAISE GOD. — *Watts.*

Sweet flocks, whose soft, enamelled wing
Swift and gently cleaves the sky,
Whose charming notes address the spring
  With an artless harmony;
  Lovely minstrels of the field,

Who in leafy shadows sit,
And your wondrous structures build,
Awake your tuneful voices with the dawning light;
To nature's God your first devotions pay,
Ere you salute the rising day; —
'T is He calls up the sun, and gives him every ray.

Serpents, who o'er the meadows slide,
And wear upon your shining back
Numerous ranks of gaudy pride,
Which thousand mingling colors make;
Let the fierce glances of your eyes
Rebate their baleful fire;
In harmless play, twist and unfold
The volumes of your scaly gold;
That rich embroidery of your gay attire
Proclaims your Maker kind and wise.

Insects and mites of mean degree,
That swarm in myriads o'er the land,
Moulded by Wisdom's artful hand,
And curled and painted with a various dye;
In your innumerable forms
Praise Him that wears the ethereal crown,
And bends his lofty counsels down
To despicable worms.

TO THE EVENING WIND. — *Bryant.*

Spirit that breathest through my lattice, thou
That cool'st the twilight of the sultry day,
Gratefully flows thy freshness round my brow;
Thou hast been out upon the deep at play,

Riding all day the wild blue waves till now,
  Roughening their crests, and scattering high their spray,
And swelling the white sail. I welcome thee
To the scorched land, thou wanderer of the sea

Nor I alone; — a thousand bosoms round
  Inhale thee in the fulness of delight;
And languid forms rise up, and pulses bound
  Livelier, at coming of the wind of night;
And, languishing to hear thy grateful sound,
  Lies the vast inland stretched beyond the sight.
Go forth into the gathering shade; go forth,
God's blessing breathed upon the fainting earth!

Go, rock the little wood-bird in his nest,
  Curl the still waters, bright with stars, and rouse
The wide old wood from his majestic rest,
  Summoning from the innumerable boughs
The strange, deep harmonies that haunt his breast;
  Pleasant shall be thy way where meekly bows
The shutting flower, and darkling waters pass,
And 'twixt the o'ershadowing branches and the grass.

The faint old man shall lean his silver head
  To feel thee; thou shalt kiss the child asleep,
And dry the moistened curls that overspread
  His temples, while his breathing grows more deep;
And they who stand about the sick man's bed
  Shall joy to listen to thy distant sweep,
And softly part his curtains to allow
Thy visit, grateful to his burning brow.

Go, — but the circle of eternal change,
  Which is the life of nature, shall restore,
With sounds and scents from all thy mighty range,
  Thee to thy birthplace of the deep once more;

Sweet odors in the sea-air, sweet and strange,
  Shall tell the homesick mariner of the shore;
And, listening to thy murmur, he shall deem
He hears the rustling leaf and running stream.

THE ERL KING.

FROM THE GERMAN OF GOETHE.

Who rideth so late through the night-wind wild?
It is the father with his child;
He has the little one well in his arm;
He holds him safe, and he folds him warm.

"My son, why hidest thy face so shy?"
"Seest thou not, father, the Erl King nigh?
The Erlen King, with train and crown?"
"It is a wreath of mist, my son."

"Come, lovely boy, come, go with me;
Such merry plays I will play with thee;
Many a bright flower grows on the strand,
And my mother has many a gay garment at hand."

"My father, my father, and dost thou not hear
What the Erl King whispers in my ear?"
"Be quiet, my darling, — be quiet, my child;
Through withered leaves the wind howls wild."

"Come, lovely boy, wilt thou go with me?
My daughters fair shall wait on thee;
My daughters their nightly revels keep;
They 'll sing, and they 'll dance, and they 'll rock
  thee to sleep."

"My father, my father, and seest thou not
The Erl King's daughters in yon dim spot?'
"My son, my son, I see and I know
'T is the old gray willow that shimmers* so."

"I love thee; thy beauty has ravished my sense;
And, willing or not, I will carry thee hence."
"O father, the Erl King now puts forth his arm!
O father, the Erl King has done me harm!"

The father shudders; he hurries on;
And faster he holds his moaning son;
He reaches his home with fear and dread,
And lo! in his arms the child was dead!

LAMENT OF MARY QUEEN OF SCOTS.—*Burns.*

Now nature hangs her mantle green
  On every blooming tree,
And spreads her sheets o' daisies white
  Out o'er the grassy lea;
Now Phœbus cheers the crystal streams,
  And glads the azure skies;
But nought can glad the weary wight
  That fast in durance lies.

Now lav'rocks wake the merry morn,
  Aloft on dewy wing;
The merle, in his noontide bower,
  Makes woodland-echoes ring;

* Gleams with an uncertain light.

The mavis wild, wi' many a note,
Sings drowsy day to rest;
In love and freedom they rejoice,
Wi' care nor thrall opprest.

Now blooms the lily by the bank,
The primrose down the brae;
The hawthorn 's budding in the glen,
And milk-white is the slae;
The meanest hind in fair Scotland
May rove their sweets among;
But I, the queen of a' Scotland,
Maun lie in prison strong.

I was the queen o' bonnie France,
Where happy I hae been;
Full lightly rose I in the morn,
As blithe lay down at e'en;
And I 'm the sovereign of Scotland,
And mony a traitor there;
Yet here I lie, in foreign bands,
And never-ending care.

But as for thee, thou false woman,*
My sister and my foe!
Grim vengeance, yet, shall whet a sword
That through thy soul shall go;
The weeping blood in woman's breast
Was never known to thee;
Nor the balm that drops on wounds of woe
Frae woman's pitying e'e.

---

* Elizabeth, Queen of England, who unjustly detained her in prison.

My son !* my son ! may kinder stars
  Upon thy fortune shine ;
And may those pleasures gild thy reign
  That ne'er wad blink on mine !
God keep thee frae thy mother's foes,
  Or turn their hearts to thee ;
And where thou meet'st thy mother's friend,
  Remember him for me !

O, soon, to me, may summer suns
  Nae mair light up the morn !
Nae mair, to me, the autumn winds
  Wave o'er the yellow corn !
And in the narrow house of death
  Let winter round me rave ;
And the next flowers that deck the spring
  Bloom on my peaceful grave.

AVARICE. — *George Herbert.*

Money, thou bane of bliss, and source of woe,
Whence comest thou, that thou art so fresh and fine
I know thy parentage is base and low ;
Man found thee poor and dirty in a mine.

Surely thou didst so little contribute
To this great kingdom which thou now hast got,
That he was fain, when thou wast destitute,
To dig thee out of thy dark cave and grot.

* James the First, King of England.

Then forcing thee by fire he made thee bright;
Nay, thou hast got the face of man; for we
Have with our stamp and seal transferred our right —
Thou art the man, and man but dross to thee.

Man calleth thee his wealth, who made thee rich,
And, while he digs out thee, falls in the ditch.

THE TRUMPET. — *Mrs. Hemans.*

The trumpet's voice hath roused the land; —
  Light up the beacon-pyre! —
A hundred hills have seen the brand,
  And waved the sign of fire.
A hundred banners to the breeze
  Their gorgeous folds have cast, —
And hark! — was that the sound of seas? -
  A king to war went past.

The chief is arming in his hall,
  The peasant by his hearth;
The mourner hears the thrilling call,
  And rises from the earth.
The mother on her first-born son
  Looks with a boding eye, —
They come not back, though all be won,
  Whose young hearts leap so high.

The bard hath ceased his song, and bound
  The falchion to his side;
E'en for the marriage-altar crowned,
  The lover quits his bride.

And all this haste, and change, and fear,
By *earthly* clarion spread! —
How will it be when kingdoms hear
The blast that wakes the dead!

FAREWELL TO THE MUSE. — *Sir W. Scott.*

Enchantress, farewell! who so oft has decoyed me,
At the close of the evening, through woodlands to roam,
Where the forester, lated, with wonder espied me
Explore the wild scenes he was quitting for home.
Farewell! and take with thee thy numbers wild speaking,
The language alternate of rapture and woe;
O, none but some lover, whose heart-strings are breaking,
The pang that I feel at our parting can know!

Each joy thou couldst double, and when there came sorrow,
Or pale disappointment, to darken my way,
What voice was like thine, that could sing of to-morrow
Till forgot in the strain was the grief of to-day!
But when friends drop around us in life's weary waning,
The grief, queen of numbers, thou canst not assuage;
Nor the gradual estrangement of those yet remaining,
The languor of pain, and the chillness of age.

'T was thou that once taught me, in accents bewailing,
To sing how a warrior lay stretched on the plain,
And a maiden hung o'er him with aid unavailing,
And held to his lips the cold goblet in vain;

As vain those enchantments, O queen o wild numbers,
  To a bard when the reign of his fancy is o'er,
And the quick pulse of feeling in apathy slumbers; —
  Farewell, then, enchantress! I meet thee no more!

TRUE RICHES. — *Watts.*

I AM not concerned to know
What, to-morrow, fate will do;
'T is enough that I can say
I 've possessed myself to-day;
Then, if haply midnight death
Seize my flesh and stop my breath,
Yet to-morrow I shall be
Heir to the best part of me.
  Glittering stones, and golden things,
Wealth and honors that have wings,
Ever fluttering to be gone,
I could never call my own;
Riches that the world bestows
She can take, and I can lose;
But the treasures that are mine
Lie afar beyond her line.
When I view my spacious soul,
And survey myself a whole,
And enjoy myself alone,
I 'm a kingdom of my own.
  I 've a mighty part within,
That the world hath never seen;
Rich as Eden's happy ground,
And with choicer plenty crowned.
Here, on all the shining boughs,
Knowledge fair and useful grows;

On the same young, flowery tree
All the seasons you may see;
Notions in the bloom of light,
Just disclosing to the sight;
Here are thoughts of larger growth,
Ripening into solid truth;
Fruits refined, of noble taste;
Seraphs feed on such repast.
Here, in a green and shady grove,
Streams of pleasure mix with love;
There, beneath the smiling skies,
Hills of contemplation rise;
Now upon some shining top
Angels light, and call me up;
I rejoice to raise my feet,
Both rejoice when there we meet.
There are endless beauties more
Earth hath no resemblance for;
Nothing like them round the pole,
Nothing can describe the soul;
'T is a region half unknown,
That has treasures of its own,
More remote from public view
Than the bowels of Peru;
Broader 't is, and brighter far,
Than the golden Indies are;
Ships that trace the watery stage
Cannot coast it in an age!
Harts, or horses, strong and fleet,
Had they wings to help their feet,
Could not run it half way o'er
In ten thousand days or more.
Yet the silly, wandering mind,
Loth to be too much confined,
Roves and takes her daily tours,
Coasting round the narrow shores.

Narrow shores of flesh and sense,
Picking shells and pebbles thence;
Or she sits at Fancy's door,
Calling shapes and shadows to her,
Foreign visits still receiving,
And to herself a stranger living.
Never, never, would she buy
Indian dust, or Tyrian dye,
Never trade abroad for more,
If she saw her native store;
If her inward worth were known,
She might ever live alone.

THE MOSS ROSE.

The Angel of the flowers one day
Beneath a rose-tree sleeping lay,—
That spirit to whose charge is given
To bathe young buds in dew from heaven.
Awakening from his slight repose,
The Angel whispered to the Rose,—
"O fondest object of my care,
Still fairest found where all is fair,
For the sweet shade thou hast given me,
Ask what thou wilt, 't is granted thee."
Then said the Rose, with deepened glow,—
"On me another grace bestow;"—
The Angel paused in silent thought,—
What grace was there the flower had not?
'T was but a moment,—o'er the Rose
A veil of moss the Angel throws,
And, robed in Nature's simplest weed,
Could there a flower that Rose exceed?

A MONARCH'S DEATH-BED.—*Mrs. Hemans.*

A MONARCH* on his death-bed lay,—
  Did censers waft perfume,
And soft lamps, from their silvery ray,
  Through his proud chambers gloom?
He lay upon a greensward bed,
  Beneath a darkening sky,—
A lone tree waving o'er his head,
  A swift stream rolling by.

Had he then fallen as warriors fall,
  Where spear strikes fire from spear?
Was there a banner for his pall,
  A buckler for his bier?
Not so,—nor cloven shields nor helms
  Had strewn the bloody sod,
Where he, the helpless lord of realms,
  Yielded his soul to God.

Were there not friends, with words of cheer,
  And friendly vassals, nigh?
And priests, the crucifix to rear
  Before the fading eye?—
A peasant-girl that royal head
  Upon her bosom laid;
And, shrinking not for woman's dread,
  The face of death surveyed.

Alone she sat,—from hill and wood
  Red sank the mournful sun;
Fast gushed the fount of noble blood,
  Treason its worst had done!

---

* Albert of Hapsburg, Emperor of Germany, who was assassinated by his nephew, was left to die by the way-side, and was supported in his last moments by a peasant-girl, who happened to be passing.

With her long hair she vainly pressed
The wounds, to stanch their tide,—
Unknown, on that meek, humble breast,
Imperial Albert died.

ON TIME.

Say, is there aught that can convey
An image of its transient stay?
'T is an hand's-breath; 't is a tale;
'T is a vessel under sail;
'T is a conqueror's straining steed;
'T is a shuttle in its speed;
'T is an eagle in its way,
Darting down upon its prey;
'T is an arrow in its flight,
Mocking the pursuing sight;
'T is a vapor in the air;
'T is a whirlwind rushing there;
'T is a short-lived, fading flower;
'T is a rainbow on a shower;
'T is a momentary ray,
Smiling in a winter's day;
'T is a torrent's troubled stream;
'T is a shadow 't is a dream;
'T is the closing watch of night,
Dying at approaching light;
'T is a landscape vainly gay,
Painted upon crumbling clay;
'T is a lamp that wastes its fires;
'T is a smoke that quick expires;
'T is a bubble; 't is a sigh;
Be prepared, O man, to die!

VIRTUE. — *George Herbert.*

Sweet day! so cool, so calm, so bright,
The bridal of the earth and sky,
The dew shall weep thy fall to-night;
For thou must die.

Sweet rose! whose hue, angry and brave,
Bids the rash gazer wipe his eye,
Thy root is ever in its grave,
And thou must die.

Sweet spring! full of sweet days and roses,
A box where sweets compacted lie,
Thy music shows ye have your closes,
And all must die.

Only a sweet and virtuous soul,
Like seasoned timber, never gives;
But, though the whole world turn to coal,
Then chiefly lives.

TO A SKYLARK. — *Wordsworth.*

Ethereal minstrel! pilgrim of the sky!
Dost thou despise the earth, where cares abound?
Or, while the wings aspire, are heart and eye
Both with thy nest upon the dewy ground?
Thy nest, which thou canst drop into at will,
Those quivering wings composed, that music still!

To the last point of vision and beyond,
Mount, daring warbler! — that love-prompted strain
('Twixt thee and thine a never-failing bond)
Thrills not the less the bosom of the plain;

Yet might'st thou seem, proud privilege! to sing
All independent of the leafy spring.

Leave to the nightingale her shady wood,—
A privacy of glorious light is thine;
Whence thou dost pour upon the world a flood
Of harmony, with instinct more divine;
Type of the wise, who soar, but never roam;
True to the kindred points of heaven and home:

TO THE BRAMBLE-FLOWER.—*Elliot.*

Thy fruit full well the schoolboy knows,
  Wild bramble of the brake!
So put forth thy small, white rose;
  I love it for his sake.
Though woodbines flaunt, and roses glow,
  O'er all the fragrant bowers,
Thou need'st not be ashamed to show
  Thy satin-threaded flowers;
For dull the eye, the heart is dull,
  That cannot feel how fair,
Amid all beauty beautiful,
  Thy tender blossoms are!
How delicate thy gauzy frill!
  How rich thy branchy stem!
How soft thy voice, when woods are still,
  And thou sing'st hymns to them;
While silent showers are falling slow,
  And, 'mid the general hush,
A sweet air lifts the little bough,
  Lone whispering through the bush!
The primrose to the grave is gone;
  The hawthorn flower is dead;

The violet by the mossed gray stone
  Hath laid her weary head;
But thou, wild bramble! back dost bring,
  In all thy beauteous power,
The fresh, green days of life's fair spring,
  And boyhood's blossomy hour.
Scorned bramble of the brake! once more
  Thou bidd'st me be a boy,
To gad with thee the woodlands o'er,
  In freedom and in joy.

LINES WRITTEN IN A HIGHLAND GLEN.—*Wilson.*

To whom belongs this valley fair,
That sleeps beneath the filmy air,
  Even like a living thing?
Silent—as infant at the breast—
Save a still sound that speaks of rest,
  That streamlet's murmuring!

The heavens appear to love this vale;
Here clouds with scarce-seen motion sail,
  Or 'mid the silence lie!
By that blue arch, this beauteous earth,
'Mid evening's hour of dewy mirth,
  Seems bound unto the sky.

O, that this lovely vale were mine!
Then, from glad youth to calm decline,
  My years would gently glide;
Hope would rejoice in endless dreams,
And memory's oft returning gleams
  By peace be sanctified.

There would unto my soul be given,
From presence of that gracious heaven,
A piety sublime!
And thoughts would come of mystic mood,
To make in this deep solitude
Eternity of time!

And did I ask to whom belonged
This vale? I feel that I have wronged
Nature's most gracious soul!
She spreads her glories o'er the earth,
And all her children, from their birth,
Are joint heirs of the whole!

Yea, long as Nature's humblest child
Hath kept her temple undefiled
By sinful sacrifice;
Earth's fairest scenes are all his own;
He is the monarch, and his throne
Is built amid the skies!

THE EVENING RAINBOW.—*Southey.*

Mild arch of promise! on the evening sky
Thou shinest fair, with many a lovely ray,
Each in the other melting. Much mine eye
Delights to linger on thee; for the day,
Changeful and many-weathered, seemed to smile,
Flashing brief splendor through his clouds a while,
That deepened dark anon, and fell in rain.
But pleasant is it now to pause, and view
Thy various tints of frail and watery hue,
And think the storm shall not return again.

Such is the smile that piety bestows
On the good man's pale cheek, when he in peace,
Departing gently from a world of woes,
Anticipates the realm where sorrows cease.

BOOK OF THE WORLD.—*Drummond.*

Of this fair volume which we "World" do name,
If we the sheets and leaves could turn with care,
Of Him who it corrects, and did it frame,
We clear might read the art and wisdom rare,—
Find out his power,—which wildest powers doth tame,—
His providence,—extending everywhere,—
His justice,—which proud rebels doth not spare,—
In every page,—no period of the same!
But silly we, like foolish children, rest
Well pleased with colored vellum, leaves of gold,
Fair, dangling ribands, leaving what is best,
On the great Writer's sense ne'er taking hold;
Or if by chance we stay our minds on aught,
It is some picture on the margin wrought.

THE SKYLARK.—*Hogg.*

Bird of the wilderness,
Blithesome and cumberless,
Sweet be thy matin o'er moorland and lea!
Emblem of happiness,
Blest is thy dwelling-place,—
O, to abide in the desert with thee!

Wild is thy lay, and loud,
Far in the downy cloud,
Love gives it energy, love gave it birth.
Where, on the dewy wing,
Where art thou journeying?
Thy lay is in heaven, thy love is on earth.
O'er fell and fountain sheen,
O'er moor and mountain green,
O'er the red streamer that heralds the day,
Over the cloudlet dim,
Over the rainbow's rim,
Musical cherub, soar, singing away!
Then, when the gloaming comes,
Low in the heather-blooms
Sweet will thy welcome and bed of love be;
Emblem of happiness,
Blest is thy dwelling-place,—
O, to abide in the desert with thee!

TO DAFFODILS.—*Herrick.**

Fair Daffodils, we weep to see
You waste away so soon;
As yet the early-rising sun
Has not attained his noon;
Stay, stay,
Until the hast'ning day
Has run
But to the even-song;
And, having prayed together, we
Will go with you along!

---

* Born in 1591.

We have short time to stay, as you;
We have as short a spring,
As quick a growth to meet decay,
  As you, or anything;
      We die,
  As your hours do; and dry
      Away
Like to the summer's rain;
Or as the pearls of morning dew,
  Ne'er to be found again.

THE HERMIT. — *Beattie.*

At the close of the day, when the hamlet is still,
  And mortals the sweets of forgetfulness prove,
When nought but the torrent is heard on the hill,
  And nought but the nightingale's song in the grove;
T was then, by the cave of the mountain reclined,
  A hermit his nightly complaint thus began;
Though mournful his numbers, his soul was resigned;
  He thought as a sage, though he felt as a man.

"Ah! why thus abandoned to darkness and woe,
  Why thus, lonely Philomel, flows thy sad strain?
For spring shall return, and a lover bestow,
  And thy bosom no trace of misfortune retain.
Yet, if pity inspire thee, O, cease not thy lay!
  Mourn, sweetest companion! man calls thee to mourn;
O, soothe him, whose pleasures, like thine, pass away,
  Full quickly they pass, but they never return!

"Now, gliding remote on the verge of the sky,
The moon, half extinct, a dim crescent displays;
But lately I marked when, majestic, on high
She shone, and the planets were lost in her blaze.
Roll on, then, fair orb, and with gladness pursue
The path that conducts thee to splendor again;
But man's faded glory no change shall renew;
Ah, fool! to exult in a glory so vain!

"'T is night, and the landscape is lovely no more;
I mourn; but, ye woodlands, I mourn not for you;
For morn is approaching, your charms to restore,
Perfumed with fresh fragrance, and glittering with dew.
Nor yet for the ravage of winter I mourn,
Kind Nature the embryo-blossom shall save;
But when shall spring visit the mouldering urn?
O, when shall it dawn on the night of the grave?"

'T was thus, by the glare of false science betrayed,
That leads to bewilder and dazzles to blind;
My thoughts wont to roam from shade onward to shade,
Destruction before me, and sorrow behind.
"O, pity, great Father of light!" then I cried,
"Thy creature, who fain would not wander from thee;
Lo! humbled in dust, I relinquish my pride;
From doubt and from darkness thou only canst free."

And darkness and doubt are now flying away;
No longer I roam in conjecture forlorn;
So breaks on the traveller, faint and astray,
The bright and the balmy effulgence of morn;

See Truth, Love, and Mercy, in triumph descending,
  And Nature all glowing in Eden's first bloom!
On the cold cheek of Death smiles and roses are
      blending,
  And Beauty immortal awakes from the tomb.

SONG OF THE SILENT LAND.

TRANSLATED FROM THE GERMAN OF SALIS, BY LONGFELLOW.

Into the Silent Land!
Ah! who shall lead us thither?
Clouds in the evening sky more darkly gather,
And shattered wrecks lie thicker on the strand.
Who leads us with a gentle hand
Thither, O thither,
Into the Silent Land?

Into the Silent Land!
To you, ye boundless regions
Of all perfection! Tender morning-visions
Of beauteous souls! The Future's pledge and band
Who in Life's battle firm doth stand
Shall bear Hope's tender blossoms
Into the Silent Land!

O Land! O Land!
For all the broken-hearted
The mildest herald by our fate allotted
Beckons, and with inverted torch doth stand
To lead us with a gentle hand
Into the land of the great departed,
Into the Silent Land!

ODE. — *Collins.*

How sleep the brave, who sink to rest
By all their country's wishes blest!
When Spring, with dewy fingers cold,
Returns to deck the hallowed mould,
She there shall dress a sweeter sod
Than Fancy's feet have ever trod.

By fairy hands their knell is rung,
By forms unseen their dirge is sung;
There Honor comes, a pilgrim gray,
To bless the turf that wraps their clay;
And Freedom shall a while repair
To dwell a weeping hermit there!

TO OUR ELDEST HEIR. — *Mrs. Henry Coleridge.*

Deem not that our eldest heir
Wins too much of love and care;
What a parent's heart can spare,
Who can measure truly?
Early crops were never found
To exhaust that fertile ground,
Still with riches 't will abound,
Ever springing newly.

See in yonder plot of flowers
How the tallest lily towers,
Catching beams and kindly showers
Which the heavens are shedding.
While the younger plants below
Less of sun and breezes know,
Till beyond the shade they grow,
High and richly spreading.

She that latest leaves the nest,
Little fledgling much carest,
Is not therefore loved the best,
    Though the most protected;
Nor the gadding, daring child,
Oft reproved for antics wild,
Of our tenderness beguiled,
    Or in thought neglected.

'Gainst the islet's rocky shore
Waves are beating evermore,
Yet with blooms it 's scattered o'er,
    Decked in softest lustre;
Nature favors it no less
Than the guarded, still recess,
Where the birds for shelter press,
    And the harebells cluster.

THE HUSBANDMAN. — *Sterling.*

Earth, of man the bounteous mother,
  Feeds him still with corn and wine;
He who best would aid a brother
  Shares with him these gifts divine.

Many a power within her bosom
  Noiseless, hidden, works beneath;
Hence are seed, and leaf, and blossom,
  Golden ear and clustered wreath.

These to swell with strength and beauty
  Is the royal task of man;
Man 's a king, his throne is Duty,
  Since his work on earth began.

Bud and harvest, bloom and vintage,
  These, like man, are fruits of earth;
Stamped in clay, a heavenly mintage,
  All from dust receive their birth.

Barn, and mill, and wine-vat's treasures,
  Earthly goods for earthly lives,
These are Nature's ancient pleasures,
  These her child from her derives.

What the dream, but vain rebelling,
  If from earth we sought to flee?
'T is our stored and ample dwelling,
  'T is from it the skies we see.

Wind and frost, and hour and season,
  Land and water, sun and shade, —
Work with these, as bids thy reason,
  For they work thy toil to aid.

Sow thy seed and reap in gladness!
  Man himself is all a seed;
Hope and hardship, joy and sadness,
  Slow the plant to ripeness lead.

HELLVELLYN. — *Sir W. Scott.*

In 1805, a young gentleman, who was fond of wandering amidst the romantic scenery of the "Lake District," in the counties of Westmoreland and Cumberland, in England, lost his way on the Hellvellyn Mountains, and perished there. Three months afterwards his remains were found, guarded by a faithful terrier-dog, the sole companion of his rambles.

I CLIMBED the dark brow of the mighty Hellvellyn,
  Lakes and mountains beneath me gleamed misty
      and wide;

All was still, save by fits, when the eagle was yelling,
And starting around me the echoes replied.
On the right, Striden-edge* round the Red-tarn was bending,
And Catchedicam* its left verge was defending,
One huge, nameless rock in the front was ascending,
When I marked the sad spot where the wanderer had died.

Dark green was the spot, 'mid the brown mountain heather,
Where the pilgrim of nature lay stretched in decay,
Like the corpse of an outcast abandoned to weather,
Till the mountain winds wasted the tenantless clay.
Nor yet quite deserted, though lonely extended,
For, faithful in death, his mute favorite attended,
The much-loved remains of her master defended,
And chased the hill-fox and the raven away.

How long didst thou think that his silence was slumber?
When the wind waved his garment, how oft didst thou start?
How many long days and long weeks didst thou number,
Ere he faded before thee, the friend of thy heart?
And, O, was it meet, that — no requiem read o'er him,
No mother to weep, and no friend to deplore him,
And thou, little guardian, alone stretched before him —
Unhonored the pilgrim from life should depart?

When a prince to the fate of a peasant has yielded
The tapestry waves dark round the dim-lighted hall;
With scutcheons of silver the coffin is shielded,
And pages stand mute by the canopied pall;

* Hills in the Lake District.

Through the courts, at deep midnight, the torches are gleaming,
In the proudly-arched chapel the banners are beaming,
Far down the long aisle sacred music is streaming,
Lamenting a chief of the people should fall.

But meeter for thee, gentle lover of nature,
To lay down thy head like the meek mountain lamb;
When, wildered, he drops from some cliff huge in stature,
And draws his last sob by the side of his dam;
And more stately thy couch by this desert lake lying,
Thy obsequies sung by the gray plover flying,
With one faithful friend but to witness thy dying,
In the arms of Hellvellyn and Catchedicam.

THE REAPER AND THE FLOWERS. — *Longfellow.*

There is a reaper, whose name is Death,
And, with his sickle keen,
He reaps the bearded grain at a breath,
And the flowers that grow between.

"Shall I have nought that is fair?" saith he;
"Have nought but the bearded grain?
Though the breath of these flowers is sweet to me,
I will give them all back again."

He gazed at the flowers with tearful eyes,
He kissed their drooping leaves;
It was for the Lord of Paradise
He bound them in his sheaves

"My Lord has need of these flowerets gay,"
The reaper said, and smiled;
"Dear tokens of the earth are they,
Where he was once a child.

"They shall all bloom in fields of light,
Transplanted by my care,
And saints, upon their garments white,
These sacred blossoms wear."

And the mother gave, in tears and pain,
The flowers she most did love;
She knew she should find them all again
In the fields of light above.

O, not in cruelty, not in wrath,
The reaper came that day;
'T was an angel visited the green earth,
And took the flowers away.

THE FLOWERS OF THE FOREST. — *Mrs. Cockburn.*

I 've seen the smiling of Fortune beguiling,
I 've felt all its favors, and found its decay;
Sweet is her blessing, and kind her caressing,
But soon it is fled, — it is fled far away.

I 've seen the forest adorned of the foremost
With flowers of the fairest, both pleasant and gay
Full sweet was their blooming, their scent the air per
fuming;
But now they are withered, and a' wede away.

I 've seen the morning with gold the hills adorning,
  And loud tempest storming before the mid-day; —
I 've seen Tweed's silver streams, glittering in the sunny beams,
  Grow drumly* and dark, as he rolled on his way.

O fickle fortune! why this cruel sporting?
  O, why thus perplex us poor sons of a day?
No more your smiles can cheer me, no more your frowns can fear me,
  Since the flowers of the forest are a' wede away.

THE TRAGEDY OF THE LAC DE GAUBE. — *Milnes.*

THE marriage-blessing on their brows,
  Across the channel seas,
And lands of gay Garonne, they reach
  The pleasant Pyrenees;
He into boyhood born again,
  A child of joy and life;
And she a happy English girl,
  A happier English wife.

They loiter not where Argeles,
  The chestnut-crested plain,
Unfolds its robe of green and gold
  In pasture, grape, and grain;
But on and up, where nature's heart
  Beats strong amid the hills,
They pause, — contented with the wealth
  That either bosom fills.

* Discolored.

There is a lake, a small, round lake,
 High on the mountain's breast;
The child of rains and melted snows,
 The torrent's summer rest.
A mirror, where the veteran rocks
 May glass their peaks and scars;
A nether sky where breezes break
 The sunlight into stars.

O, gayly shone that little lake,
 And nature, sternly fair,
Put on a sparkling countenance
 To greet that merry pair;
How light from stone to stone they leapt!
 How trippingly they ran!
To scale the rock and gain the marge
 Was all a moment's span!

" See, dearest, this primeval boat,
 So quaint and rough, — I deem
Just such an one did Charon ply
 Across the Stygian stream;
Step in, — I will your Charon be,
 And you a spirit bold;
I was a famous rower once,
 In college days of old.

' The clumsy oar! the laggard boat!
 How slow we move along!
The work is harder than I thought,
 A song, my love, a song!"
Then, standing up, she carolled out
 So blithe and sweet a strain,
That the long-silent cliffs were glad
 To peal it back again.

He, tranced in joy, the oar laid down,
  And rose in careless pride,
And swayed, in cadence to the song,
  The boat from side to side;
Then, clasping hand in loving hand,
  They danced a childish round,
And felt as safe in that mid-lake
  As on the firmest ground.

One poise too much! he headlong fell, —
  She, stretching out to save
A feeble arm, was borne adown
  Within that glittering grave;
One moment, and the gush went forth
  Of music-mingled laughter;
The struggling splash and deathly shriek
  Were there the instant after.

Her weaker head above the flood,
  That quick engulfed the strong,
Like some enchanted water-flower,
  Waved pitifully long;
Long seemed the low and lonely wail
  Athwart the tide to fade;
Alas! that there were some to hear,
  But never one to save.

Yet not alas! if Heaven revered
  The freshly spoken vow,
And willed that what was then made one
  Should not be sundered now;
If she was spared, by that sharp stroke,
  Love's most unnatural doom,
The future lorn and unconsoled,
  The unavoided tomb!

But weep, ye very rocks, for those,
Who, on their native shore,
Await the letters of dear news,
That shall arrive no more!
One letter from a stranger hand,—
Few words are all the need;—
And then the funeral of the heart,
The course of useless speed!

The presence of the cold, dead wood,
The single mark and sign
Of all so loved and beautiful,—
The handiwork divine!
The weary search for his fine form,
That in the depth would linger,
And late success,—O, leave the ring
Upon that faithful finger!

And if in life there lie the seed
Of real enduring being,
If love and truth be not decreed
To perish unforeseeing,
This youth the seal of death has stamped,
Now time can wither never,
This hope, that sorrow might have damped,
Is flowering fresh forever.

AUTUMN MUSINGS.—*Burns.*

The lazy mist hangs from the brow of the hill,
Concealing the course of the dark, winding rill
How languid the scenes, late so sprightly, appea
As autumn to winter resigns the pale year!

The forests are leafless, the meadows are brown,
And all the gay foppery of summer is flown;
Apart let me wander, apart let me muse,
How quick Time is flying, how keen fate pursues!

How long I have lived, — but how much lived in vain, —
How little of life's scanty span may remain!
What aspects old Time in his progress has worn!
What ties cruel Fate in my bosom has torn!

How foolish, or worse, till our summit is gained;
And downward, how weakened, how darkened, how pained!
Life is not worth having, with all it can give;
For something beyond it poor man sure must live.

ON THE SHORTNESS OF HUMAN LIFE. — *Wastell.* *

LIKE as the damask rose you see,
Or like the blossom on the tree,
Or like the dainty flower of May,
Or like the morning to the day,
Or like the sun, or like the shade,
Or like the gourd which Jonah had,
E'en such is man; — whose thread is spun,
Drawn out and cut, and so is done.
Withers the rose, the blossom blasts,
The flower fades, the morning hastes,
The sun doth set, the shadow flies,
The gourd consumes, — and man, he dies!

Like to the grass that 's newly sprung,
Or like a tale that 's new begun,

* Born about 1565.

Or like the bird that 's here to-day,
Or like the pearlèd dew of May,
Or like an hour, or like a span,
Or like the singing of a swan,
E'en such is man; — who lives by breath,
Is here, now there, in life and death.
The grass decays, the tale is ended,
The bird is flown, the dew 's ascended,
The hour is short, the span not long,
The swan 's near death, — man's life is done!

Like to the bubble in the brook,
Or in a glass much like a look,
Or like the shuttle in the hand,
Or like the writing in the sand,
Or like a thought, or like a dream,
Or like the gliding of the stream,
E'en such is man; — who lives by breath,
Is here, now there, in life and death.
The bubble 's burst, the look 's forgot,
The shuttle 's flung, the writing 's blot,
The thought is past, the dream is gone,
The water glides, — man's life is done!

SENSIBILITY. — *Burns.*

Sensibility, how charming,
  Thou, my friend, canst truly tell
But distress, with horrors arming,
  Thou hast also known too well.

Fairest flower! behold the lily
  Blooming in the sunny ray;
Let the blast sweep o'er the valley,
  See it prostrate on the clay.

Hear the wood-lark charm the forest,
Telling o'er his little joys;
Hapless bird! a prey the surest
To each pirate of the skies.

Dearly bought the hidden treasure
Finer feelings can bestow;
Chords that vibrate sweetest pleasure
Thrill the deepest notes of woe.

TO BLOSSOMS.—*Herrick.*

FAIR pledges of a fruitful tree,
Why do ye fall so fast?
Your date is not so past,
But you may stay yet here a while
To blush and gently smile,
Then go at last.

What! were ye born to be
An hour or half's delight,
And so to bid good-night?
'T was pity Nature brought ye forth
Merely to show your worth,
And lose you quite.

But you are lovely leaves, where we
May read how soon things have
Their end, though ne'er so brave;
And after they have shown their pride,
Like you, a while, they glide
Into the grave.

LOVE. — *Milnes.*

THERE are gold-bright suns in worlds above,
And blazing gems in worlds below,
Our world has Love and only Love,
For living warmth and jewel glow;
God's love is sunlight to the good,
And Woman's pure as diamond sheen,
And Friendship's mystic brotherhood
In twilight beauty lies between.

BURIAL OF THE MINNISINK. — *Longfellow.*

ON sunny slope and beechen swell
The shadowed light of evening fell;
And, where the maple's leaf was brown,
With soft and silent lapse came down
The glory that the wood receives,
At sunset, in its brazen leaves.

Far upward in the mellow light
Rose the blue hills. One cloud of white,
Around a far-uplifted cone,
In the warm blush of evening shone;
An image of the silver lakes
By which the Indian's soul awakes.

But soon a funeral hymn was heard
Where the soft breath of evening stirred
The tall, gray forest; and a band
Of stern in heart, and strong in hand,
Came winding down beside the wave,
To lay the red chief in his grave.

They sang, that by his native bowers
He stood, in the last moon of flowers,
And thirty snows had not yet shed
Their glory on the warrior's head;
But, as the summer fruit decays,
So died he in those naked days.

A dark cloak of the roebuck's skin
Covered the warrior, and within
Its heavy folds the weapons, made
For the hard toils of war, were laid;
The cuirass, woven of plaited reeds,
And the broad belt of shells and beads.

Before, a dark-haired virgin train
Chanted the death-dirge of the slain;
Behind, the long procession came
Of hoary men and chiefs of fame,
With heavy hearts, and eyes of grief,
Leading the war-horse of their chief.

Stripped of his proud and martial dress,
Uncurbed, unreined, and riderless,
With darting eye, and nostril spread,
And heavy and impatient tread,
He came; and oft that eye so proud
Asked for his rider in the crowd.

They buried the dark chief; they freed
Beside the grave his battle steed;
And swift an arrow cleaved its way
To his stern heart! One piercing neigh
Arose, — and, on the dead man's plain,
The rider grasps his steed again.

HEAVEN.—*From Festus.*

Is heaven a place where pearly streams
Glide over silver sand?
Like childhood's rosy, dazzling dreams
Of some far fairy land?

Is heaven a clime where diamond dews
Glitter on fadeless flowers,
And mirth and music ring aloud
From amaranthine bowers?

Ah no; not such, not such is heaven!
Surpassing far all these;
Such cannot be the guerdon given
Man's wearied soul to please.

For saints and sinners here below,
Such vain to be have proved;
And the pure spirit will despise
What'er the sense has loved.

There shall we dwell with Sire and Son,
And with the Mother-maid,
And with the Holy Spirit, one,
In glory like arrayed;

And not to one created thing
Shall one embrace be given;
But all our joy shall be in God,
For only God is heaven.

ARNOLD WINKELRIED. — *Montgomery.*

"Make way for liberty!" he cried;
Made way for liberty, and died! —

It must not be; this day, this hour,
Annihilates the oppressor's power!
All Switzerland is in the field,
She will not fly, she cannot yield, —
She must not fall; her better fate
Here gives her an immortal date.
Few were the numbers she could boast;
But every freeman was a host,
And felt as though himself were he
On whose sole arm hung victory.
It did depend on one indeed;
Behold him, — Arnold Winkelried!
There sounds not to the trump of fame
The echo of a nobler name.
Unmarked he stood amid the throng,
In rumination deep and long,
Till you might see, with sudden grace,
The very thought come o'er his face;
And, by the motion of his form,
Anticipate the rising storm;
And, by the uplifting of his brow,
Tell where the bolt would strike, and how.
But 't was no sooner thought than done!
The field was in a moment won: —
"Make way for liberty!" he cried,
Then ran, with arms extended wide,
As if his dearest friend to clasp;
Ten spears he swept within his grasp:
"Make way for liberty!" he cried
Their keen points met from side to side;

He bowed amongst them like a tree,
And thus made way for liberty.
  Swift to the breach his comrades fly;
"Make way for liberty!" they cry,
And through the Austrian phalanx dart,
As rushed the spears through Arnold's heart;
While, instantaneous as his fall,
Rout, ruin, panic, scattered all;
An earthquake could not overthrow
A city with a surer blow
  Thus Switzerland again was free;
Thus death made way for liberty!

ON MYSELF. — *Cowley.*

THIS only grant me, that my means may lie
Too low for envy, for contempt too high.
    Some honor I would have,
Not from great deeds, but good alone;
The unknown are better than ill known;
    Rumor can ope the grave.
Acquaintance I would have, but when 't depends
Not on the number, but the choice, of friends.

Books should, not business, entertain the light,
And sleep, as undisturbed as death, the night.
    My house a cottage more
Than palace; and should fitting be
For all my use, no luxury.
    My garden painted o'er
With Nature's hand, not Art's; and pleasures yiel
Horace might envy in his Sabine field.

Thus would I double my life's fading space;
For he that runs it well twice runs his race.
        And in this true delight,
These unbought sports, this happy state,
I would not fear, nor wish, my fate;
        But boldly say, each night,
To-morrow let my sun his beams display,
Or in clouds hide them; I have lived to-day.

THE GRASSHOPPER. — *Tennyson.*

Voice of the summer wind,
Joy of the summer plain,
Life of the summer hours,
Carol clearly, bound along.
No Tithon* thou, as poets feign,
(Shame fall 'em, they are deaf and blind,)
But an insect lithe and strong,
Bowing the seeded summer flowers.
Prove their falsehood and their quarrel,
Vaulting on thy airy feet,
Clap thy shielded sides and carol,
Carol clearly, chirrup sweet.
Thou art a mailed warrior, in youth and strength
    complete.

---

* Among the many beautiful fables of the ancient Greeks was this one. The beauty of Tithonus, son of a king of Troy, gained for him the affection of one of the goddesses. He begged her, as a favor, to make him immortal, and his request was granted. But, as he had forgotten to ask to retain the vigor and beauty of youth, he soon became infirm and decrepid; and, as life became insupportable to him, he begged the goddess to remove him from the world. As he could not die, she changed him into a grasshopper.

Armed cap-a-pie,
Full fair to see;
Unknowing fear,
Undreading loss.
A gallant cavalier,
" Sans peur et sans reproche," *
In sunlight and in shadow,
The Bayard of the meadow.
I would dwell with thee,
  Merry grasshopper,
Thou art so glad and free,
  And as light as air;
Thou hast no sorrow or tears,
Thou hast no compt of years,
No withered immortality,
But a short youth, sunny and free.
Carol clearly, bound along,
  Soon thy joy is over.
A summer of loud song,
  And slumbers in the clover,
What hast thou to do with evil
In thine hour of love and revel,
  In thy heat of summer pride
  Pushing the thick roots aside
  Of the singing, flowered grasses,
  That brush thee with their silken tresses?
What hast thou to do with evil,
Shooting, singing, ever springing
  In and out the emerald glooms;
Ever leaping, ever singing,
  Lighting on the golden blooms?

---

* *Without fear and without reproach;* an epithet applied to Bayard, a French knight distinguished for his courage and his integrity He died in 1524.

A GRECIAN ANECDOTE. — *Milnes.*

How Sparta thirsted after orient gold,
And bartered faith for wealth she dared not use,
Is as severe a tale as e'er was told
The pride of man to conquer and confuse.

Therefore forget not what that nature was,
That once availed the base desire to foil,
When sought the Ionian Aristagoras
To mingle Sparta in his distant broil.

How thick the perils of that far emprise,
How dim the vista cunningly displayed,
The king discerned, with clear and practised eyes,
And bade the stranger court Athenian aid.

To people as to prince, appeal was vain, —
Vain the dark menace, — vain the shadowy gibe, —
But the wise envoy would not bend again
His homeward steps till failed the wonted bribe.

A suppliant at the regal hearth he stood,
Nor ever thought that proffer to withhold
Because about them, in her careless mood,
Played the king's child, — a girl some nine years old.

Ten — twenty — forty talents rose the bait; —
Strange feeling glistened in those infant eyes,
That gazed attentive on the grave debate,
And seemed to search its meaning in surprise.

Yet fifty now had well secured the prey,
Had not a little hand tight clasped his arm,
And a quick spirit uttered, "Come away,
Father, — that man is there to do you harm."

Not unaccepted such pure omen came;
  That gentle voice the present God revealed,—
And back the Ionian chief returned in shame,
  Checked by the virtue of that simple shield.

THE DEATH OF THE FLOWERS.—*Bryant.*

The melancholy days have come, the saddest of the year,
Of wailing winds, and naked woods, and meadows brown and sear.
Heaped in the hollows of the grove, the withered leaves lie dead;
They rustle to the eddying gust, and to the rabbit's tread.
The robin and the wren are flown, and from the shrubs the jay,
And from the wood-top calls the crow, through all the gloomy day.

Where are the flowers, the fair young flowers, that lately sprang and stood
In brighter light and softer airs, a beauteous sisterhood?
Alas! they all are in their graves; the gentle race of flowers
Are lying in their lowly beds, with the fair and good of ours.
The rain is falling where they lie, but the cold November rain
Calls not, from out the gloomy earth, the lovely ones again.

The wind-flower and the violet, they perished long ago,
And the brier-rose and the orchis died amid the summer glow;
But on the hill the golden-rod, and the aster in the wood,
And the yellow sunflower by the brook, in autumn beauty stood,
Till fell the frost from the clear, cold heaven, as falls the plague on men,
And the brightness of their smile was gone, from upland, glade, and glen.

And now, when comes the calm, mild day, as still such days will come,
To call the squirrel and the bee from out their winter home,
When the sound of dropping nuts is heard, though all the trees are still,
And twinkle in the smoky light the waters of the rill,
The south wind searches for the flowers whose fragrance late he bore,
And sighs to find them in the wood and by the stream no more.

And then I think of one who in her youthful beauty died,
The fair, meek blossom that grew up and faded by my side:
In the cold, moist earth we laid her, when the forest cast the leaf,
And we wept that one so lovely should have a life so brief;
Yet not unmeet it was that one, like that young friend of ours,
So gentle, and so beautiful, should perish with the flowers.

THE CORAL GROVE.—*Percival.*

DEEP in the wave is a coral grove,
Where the purple mullet and gold-fish rove;
Where the sea-flower spreads its leaves of blue,
That never are wet with falling dew,
But in bright and changeful beauty shine,
Far down in the green and grassy brine.
The floor is of sand, like the mountain drift,
And the pearl-shells spangle the flinty snow;
From coral rocks the sea-plants lift
Their boughs, where the tides and billows flow;
The water is calm and still below,
For the winds and the waves are absent there,
And the sands are bright as the stars that glow
In the motionless fields of upper air;
There, with its waving blade of green,
The sea-flag streams through the silent water,
And the crimson leaf of the dulse is seen
To blush like a banner bathed in slaughter;
There, with a light and easy motion,
The fan-coral sweeps through the clear, deep sea;
And the yellow and scarlet tufts of ocean
Are bending like corn on the upland lea:
And life, in rare and beautiful forms,
Is sporting amid those bowers of stone,
And is safe, when the wrathful spirit of storms
Has made the top of the waves his own.
And when the ship from his fury flies,
When the myriad voices of ocean roar,
When the wind-god frowns in the murky skies,
And demons are waiting the wreck on the shore;
Then, far below, in the peaceful sea,
The purple mullet and gold-fish rove
Where the waters murmur tranquilly
Through the bending twigs of the coral grove.

A HAPPY LIFE.—*Sir Henry Wotton.*

How happy is he born and taught,
That serveth not another's will;
Whose armor is his honest thought,
And simple truth his utmost skill;

Whose passions not his masters are;
Whose soul is still prepared for death,
Untied unto the world by care
Of public fame or private breath;

Who envies none that chance doth raise,
Nor vice; hath ever understood
How deepest wounds are given by praise,
Nor rules of state, but rules of good;

Who hath his life from rumors freed;
Whose conscience is his strong retreat;
Whose state can neither flatterers feed,
Nor ruin make oppressors great;

Who God doth late and early pray
More of his grace than gifts to lend;
And entertains the harmless day
With a well-chosen book or friend.

This man is freed from servile bands
Of hope to rise or fear to fall;
Lord of himself, though not of lands,
And having nothing, yet hath all.

KNOWLEDGE AND WISDOM. — *Cowper.*

Knowledge and Wisdom, far from being one,
Have oft times no connection. Knowledge dwells
In heads replete with thoughts of other men;
Wisdom, in minds attentive to their own.
Knowledge, — a rude, unprofitable mass,
The mere materials with which Wisdom builds, —
Till smoothed, and squared, and fitted to its place,
Does but encumber whom it seems to enrich!
Knowledge is proud that he has learned so much,
Wisdom is humble that he knows no more.

GOOD TEMPER. — *More.*

Since trifles make the sum of human things,
And half our misery from our foibles springs;
Since life's best joys consist in peace and ease,
And though but few can serve, yet all may please;
O, let the ungentle spirit learn from hence,
A small unkindness is a great offence!

VIRTUE. — *Old English Poetry.*

The sturdy rock, for all his strength,
By raging seas is rent in twain;
The marble stone is pierced at length
With little drops of drizzling rain;
The ox doth yield unto the yoke;
The steel obeyeth the hammer stroke.

Yea, man himself, unto whose will
  All things are bounden to obey,
For all his wit, and worthy skill,
  Doth fade at length, and fall away.
There is no thing but time doth waste;
The heavens, the earth, consume at last.

But Virtue sits, triumphing still,
  Upon the throne of glorious Fame;
Though spiteful Death man's body kill,
  Yet hurts he not his virtuous name.
By life or death, whatso betides,
The state of Virtue never slides.

CONSTANCY. — *George Herbert.*

  Who is the honest man?
He that doth still and strongly good pursue,
To God, his neighbor, and himself, most true;
  Whom neither force nor frowning can
Unpin, or wrench from giving all their due.

  Whose honesty is not
So loose or easy, that a ruffling wind
Can blow away, or glittering look it blind;
  Who rides his sure and even trot,
While the world now rides by, now lags behind.

  Who, when great trials come,
Nor seeks nor shuns them; but doth calmly stay
Till he the thing and the example weigh;
  All being brought into a sum,
What place or person calls for, he doth pay.

Whom none can work or woo
To use in anything a trick or sleight;
Far above all things he abhors deceit;
His words, and works, and fashion, too,
All of a piece, and all are clear and straight.

Who never melts or thaws
At close temptations! when the day is done
His goodness sets not, but in dark can run;
The sun to others writeth laws
And is their virtue; virtue is his sun.

Who, when he is to treat
With sick folks, women, those whom passions sway.
Allows for that, and keeps his constant way;
Whom others' faults do not defeat,
But, though men fail him, yet his part doth play.

Whom nothing can procure,
When the wide world runs bias from his will,
To writhe his limbs, and share, not mend, the ill.
This is the marksman, safe and sure,
Who still is right and prays to be so still.

TIMES GO BY TURNS. — *Southwell*, born in 1560.

THE loppéd tree in time may grow again,
Most naked plants renew both fruit and flower;
The sorriest wight may find release of pain;
The driest soil suck up some moistening shower;
Times go by turns, and chances change by course,
From foul to fair, from better hap to worse.

The sea of Fortune doth not ever flow;
She draws her favors to the lowest ebb;
Her tides have equal times to come and go;
Her loom doth weave the fine and coarsest web;
No joy so great but runneth to an end,
No hap so hard but may in fine amend.

Not always fall of leaf, nor ever spring;
Not endless night, nor yet eternal day;
The saddest birds a season find to sing;
The roughest storm a calm may soon allay;
Thus with succeeding turns God tempereth all,
That man may hope to rise, yet fear to fall.

A chance may win that by mischance was lost;
That net that holds no great, takes little fish;
In some things all, in all things none, are crossed;
Few all they need, but none have all they wish.
Unmingled joys here to no man befall;
Who least, have some; who most, have never all.

TO SORROW. — *Milnes.*

Sister Sorrow! sit beside me,
Or, if I must wander, guide me;
Let me take thy hand in mine,
Cold alike are mine and thine.

Think not, Sorrow, that I hate thee, —
Think not I am frightened at thee, —
Thou art come for some good end,
I will treat thee as a friend.

I will say that thou art bound
My unshielded soul to wound
By some force without thy will,
And art tender-minded still.

I will say thou givest scope
To the breath and light of hope;
That thy gentle tears have weight
Hardest hearts to penetrate:

That thy shadow brings together
Friends long lost in sunny weather,
With an hundred offices
Beautiful and blest as these.

Softly takest thou the crown
From my haughty temples down;
Place it on thine own pale brow,
Pleasure wears one — why not thou?

Let the blossoms glitter there
On thy long, unbanded hair,
And, when I have borne my pain,
Thou wilt give them me again.

If thou goest, sister Sorrow!
I shall look for thee to-morrow, —
I shall often see thee drest
As a masquerading guest:

And, howe'er thou hid'st the name,
I shall know thee still the same,
As thou sit'st beside me now,
With my garland on thy brow.

HUMILIBUS DAT GRATIAN.—*Peacham* about 1600.

THE mountains huge, that seem to check the sky,
  And all the world with greatness over-peer,
With heath or moss for most part barren lie;
  When valleys low doth kindly Phœbus cheer,
And with his heat in hedge and grove begets
The virgin primrose or sweet violets.

So God oft times denies unto the great
  The gifts of nature, or his heavenly grace,
And those that high in honor's chair are set
  Do feel their wants; when men of meaner place,
Although they lack the others' golden spring,
Perhaps are blest above the richest king.

ON THE DEATH OF A FRIEND.—*Milnes.*

I 'M not where I was yesterday,
Though my home be still the same,
For I have lost the veriest friend
Whom ever a friend could name;
I 'm not what I was yesterday,
Though change there be little to see,
For a part of myself has lapsed away
From Time to Eternity.

I have lost a thought, that many a year
Was most familiar food
To my inmost mind, by night or day,
In merry or plaintive mood;

I have lost a hope, that many a year
Looked far on a gleaming way,
When the walls of life were closing round,
And the sky was sombre gray.

For long, too long, in distant climes
My lot was cast, and then
A frail and casual intercourse
Was all I had with men;
But lonelily in distant climes
I was well content to roam,
And felt no void, for my heart was full
Of the friend it had left at home.

And now I was close to my native shores,
And I felt him at my side,
His spirit was in that homeward wind,
His voice in that homeward tide;
For what were to me my native shores,
But that they held the scene
Where my youth's most genial flowers had blown
And affection's root had been?

I thought, how should I see him first,
How should our hands first meet;
Within his room, — upon the stair, —
At the corner of the street?
I thought, where should I hear him first,
How catch his greeting tone? —
And thus I went up to his door,
And they told me he was gone!

O, what is life but a sum of love,
And death but to lose it all?
Weeds be for those that are left behind,
And not for those that fall;

And now how mighty a sum of love
Is lost forever for me!
No, I 'm not what I was yesterday,
Though change there be little to see.

TO A VIRTUOUS YOUNG LADY.—*Milton.*

Lady, that in the prime of earliest youth
Wisely hast shunned the broad way and the green,
And with those few are eminently seen
That labor up the hill of heavenly truth,
The better part with Mary and with Ruth
Chosen thou hast; and they that overween,
And at thy growing virtues fret their spleen,
No anger find in thee, but pity and ruth.
Thy care is fixed, and zealously attends
To fill thy odorous lamp with deeds of light,
And hope that reaps not shame. Therefore be sure
Thou, when the bridegroom with his feastful friends
Passes to bliss at the mid hour of night,
Hast gained thy entrance, virgin wise and pure.

TWENTY-SECOND SUNDAY AFTER TRINITY.—*Keble.*

"Lord, how often shall my brother sin against me, and I forgive him?"—Matthew xviii. 21.

What liberty so glad and gay,
  As where the mountain boy,
Reckless of regions far away,
  A prisoner lives in joy.

The dreary sounds of crowded earth,
  The cries of camp or town,
Never untuned his lonely mirth,
  Nor drew his visions down.

The snow-clad peaks of rosy light
  That meet his morning view,
The thwarting cliffs that bound his sight,
  They bound his fancy too.

Two ways alone his roving eye
  For age may onward go, —
Or in the azure deep on high,
  Or darksome mere below.

O blessed restraint! more blessèd range!
  Too soon the happy child
His nook of homely thought will change
  For life's seducing wild:

Too soon his altered day-dreams show
  This earth a boundless space,
With sun-bright pleasures to and fro
  Sporting in joyous race:

While of his narrowing heart each year
  Heaven less and less will fill,
Less keenly through his grosser ear
  The tones of mercy thrill.

It must be so; else wherefore falls
  The Saviour's voice unheard,
While from his pardoning cross he calls,
  "O, spare, as I have spared?"

By our own niggard rule we try
  The hope to suppliants given;
We mete out love, as if our eye
  Saw to the end of heaven.

Yes, ransomed sinner! wouldst thou know
  How often to forgive,
How dearly to embrace thy foe,
  Look where thou hop'st to live:

When thou hast told those isles of light,
  And fancied all beyond,
Whatever owns, in depth or height,
  Creation's wondrous bond;

Then in their solemn pageant learn
  Sweet mercy's praise to see;
Their Lord resigned them all, to earn
  The bliss of pardoning thee.

THE BEGGAR.—*J. R. Lowell.*

A BEGGAR through the world am I,
From place to place I wander by;
Fill up my pilgrim's scrip for me,
For Christ's sweet sake and charity!
  A little of thy steadfastness,
Rounded with leafy gracefulness,
Old oak, give me,—
That the world's blasts may round me blow,
And I yield gently to and fro,
While my stout-hearted trunk below
And firm-set roots, unmovéd be.

Some of thy stern, unyielding might,
Enduring still through day and night
Rude tempest-shock and withering blight, —
That I may keep at bay
The changeful April sky of chance,
And the strong tide of circumstance, —
Give me, old granite gray.
Some of thy mournfulness serene,
Some of thy never-dying green,
Put in this scrip of mine, —
That grief may fall like snow-flakes light,
And deck me in a robe of white,
Ready to be an angel bright, —
O sweetly mournful pine.
A little of thy merriment,
Of thy sparkling, light content,
Give me, my cheerful brook, —
That I may still be full of glee
And gladsomeness, where'er I be,
Though fickle fate hath prisoned me
In some neglected nook.
Ye have been very kind and good
To me, since I have been in the wood;
Ye have gone nigh to fill my heart;
But good-by, kind friends, every one,
I 've far to go ere set of sun;
Of all good things I would have part,
The day was high ere I could start,
And so my journey 's scarce begun.
Heaven help me! how could I forget
To beg of thee, dear violet!
Some of thy modesty,
That flowers here as well, unseen,
As if before the world thou 'dst been,
O, give, to strengthen me.

ODE TO DUTY. — *Wordsworth.*

STERN daughter of the voice of God!
O Duty! if that name thou love,
Who art a light to guide, a rod
To check the erring, and reprove;
Thou, who art victory and law
When empty terrors overawe,
From vain temptations dost set free,
And calm'st the weary strife of frail humanity!

There are who ask not if thine eye
Be on them; who, in love and truth,
Where no misgiving is, rely
Upon the genial sense of youth;
Glad hearts! without reproach or blot;
Who do thy work and know it not;
Long may the kindly impulse last!
But thou, if they should totter, teach them to stand fast!

Serene will be our days and bright,
And happy will our nature be,
When love is an unerring light,
And joy its own security.
And they a blissful course may hold,
Even now, who, not unwisely bold,
Live in the spirit of this creed;
Yet find that other strength, according to their need.

I, loving freedom, and untried,
No sport of every random gust,
Yet being to myself a guide,
Too blindly have reposed my trust;

And oft, when in my heart was heard
Thy timely mandate, I deferred
The task, in smoother walks to stray;
But thee I now would serve more strictly, if I may.

Through no disturbance of my soul,
Or strong compunction in me wrought,
I supplicate for thy control;
But in the quietness of thought:
Me this unchartered freedom tires;
I feel the weight of chance desires:
My hopes no more must change their name,
I long for a repose that ever is the same.

Stern Lawgiver! yet thou dost wear
The Godhead's most benignant grace;
Nor know we anything so fair
As is the smile upon thy face;
Flowers laugh before thee on their beds;
And Fragrance in thy footing treads;
Thou dost preserve the stars from wrong;
And the most ancient heavens, through thee, are
fresh and strong.

To humbler functions, awful Power!
I call thee; I myself commend
Unto thy guidance, from this hour;
O, let my weakness have an end!
Give unto me, made lowly, wise,
The spirit of self-sacrifice;
The confidence of reason give;
And in the light of truth thy bondman let me live!

FAMILIAR LOVE. — *Milnes.*

We read together, reading the same book,
Our heads bent forward in a half embrace,
So that each shade that either spirit took
Was straight reflected in the other's face;
We read, not silent, nor aloud, but each
Followed the eye that passed the page along,
With a low murmuring sound, that was not speech,
        Yet with so much monotony
        In its half slumbering harmony,
        You might not call it song;
        More like a bee, that in the noon rejoices,
Than any customed mood of human voices.
Then if some wayward or disputed sense
Made cease a while that music, and brought on
A strife of gracious-worded difference,
Too light to hurt our souls' dear unison,
We had experience of a blissful state,
In which our powers of thought stood separate,
Each, in its own high freedom, set apart,
But both close folded in one loving heart;
So that we seemed, without conceit, to be
Both one and two in our identity.

DEATH'S FINAL CONQUEST. — *Shirley.*

The glories of our birth and state
    Are shadows, not substantial things;
There is no armor against fate;
    Death lays his icy hand on kings.

Sceptre and crown
Must tumble down,
And in the dust be equal made
With the poor, crooked scythe and spade.

Some men with swords may reap the field,
And plant fresh laurels where they kill;
But their strong nerves at last must yield;
They tame but one another still:
Early or late
They stoop to fate,
And must give up their murmuring breath,
When they pale captives creep to Death.

The garlands wither on your brow;
Then boast no more your mighty deeds;
Upon Death's purple altar now
See where the victor victim bleeds;
All hands must come
To the cold tomb,
Only the actions of the just
Smell sweet and blossom in the dust.

THE WIDOW TO HER HOUR-GLASS.—*Bloomfield.*

Come, friend, I 'll turn thee up again;
Companion of the lonely hour!
Spring thirty times hath fed with rain
And clothed with leaves my humble bower,
Since thou hast stood,
In frame of wood,
On chest or window by my side;
At every birth still thou wert near,
Still spoke thine admonitions clear,—
And when my husband died.

I 've often watched thy streaming sand,
And seen the growing mountain rise,
And often found life's hopes to stand
On props as weak in Wisdom's eyes;
    Its conic crown
    Still sliding down,
Again heaped up, then down again;
The sand above more hollow grew,
Like days and years still filtering through,
    And mingling joy and pain.

While thus I spin and sometimes sing,
(For now and then my heart will glow,)
Thou measur'st Time's expanding wing;
By thee the noontide hour I know;
    Though silent thou,
    Still shalt thou flow,
And jog along thy destined way;
But when I glean the sultry fields,
When earth her yellow harvest yields,
    Thou gett'st a holiday.

Steady as truth, on either end
Thy daily task performing well,
Thou 'rt Meditation's constant friend,
And strik'st the heart without a bell:
    Come, lovely May!
    Thy lengthened day
Shall gild once more my native plain;
Curl inward here, sweet woodbine-flower·
Companion of the lonely hour,
    I 'll turn thee up again.

HYMN TO DIANA.—*Jonson*, born in 1574.

QUEENE, and huntresse, chaste, and faire,
Now the sun is laid to sleepe,
Seated, in thy silver chaire,
State in wonted manner keepe:
Hesperus intreats thy light,
Goddesse, excellently bright.

Earth, let not thy impious shade
Dare itself to interpose:
Cynthia's shining orbe was made
Heaven to cheere, when day did close;
Bless us, then, with wishéd sight,
Goddesse, excellently bright.

Lay thy bow of pearle apart,
And thy cristall-shining quiver;
Give unto the flying hart
Space to breathe, how short soever:
Thou that mak'st a day of night,
Goddesse, excellently bright.

THE MEN OF OLD.—*Milnes*.

I KNOW not that the men of old
Were better than men now,
Of heart more kind, of hand more bold,
Of more ingenuous brow;
I heed not those who pine perforce
A ghost of Time to raise,
As if they could check the course
Of these appointed days.

Still it is true, and over true,
That I delight to close
This book of life, self-wise and new,
And let my thoughts repose
On all that humble happiness
The world has since foregone, —
The daylight of contentedness
That on those faces shone!

With rights, though not too closely scanned,
Enjoyed as far as known, —
With will by no reverse unmanned, —
With pulse of even tone, —
They from to-day and from to-night
Expected nothing more
Than yesterday and yesternight
Had proffered them before.

To them was life a simple art
Of duties to be done,
A game where each man took his part,
A race where all must run;
A battle whose great scheme and scope
They little cared to know,
Content, as men-at-arms, to cope
Each with his fronting foe.

Man now his virtue's diadem
Puts on and proudly wears;
Great thoughts, great feelings, came to them,
Like instincts, unawares:
Blending their souls' sublimest needs
With tasks of every day,
They went about their gravest deeds
As noble boys at play.

And what if Nature's fearful wound
They did not probe and bare, —
For that their spirits never swooned
To watch the misery there, —
For that their love but flowed more fast,
Their charities more free,
Not conscious what mere drops they cast
Into the evil sea.

A man's best things are nearest him,
Lie close about his feet;
It is the distant and the dim
That we are sick to greet:
For flowers that grow our hands beneath,
We struggle and aspire, —
Our hearts must die, except they breathe
The air of fresh Desire.

Yet, Brothers, who up Reason's hill
Advance with hopeful cheer, —
O, loiter not! those heights are chill, —
As chill as they are clear;
And still restrain your haughty gaze,
The loftier that ye go,
Remembering distance leaves a haze
On all that lies below.

THE WORTH OF HOURS. — *Milnes.*

BELIEVE not that your inner eye
Can ever in just measure try
The worth of Hours as they go by:

For every man's weak self, alas!
Makes him to see them, while they pass,
As through a dim or tinted glass:

But if in earnest care you would
Mete out to each its part of good,
Trust rather to your after-mood.

Those surely are not fairly spent,
That leave your spirit bowed and bent
In sad unrest and ill-content:

And more, — though free from seeming harm,
You rest from toil of mind or arm,
Or slow retire from Pleasure's charm, —

If then a painful sense comes on
Of something wholly lost and gone,
Vainly enjoyed, or vainly done, —

Of something from your being's chain
Broke off, nor to be linked again
By all mere Memory can retain, —

Upon your heart this truth may rise, —
Nothing that altogether dies
Suffices Man's just destinies:

So should we live, that every Hour
May die as dies the natural flower, —
A self-reviving thing of power;

That every Thought and every Deed
May hold within itself the seed
Of future good and future need;

Esteeming Sorrow, whose employ
Is to develop, not destroy,
Far better than a barren Joy.

ABOU BEN ADHEM AND THE ANGEL. — *Leigh Hunt.*

Abou Ben Adhem (may his tribe increase !)
Awoke one night from a deep dream of peace,
And saw, within the moonlight in his room,
Making it rich, and like a lily in bloom,
An angel, writing in a book of gold;
Exceeding peace had made Ben Adhem bold;
And to the presence in the room he said,
" What writest thou ? " The vision raised his head,
And, with a look made all of sweet accord,
Answered, " The names of those who love the Lord."
" And is mine one ? " said Abou. " Nay, not so,"
Replied the angel. Abou spoke more low,
But cheerly still; and said, " I pray thee, then,
Write me as one that loves his fellow-men."
The angel wrote and vanished. The next night
It came again with great awakening light,
And showed the names whom love of God had blessed,
And lo ! Ben Adhem's name led all the rest.

THE VIOLET-GIRL. — *Milnes.*

When Fancy will continually rehearse
Some painful scene once present to the eye,
'T is well to mould it into gentle verse,
That it may lighter on the spirit lie.

Home yester-eve I wearily returned,
Though bright my morning mood and short my way;
But sad experience, in one moment earned,
Can crush the heaped enjoyments of the day.

Passing the corner of a populous street,
I marked a girl whose wont it was to stand,
With pallid cheek, torn gown, and naked feet,
And bunches of fresh violets in each hand.

There her small commerce, in the chill March weather
She plied with accents miserably mild;
It was a frightful thought to set together
Those blooming blossoms and that fading child: —

Those luxuries and largess of the earth,
Beauty and pleasure to the sense of man,
And this poor sorry weed, cast loosely forth
On life's wild waste, to struggle as it can!

To me that odorous purple ministers
Hope-bearing memories and inspiring glee;
While meanest images alone are hers, —
The sordid wants of base humanity.

Think, after all this lapse of hungry hours
In the disfurnished chamber of dim cold,
How she must loathe the very scented flowers
That on the squalid table lie unsold!

Rest on your woodland banks and wither there,
Sweet preluders of spring! far better so
Than live misused to fill the grasp of care,
And serve the piteous purposes of woe.

FROM ELEONORA. — *Dryden.*

As precious gums are not for lasting fire,
They but perfume the temple, and expire;
So was she soon exhaled, and vanished hence;
A short, sweet odor, of a vast expense.

She vanished, we can scarcely say she died,
For but a now did heaven and earth divide:
She passed serenely with a single breath;
This moment perfect health, the next was death:
One sigh did her eternal bliss assure;
So little penance needs, when souls are almost pure
As gentle dreams our waking thoughts pursue;
Or, one dream passed, we slide into a new;
So close they follow, such wild order keep,
We think ourselves awake, and are asleep:
So softly death succeeded life in her:
She did but dream of heaven, and she was there.

THE DESERTED HOUSE. — *Tennyson.*

Life and thought have gone away,
Side by side,
Leaving door and windows wide;
Careless tenants they!
All within is dark as night!
In the windows is no light;
And no murmur at the door,
So frequent on its hinge before.

Close the door, the shutters close,
Or through the windows we shall see
The nakedness and vacancy
Of the dark, deserted house.
Come away! no more of mirth
Is here or merry-making sound;
The house was builded of the earth,
And shall fall again to ground.

Come away! for Life and Thought
Here no longer dwell;
But in a city glorious —
A great and distant city — have bought
A mansion incorruptible.
Would they could have stayed with us!

A PSALM OF LIFE. — *Longfellow.*

Tell me not, in mournful numbers,
"Life is but an empty dream!"
For the soul is dead that slumbers,
And things are not what they seem.

Life is real! Life is earnest!
And the grave is not its goal;
"Dust thou art, to dust returnest,"
Was not spoken of the soul.

Not enjoyment, and not sorrow,
Is our destined end or way;
But to act, that each to-morrow
Find us further than to-day.

Art is long, and Time is fleeting,
And our hearts, though stout and brave,
Still, like muffled drums, are beating
Funeral marches to the grave.

In the world's broad field of battle,
In the bivouac of Life,
Be not like dumb, driven cattle!
Be a hero in the strife!

Trust no Future, howe'er pleasant!
  Let the dead Past bury its dead!
Act, — act in the living Present!
  Heart within, and God o'erhead!

Lives of great men all remind us
  We can make our lives sublime,
And, departing, leave behind us
  Footsteps on the sands of time;

Footprints, that perhaps another,
  Sailing o'er life's solemn main,
A forlorn and shipwrecked brother,
  Seeing, shall take heart again.

Let us, then, be up and doing,
  With a heart for any fate;
Still achieving, still pursuing,
  Learn to labor and to wait.

BERMUDAS. — *Marvell.*

Where the remote Bermudas ride,
In the ocean's bosom unespied;
From a small boat that rowed along,
The list'ning winds received this song.

" What should we do but sing His praise,
That led us through the watery maze
Unto an isle so long unknown,
And yet far kinder than our own?
Where He the huge sea-monsters wracks,
That lift the deep upon their backs.

He lands us on a glassy stage,
Safe from the storms, and prelate's rage.
He gave us this eternal spring,
Which here enamels everything;
And sends the fowls to us in care,
On daily visits through the air.
He hangs in shades the orange bright,
Like golden lamps in a green night;
And does in the pomegranates close
Jewels more rich than Ormus shows.
He makes the figs our mouths to meet;
And throws the melons at our feet.
But apples plants of such a price,
No tree could ever bear them twice.
With cedars, chosen by His hand
From Lebanon, He stores the land;
And makes the hollow seas, that roar,
Proclaim the Ambergris on shore.
He cast (of which we rather boast)
The gospel's pearl upon our coast;
And in these rocks for us did frame
A temple, where to sound His name.
O, let our voice His praise exalt,
Till it arrive at heaven's vault!
Which, thence (perhaps) rebounding, may
Echo beyond the Mexique bay."

Thus sung they, in the English boat,
An holy and a cheerful note;
And all the way, to guide their chime,
With falling oars they kept the time.

TWENTY-FOURTH SUNDAY AFTER TRINITY.—*Keble.*

"The heart knoweth his own bitterness; and a stranger doth no intermeddle with his joy."—PROVERBS xiv. 10.

WHY should we faint and fear to live alone,
  Since all alone—so Heaven has willed—we die,
Nor even the tenderest heart, and next our own,
  Knows half the reasons why we smile or sigh?

Each in its hidden sphere of joy or woe,
  Our hermit spirits dwell, and range apart;
Our eyes see all around,—in gloom or glow,—
  Hues of their own, fresh borrowed from the heart.

And well it is for us our God should feel
  Alone our secret throbbings; so our prayer
May readier spring to heaven, nor spend its zeal
  On cloud-born idols of this lower air.

For if one heart in perfect sympathy
  Beat with another, answering love for love,
Weak mortals all entranced on earth would lie,
  Nor listen for those purer strains above.

Or what if Heaven for once its searching light
  Lent to some partial eye, disclosing all
The rude, bad thoughts that in our bosom's night
  Wander at large, nor heed Love's gentle thrall?

Who would not shun the dreary, uncouth place?
  As if, fond leaning where her infant slept,
A mother's arm a serpent should embrace;
  So might we friendless live, and die unwept.

Then keep the softening veil in mercy drawn,
Thou who canst love us, though thou read'st us true!
As on the bosom of the aerial dawn
Melts in dim haze each coarse, ungentle hue.

A SONNET.— *Wordsworth.*

Scorn not the Sonnet; critic, you have frowned,
Mindless of its just honors; with this key
Shakspeare unlocked his heart; the melody
Of this small lute gave ease to Petrarch's wound;
A thousand times this pipe did Tasso sound;
Camoens soothed with it an exile's grief;
The Sonnet glittered a gay myrtle-leaf
Amid the cypress with which Dante crowned
His visionary brow; a glow-worm lamp,
It cheered mild Spenser, called from Faery-land
To struggle through dark ways; and, when a damp
Fell round the path of Milton, in his hand
The thing became a trumpet, whence he blew
Soul-animating strains,—alas, too few!

EXPERIENCE.—*Jane Taylor.*

How false is found, as on in life we go,
Our early estimate of bliss and woe!
Some sparkling joy attracts us, that we fain
Would sell a precious birthright to obtain.

There all our hopes of happiness are placed;
Life looks without it like a joyless waste;
No good is prized, no comfort sought beside,
Prayers, tears, implore, and will not be denied.
Heaven pitying hears the intemperate, rude appeal,
And suits its answer to our truest weal;
The self-sought idol, if at last bestowed,
Proves what our wilfulness required, — a goad.
Ne'er but as needful chastisement is given
The wish thus forced, and torn, and stormed from Heaven.
  But if withheld, in pity, from our prayer,
We rave a while of torment and despair, —
Refuse each proffered comfort with disdain,
And slight the thousand blessings that remain.
Meantime Heaven bears the grievous wrong, and waits,
In patient pity, till the storm abates;
Applies with gentlest hand the healing balm,
Or speaks the ruffled mind into a calm;
Deigning, perhaps, to show the mourner soon
'T was special mercy that denied the boon.
  Our blasted hopes, our aims and wishes crost,
Are worth the tears and agonies they cost,
When the poor mind, by fruitless efforts spent,
With food and raiment learns to be content.
Bounding with youthful hope, the restless mind
Leaves that divine monition far behind;
And, tamed at length by suffering, comprehends
The tranquil happiness to which it tends;
Perceives the high-wrought bliss it aimed to share,
Demands a richer soil, a purer air, —
That 't is not fitted, and would strangely grace
The mean condition of our mortal race;
And all we need in this terrestrial spot
Is calm contentment with "the common lot."

SAY, HENRY, SHOULD A MAN OF MIND.

Say, Henry, should a man of mind
  Sigh o'er his brittle crust,
Or grieve because he is not joined
  To fibres more robust?

Look round, with philosophic ken,
  Through Nature's works below,
From very atoms up to men
  We find it ordered so —

That much of all we finest hold,
  Admire with one acclaim,
Is of a delicater mould,
  And of a feebler frame.

Look at bent lilies as you walk,
  How elegantly thin!
Yet well the fragrance from that stalk
  Proclaims the power within.

Look at the bird with glossiest wings,
  Yet sweeter taste than plume,
That scuds, that murmurs, sips, and sings,
  And feasts upon perfume.

Look at the rose his bill invades
  With eager, wanton strife!
On what a slender stalk it fades
  And blushes out its life.

Look at the sex, whose form may vaunt
 More grace than bird or rose;
What fine infirmities enchant,
 What frailty charms, in those!

Great minds with energetic thought
 Wear out their shell of clay,
Yet at each crevice light is caught,
 Till all is mental day.

Then, Henry, let no man of mind
 Sigh o'er his brittle crust,
Or grieve because he is not joined
 To fibres more robust.

SONNET. — *J. R. Lowell.*

Through suffering and sorrow thou hast past,
To show us what a woman true may be;
They have not taken sympathy from thee,
Nor made thee any other than thou wast;
Save as some tree, which, in a sudden blast,
Sheddeth those blossoms that were weakly grown
Upon the air, but keepeth every one
Whose strength gives warrant of good fruit at last
So thou hast shed some blooms of gayety,
But never one of steadfast cheerfulness,
Nor hath thy knowledge of adversity
Robbed thee of any faith in happiness,
But rather cleared thine inner eyes to see
How many simple ways there are to bless.

THE FORERUNNERS. — *R. W. Emerson.*

Long I followed happy guides,
I could never reach their sides.
Their step is forth, and ere the day
Breaks up their leaguer and away.
Keen my sense, my heart was young,
Right good-will my sinews strung,
But no speed of mine avails
To hunt upon their shining trails.
On and away, their hasting feet
Make the morning proud and sweet.
Flowers they strew, I catch the scent,
Or tone of silver instrument
Leaves on the wind melodious trace,
Yet I could never see their face.
On eastern hills I see their smokes
Mixed with mist by distant lochs.
I met many travellers,
Who the road had surely kept,
They saw not my fine revellers,
These had crossed them while they slept.
Some had heard their fine report,
In the country or the court.
Fleetest couriers alive
Never yet could once arrive,
As they went or they returned,
At the house where these sojourned.
Sometimes their strong speed they slacken,
Though they are not overtaken;
In sleep their jubilant troop is near,
I tuneful voices overhear,
It may be in wood or waste, —
At unawares 't is come and passed.

Their near camp my spirit knows
By signs gracious as rainbows.
I thenceforward, and long after,
Listen for their harp-like laughter,
And carry in my heart for days
Peace that hallows rudest ways.

THE SUMMER EVENING. — *Clare.*

The sinking sun is taking leave,
And sweetly gilds the edge of eve,
While huddling clouds of purple dye
Gloomy hang the western sky;
Crows crowd croaking overhead,
Hastening to the woods to bed;
Cooing sits the lonely dove,
Calling home her absent love;
From the hay-cock's moistened heaps,
Startled frogs take vaulting leaps,
And along the shaven mead,
Jumping travellers, they proceed;
Quick the dewy grass divides,
Moistening sweet their speckled sides.
From the grass or floweret's cup,
Quick the dew-drop bounces up.
Now the blue fog creeps along,
And the bird's forgot his song;
Flowers now sleep within their hoods,
Daisies button into buds;
From soiling dew the buttercup
Shuts his golden jewels up;
And the rose and woodbine, they
Wait again the smiles of May.

'Neath the willow's wavy boughs,
Dolly, singing, milks her cows;
While the brook, as bubbling by,
Joins in murmuring melody.
Swains to fold their sheep begin,
Dogs, loud barking, drive them in.
Hedgers now along the road
Homeward bend beneath their load;
And, from the long, furrowed seams,
Ploughmen loose their weary teams;
Ball, with urging lashes mealed,
Still so slow to drive afield,
Eager blundering from the plough,
Wants no whip to drive him now;
At the stable-door he stands,
Looking round for friendly hands
To loose the door its fastening pin,
And let him with his corn begin.
The night-wind now, with sooty wings,
In the cotter's chimney sings;
Now, as stretching o'er the bed,
Soft I raise my drowsy head,
Listening to the ushering charms
That shake the elm-tree's massy arms,
Till sweet slumbers stronger creep,
Deeper darkness stealing round;
Then, as rocked, I sink to sleep,
'Mid the wild winds' lulling sound.

TO THE RAINBOW. — *Campbell.*

TRIUMPHAL arch, that fill'st the sky
  When storms prepare to part,
I ask not proud Philosophy
  To teach me what thou art.

Still seem as to my childhood's sight,—
  A midway station given,
For happy spirits to alight
  Betwixt the earth and heaven.

Can all that Optics teach unfold
  Thy form to please me so,
As when I dreamed of gems and gold
  Hid in thy radiant bow?

When Science from creation's face
  Enchantment's veil withdraws,
What lovely visions yield their place
  To cold, material laws!

And yet, fair bow, no fabling dreams,
  But words of the Most High,
Have told why first thy robe of beams
  Was woven in the sky.

When o'er the green, undeluged earth,
  Heaven's covenant thou didst shine.
How came the world's gray fathers forth,
  To watch thy sacred sign?

And when its yellow lustre smiled
  O'er mountains yet untrod,
Each mother held aloft her child,
  To bless the bow of God.

Methinks, thy jubilee to keep,
  The first-made anthem rang
On earth, delivered from the deep,
  And the first poet sang.

Nor ever shall the Muse's eye
  Unraptured greet thy beam;
Theme of primeval prophecy,
  Be still the poet's theme!

The earth to thee her incense yields,
  The lark thy welcome sings, —
When, glittering in the freshened fields
  The snowy mushroom springs.

How glorious is thy girdle cast
  O'er mountain, tower, and town;
Or mirrored in the ocean vast,
  A thousand fathoms down!

As fresh as yon horizon dark,
  As young thy beauties seem,
As when the eagle from the ark
  First sported in thy beam.

For, faithful to its sacred page,
  Heaven still rebuilds thy span;
Nor lets the type grow pale with age,
  That first spoke peace to man.

HYMN OF THE CHEROKEE INDIAN. — *I. McLellan, Jr.*

Like the shadows in the stream,
Like the evanescent gleam
Of the twilight's failing blaze,
Like the fleeting years and days,
Like all things that soon decay,
Pass the Indian tribes away.

Indian son and Indian sire!
Lo! the embers of your fire
On the wigwam hearth burn low,
Never to revive its glow!
And the Indian's heart is ailing,
And the Indian's blood is failing.

Now the hunter's bow 's unbent,
And his arrows all are spent!
Like a very little child
Is the red man of the wild;
To his day there 'll dawn no morrow;
Therefore is he full of sorrow.

From his hills the stag is fled,
And the fallow deer are dead,
And the wild beasts of the chase
Are a lost and perished race;
And the birds have left the mountain,
And the fishes the clear fountain.

Indian woman, to thy breast
Closer let thy babe be pressed,
For thy garb is thin and old,
And the winter wind is cold;
On thy homeless head it dashes,
Round thee the grim lightning flashes.

We, the rightful lords of yore,
Are the rightful lords no more;
Like the silver mist we fail,
Like the red leaves in the gale,—
Fail like shadows, when the dawning
Waves the bright flag of the morning.

By the river's lonely marge
Rotting is the Indian barge;

And his hut is ruined now
On the rocky mountain-brow;
The fathers' bones are all neglected,
And the children's hearts dejected.

Therefore, Indian people, flee
To the furthest western sea;
Let us yield our pleasant land
To the stranger's stronger hand;
Red men and their realms must sever;
They forsake them, and forever!

CHIDHAR THE PROPHET.

FROM THE GERMAN OF RÜCKERT, BY MILNES.

CHIDHAR THE PROPHET, ever young,
Thus loosed the bridle of his tongue.

I journeyed by a goodly town,
Beset with many a garden fair,
And asked with one who gathered down
Large fruit how long the town was there.
He spoke, nor chose his hand to stay, —
"The town has stood for many a day,
And will be here forever and aye."

A thousand years went by, and then
I went the selfsame road again.

No vestige of that town I traced, —
But one poor swain his horn employed, —
His sheep unconscious browsed and grazed,
I asked, "When was that town destroyed?"
He spoke, nor would his horn lay by,
"One thing may grow and another die,
But I know nothing of towns, — not I."

A thousand years went by, and then
I passed the self-same place again.

There in the deep of waters cast
His nets one lonely fisherman,
And as he drew them up at last,
I asked him how that lake began.
He looked at me and laughed to say,
" The waters spring forever and aye,
And fish are plenty every day."

A thousand years went by, and then
I went the self-same road again.

I found a country wild and rude,
And, axe in hand, beside a tree,
The hermit of that solitude, —
I asked how old that wood might be.
He spoke, — " I count not time at all,
A tree may rise, a tree may fall,
The forest overlives us all."

A thousand years went on, and then
I passed the self-same place again.

And there a glorious city stood,
And, 'mid tumultuous market-cry,
I asked when rose the town, where wood,
Pasture and lake, forgotten lie.
They heard me not, and little blame, —
For them the world is as it came,
And all things must be still the same.

A thousand years shall pass, and then
I mean to try that road again.

POETRY

FOR

HOME AND SCHOOL.

PART II.

SOME MURMUR, WHEN THEIR SKY IS CLEAR.—*R. C. Trench.*

Some murmur, when their sky is clear
   And wholly bright to view,
If one small speck of dark appear
   In their great heaven of blue;
And some with thankful love are filled,
   If but one streak of light,
One ray of God's good mercy, gild
   The darkness of their night.

In palaces are hearts that ask,
   In discontent and pride,
Why life is such a dreary task,
   And all good things denied;
And hearts in poorest huts admire
   How Love has in their aid
(Love that not ever seems to tire)
   Such rich provision made.

WEEP NOT FOR BROAD LANDS LOST.—*R. C. Trench.*

Weep not for broad lands lost;
Weep not for fair hopes crost:

Weep not when limbs wax old;
Weep not when friends grow cold;
Weep not that Death must part
Thine and the best loved heart;
  Yet weep, weep all thou can, —
Weep, weep, because thou art
  A sin-defilèd man.

SUNDAYS. — *Henry Vaughan.*

Bright shadows of true rest! some shoots of bliss;
      Heaven once a week;
The next world's gladness prepossessed in this;
      A day to seek;
Eternity in time; the steps by which
  We climb above all ages; lamps that light
Man through his heap of dark days; and the rich
  And full redemption of the whole week's flight;
The pulleys unto headlong man; time's bower;
      The narrow way;
Transplanted paradise; God's walking hour;
      The cool o' th' day;
The creature's jubilee; God's parle with dust;
  Heaven here; man on those hills of myrrh and flowers;
Angels descending; the returns of trust;
  A gleam of glory after six days' showers;
The church's love-feasts; time's prerogative
      And interest,
Deducted from the whole, the combs and hive,
      And home of rest;
The milky way chalked out with suns; a clue
  That guides through erring hours, and in full story
A taste of heaven on earth; the pledge and cue
  Of a full feast, and the out-courts of glory.

THE BOY OF EGREMOND.* — *Rogers.*

"SAY, what remains when hope is fled?"
She answered, "Endless weeping!"
For in the herdsman's eye she read
Who in his shroud lay sleeping.
At Embsay rung the matin-bell,
The stag was roused on Barden-fell;
The mingled sounds were swelling, dying,
And down the Wharfe a hern was flying;
When near the cabin in the wood,
In tartan clad and forest-green,
With hound in leash and hawk in hood,
The Boy of Egremond was seen.
Blithe was his song, a song of yore;
But where the rock is rent in two,
And the river rushes through,
His voice was heard no more!
'T was but a step! the gulf he past;
But that step, — it was his last!
As through the mist he winged his way
(A cloud that hovers night and day),
The hound hung back, and back he drew
The master and his merlin too.

---

* In the twelfth century, William Fitz-Duncan laid waste the valleys of Craven with fire and sword, and was afterwards established there by his uncle, David of Scotland.

He was the last of the race; his son, commonly called the Boy of Egremond, dying before him in the manner here related; when a priory was removed from Embsay to Bolton, that it might be as near as possible to the place where the accident happened. That place is still known by the name of the *Strid;* and the mother's answer, as given in the first stanza, is to this day often repeated in Wharfedale. See Whitaker's *History of Craven.*

That narrow place of noise and strife
Received their little all of life!
   There now the matin-bell is rung,
The "Miserere!" duly sung;
And holy men in cowl and hood
Are wandering up and down the wood.
But what avail they? Ruthless Lord,
Thou didst not shudder when the sword
Here on the young its fury spent,
The helpless and the innocent.
Sit now and answer groan for groan;
The child before thee is thy own.
And she who wildly wanders there,
The mother in her long despair,
Shall oft remind thee, waking, sleeping,
Of those who by the Wharfe were weeping;
Of those who would not be consoled,
When red with blood the river rolled.

LIFE AND DEATH. — *R. C. Trench.*

A PARABLE, FROM THE GERMAN OF RÜCKERT.

There went a man through Syrian land,
Leading a camel by the hand.
The beast, made wild by some alarm,
Began to threaten sudden harm,
So fiercely snorting, that the man
With all his speed escaping ran;—
He ran, and saw a well that lay,
As chance would have it, by the way.
He heard the camel snort so near,
As almost maddened him with fear,

And crawled into the well, — yet there
Fell not, but dangled in mid ai:
For from a fissure in the stone,
Which lined its sides, a bush had grown;
To this he clung with all his might,
From thence lamenting his sad plight.
He saw, what time he looked on high,
The beast's head perilously nigh,
Ready to drag him back again;
He looked into the bottom then,
And there a dragon he espied,
Whose horrid jaws were yawning wide,
Agape to swallow him alive,
As soon as he should there arrive.
But as he hung two fears between,
A third by that poor wretch was seen;
For, where the bush by which he clung
Had from the broken wall outsprung,
He saw two mice precisely there,
One black, one white, a stealthy pair; —
He saw the black one and the white,
How at the root by turns they bite,
They gnaw, they pull, they dig; and still
The earth that held its fibres spill,
Which, as it rustling downward ran,
The dragon to look up began,
Watching how soon the shrub and all
Its burden would together fall.

The man in anguish, fear, despair,
Beleaguered, threatened everywhere,
In state of miserable doubt,
In vain for safety gazed about.
But as he looked around him so,
A twig he spied, and on it grow

Ripe berries from their laden stalk;
Then his desire he could not balk.
When these did once his eye engage,
He saw no more the camel's rage,
Nor dragon in the underground,
Nor game the busy mice had found.
The beast above might snort and blow,
The Dragon watch his prey below,
The mice gnaw near him as they pleased, —
The berries eagerly he seized;
They seemed to him right good to eat;
A dainty mouthful, welcome treat,
They brought him such a keen delight,
His danger was forgotten quite.

But who, you ask, is this vain man,
Who thus forget his terror can?
Then learn, O friend, that man art thou!
Listen and I will tell thee how.
The dragon in the well beneath,
That is the yawning gulf of death.
The camel threatening overhead
Is life's perplexity and dread.
'T is thou who, life and death between,
Hangest on this world's sapling green;
And they who gnaw the root, the twain
Who thee and thy support would fain
Deliver unto death a prey, —
These names the mice have, Night and Day.
From morn to evening gnaws the white,
And would the root unfasten quite;
From evening till the morn comes back,
In deepest stillness gnaws the black;
And yet, in midst of these alarms,
The berry, Pleasure, has such charms,

That thou, the camel of life's woe,
That thou, the dragon death below,
That thou, the two mice, Night and Day,
And all forgettest, save the way
To get most berries in thy power,
And on the grave's cleft side devour.

BY GRECIAN ANNALS IT REMAINED UNTOLD.—*R. C. Trench.*

By Grecian annals it remained untold,
But may be read in Eastern legend old,
How, when great Alexander died, he bade
That his two hands uncovered might be laid
Outside the bier, for men therewith to see—
Men who had seen him in his majesty—
That he had gone the common way of all,
And nothing now his own in death might call;
Nor of the treasures of two empires aught
Within those empty hands unto the grave had brought.

FOURTH SUNDAY AFTER TRINITY.—*Keble.*

It was not, then, a poet's dream,
  An idle vaunt of song,
Such as beneath the moon's soft gleam
  On vacant fancies throng,

Which bids us see in heaven and earth,
  In all fair things around,
Strong yearnings for a blest new birth
  With sinless glories crowned;

Which bids us hear, at each sweet pause
  From care and want and toil,
When dewy eve her curtain draws
  Over the day's turmoil,

In the low chant of wakeful birds,
  In the deep weltering flood,
In whispering leaves, these solemn words, —
  "God made us all for good."

All true, all faultless, all in tune,
  Creation's wondrous choir
Opened in mystic unison,
  To last till time expire.

And still it lasts: by day and night,
  With one consenting voice,
All hymn thy glory, Lord, aright,
  All worship and rejoice!

Man only mars the sweet accord,
  O'erpowering with "harsh din"
The music of thy works and word,
  Ill matched with grief and sin.

Sin is with man at morning break,
  And through the livelong day
Deafens the ear that fain would wake
  To Nature's simple lay.

But when eve's silent footfall steals
  Along the eastern sky,
And one by one to earth reveals
  Those purer fires on high, —

When one by one each human sound
  Dies on the awful ear,
Then Nature's voice no more is drowned,
  She speaks, and we must hear.

Then pours she on the Christian heart
  That warning still and deep,
At which high spirits of old would start
  E'en from their pagan sleep,

Just guessing, through their murky blind,
  Few, faint, and baffling sight,
Streaks of a brighter heaven behind
  A cloudless depth of light.

Such thoughts, the wreck of Paradise,
  Through many a dreary age,
Upbore whate'er of good and wise
  Yet lived in bard or sage:

They marked what agonizing throes
  Shook the great mother's womb; —
But Reason's spells might not disclose
  The gracious birth to come;

Nor could the enchantress Hope forecast
  God's secret love and power;
The travail-pangs of Earth must last
  Till her appointed hour;

The hour that saw from opening heaven
  Redeeming glory stream,
Beyond the summer hues of even,
  Beyond the mid-day beam.

Thenceforth, to eyes of high desire,
The meanest things below,
As with a seraph's robe of fire
Invested, burn and glow:

The rod of heaven has touched them all,
The word from heaven is spoken:
"Rise, shine, and sing, thou captive thrall!
Are not thy fetters broken?

"The God who hallowed thee, and blest,
Pronouncing thee all good, —
Hath He not all thy wrongs redrest,
And all thy bliss renewed?

"Why mourn'st thou still as one bereft,
Now that th' eternal Son
His blessed home in heaven hath left
To make thee all his own?"

Thou mourn'st because sin lingers still
In Christ's new heaven and earth;
Because our rebel works and will
Stain our immortal birth;

Because, as Love and Prayer grow cold,
The Saviour hides his face,
And worldlings blot the temple's gold
With uses vile and base.

Hence all thy groans and travail-pains,
Hence, till thy God return,
In Wisdom's ear thy blithest strains,
O Nature, seem to mourn!

IS THERE, FOR HONEST POVERTY.—*Burns*

Is there, for honest poverty,
  That hangs his head, and a' that?
The coward-slave, we pass him by,
  We dare be poor for a' that!
For a' that, and a' that,
  Our toil 's obscure, and a' that;
The rank is but the guinea's stamp,
  The man 's the gowd for a' that!

What tho' on hamely fare we dine,
  Wear hoddin gray, and a' that;
Gie fools their silks, and knaves their wine,
  A man 's a man, for a' that!
For a' that, and a' that,
  Their tinsel show, and a' that,
The honest man, though e'er sae poor,
  Is king o' men for a' that!

Ye see yon birkie, ca'd a lord,
  Wha struts, and stares, and a' that;
Though hundreds worship at his word,
  He 's but a coof for a' that!
For a' that, and a' that,
  His riband, star, and a' that,
The man of independent mind,
  He looks and laughs at a' that!

A king can mak' a belted knight,
  A marquis, duke, and a' that;
But an honest man 's aboon his might,
  Guid faith he mauna fa' that!

For a' that, and a' that,
   Their dignities, and a' that,
The pith o' sense and pride o' worth
   Are higher ranks than a' that.

Then let us pray that come it may, —
   As come it will for a' that, —
That sense and worth, o'er a' the earth,
   May bear the gree, and a' that!
For a' that, and a' that,
   It 's comin' yet, for a' that,
That man to man, the warld o'er,
   Shall brothers be for a' that!

THE GREENWOOD SHRIFT. — *Blackwood's Magazine*

Outstretched beneath the leafy shade
Of Windsor Forest's deepest glade
   A dying woman lay;
Three little children round her stood,
And there went up from the greenwood
   A woful wail that day.

"O mother!" was the mingled cry,
"O mother! mother! do not die
   And leave us all alone."
"My blessed babes!" she tried to say,
But the faint accents died away
   In a low sobbing moan.

And then life struggled hard with death,
And fast and strong she drew her breath,
   And up she raised her head;

And peering through the deep wood's maze
With a long, sharp, unearthly gaze,
"Will he not come?" she said.

Just then, the parting boughs between,
A little maid's light form was seen,
All breathless with her speed;
And following close, a man came on
(A portly man to look upon),
Who led a panting steed.

"Mother!" the little maiden cried
Or e'er she reached the woman's side,
And kissed her clay-cold cheek,
"I have not idled in the town,
But long went wandering up and down,
The minister to seek.

"They told me here, — they told me there,
I think they mocked me everywhere;
And when I found his home,
And begged him on my bended knee
To bring his book, and come with me,
Mother! he would not come.

"I told him how you dying lay,
And could not go in peace away
Without the minister;
I begged him, for dear Christ his sake,
But O! — my heart was fit to break, —
Mother! he would not stir.

"So, though my tears were blinding me,
I ran back fast as fast could be,
To come again to you;
And here — close by — this squire I met,
Who asked (so mild!) what made me fret;
And when I told him true,

"'I will go with you, child,' he said,
'God sends me to this dying bed.'
  Mother, he 's here, hard by."
While thus the little maiden spoke,
The man, his back against an oak,
  Looked on with glistening eye.

The bridle on his neck flung free,
With quivering flank and trembling knee.
  Pressed close his bonny bay;
A statelier man, a statelier steed,
Never on greensward paced, I rede,
  Than those stood there that day.

So while the little maiden spoke
The man, his back against an oak,
  Looked on with glistening eye
And folded arms; and in his look,
Something that, like a sermon book,
  Preached, — "All is vanity."

But when the dying woman's face
Turned toward him with a wishful gaze,
  He stepped to where she lay;
And kneeling down, bent over her,
Saying, — "I am a minister, —
  My sister! let us pray."

And well, withouten book or stole
(God's words were printed on his soul),
  Into the dying ear
He breathed, as 't were an angel's strain,
The things that unto life pertain,
  And death's dark shadows clear.

He spoke of sinners' lost estate,
In Christ renewed, regenerate, —
  Of God's most blest decree,
That not a single soul should die
Who turns repentant with the cry,
  "Be merciful to me!"

He spoke of trouble, pain, and toil,
Endured but for a little while
  In patience, faith, and love, —
Sure, in God's own good time, to be
Exchanged for an eternity
  Of happiness above.

Then, as the spirit ebbed away,
He raised his hands and eyes, to pray
  That peaceful it might pass;
And then — the orphans' sobs alone
Were heard, as they knelt every one
  Close round on the green grass.

Such was the sight their wondering eyes
Beheld, in heart-struck, mute surprise,
  Who reined their coursers back,
Just as they found the long astray,
Who, in the heat of chase that day,
  Had wandered from their track.

Back each man reined his pawing steed,
And lighted down, as if agreed,
  In silence at his side;
And there, uncovered all, they stood; —
It was a wholesome sight, and good,
  That day for mortal pride.

For of the noblest of the land
Was that deep-hushed, bareheaded band;
And central in the ring,
By that dead pauper on the ground,
Her ragged orphans clinging round,
Knelt their anointed king.*

MUTABILITY. — *Shelley.*

We are as clouds that veil the midnight moon;
How restlessly they speed, and gleam, and quiver,
Streaking the darkness radiantly! — yet soon
Night closes round, and they are lost for ever;

Or like forgotten lyres, whose dissonant strings
Give various response to each varying blast,
To whose frail frame no second motion brings
One mood or modulation like the last.

We rest, — a dream has power to poison sleep;
We rise, — one wandering thought pollutes the day
We feel, conceive, or reason, laugh or weep,
Embrace fond woe, or cast our cares away;

It is the same! — for, be it joy or sorrow,
The path of its departure still is free;
Man's yesterday may ne'er be like his morrow;
Naught may endure but Mutability.

---

* George the Third of England.

TO THE MOON. — *Shelley.*

Art thou pale for weariness
Of climbing heaven, and gazing on the earth,
Wandering companionless
Among the stars that have a different birth, —
And ever-changing, like a joyless eye
That finds no object worth its constancy?

OF A CONTENTED MIND.

When all is done and said,
In th' end thus shall you find:
He most of all doth bathe in bliss,
That hath a quiet mind;
And clear from worldly cares,
To deem can be content
The sweetest time in all his life
In thinking to be spent.

The body subject is
To fickle Fortune's power,
And to a million of mishaps
Is casual every hour;
And death in time doth change
It to a clod of clay;
Whereas the mind, which is divine,
Runs never to decay.

Companion none is like
Unto the mind alone;
For many have been harmed by speech,
Through thinking, few or none.

Fear oftentimes restraineth words,
  But makes not thoughts to cease;
And he speaks best, that hath the skill
  When for to hold his peace.

Our wealth leaves us at death;
  Our kinsmen at the grave;
But virtues of the mind unto
  The heavens with us we have.
Wherefore, for virtue's sake
  I can be well content
The sweetest time of all my life
  To deem in thinking spent.

THE FRIAR OF ORDERS GRAY.—*Percy.*

It was a friar of orders gray
  Walked forth to tell his beads,
And he met with a lady fair,
  Clad in a pilgrim's weeds.

"Now Christ thee save, thou reverend friar!
  I pray thee tell to me,
If ever at yon holy shrine
  My truelove you did see."

"And how should I your truelove know
  From many another one?"
"O, by his cockle hat and staff,
  And by his sandal shoon.

"But chiefly by his face and mien,
  That were so fair to view;
His flaxen locks that sweetly curled,
  And eyes of lovely blue."

"O lady, he is dead and gone,
Lady, he 's dead and gone!
At his head a green grass turf,
And at his heels a stone.

"Within these holy cloisters long
He languished, and he died
Lamenting of a lady's love,
And 'plaining of her pride.

"Here bore him barefaced on his bier
Six proper youths and tall;
And many a tear bedewed his grave
Within yon kirkyard wall."

"And art thou dead, thou gentle youth?
And art thou dead and gone?
And didst thou die for love of me?
Break, cruel heart of stone!"

"O, weep not, lady, weep not so!
Some ghostly comfort seek;
Let not vain sorrow rive thy heart,
Nor tears bedew thy cheek."

"O, do not, do not, holy friar,
My sorrow now reprove!
For I have lost the sweetest youth
That e'er won lady's love.

"And now, alas! for thy sad loss
I 'll evermore weep and sigh;
For thee I only wished to live,
For thee I wished to die."

"Weep no more, lady, weep no more;
Thy sorrow is in vain;
For violets plucked the sweetest showers
Will ne'er make grow again.

"Our joys as winged dreams do fly;
Why, then, should sorrow last?
Since grief but aggravates thy loss,
Grieve not for what is past."

"O, say not so, thou holy friar;
I pray thee, say not so!
For since my truelove died for me,
'T is meet my tears should flow."

"Sigh no more, lady, sigh no more,
Men were deceivers ever;
One foot on sea and one on land,
To one thing constant never."

"Now say not so, thou holy friar,
I pray thee, say not so;
My love he had the truest heart;
O, he was ever true!

"And art thou dead, thou much loved youth?
And didst thou die for me?
Then farewell, home; for evermore
A pilgrim I will be.

"But first upon my truelove's grave
My weary limbs I 'll lay;
And thrice I 'll kiss the green grass turf
That wraps his breathless clay."

"Yet stay, fair lady, rest awhile
   Beneath this cloister wall;
The cold wind through the hawthorn blows,
   And drizzly rain doth fall."

"O, stay me not, thou holy friar,
   O, stay me not, I pray!
No drizzly rain that falls on me
   Can wash my fault away."

"Yet stay, fair lady, turn again,
   And dry those pearly tears;
For see, beneath this gown of gray,
   Thy own truelove appears!

"Here, forced by grief and hopeless love,
   These holy weeds I sought, —
And here, amid these lonely walls,
   To end my days I thought.

"But haply, — for my year of grace
   Is not yet passed away,—
Might I still hope to win thy love,
   No longer would I stay."

"Now farewell grief, and welcome joy
   Once more unto my heart;
For since I 've found thee, lovely youth,
   We never more will part."

SONNET ON HIS BLINDNESS.—*Milton.*

When I consider how my light is spent
Ere half my days, in this dark world and wide,
And that one talent which is death to hide
Lodged with me useless (though my soul more bent
To serve therewith my Maker, and present
My true account, lest he returning chide),
"Doth God exact day-labor, light denied?"
I fondly ask. But Patience, to prevent
That murmur, soon replies, "God doth not need
Either man's work or his own gifts; who best
Bear his mild yoke, they serve him best: his state
Is kingly; thousands at his bidding speed,
And post o'er land and ocean without rest:
They also serve who only stand and wait."

TO THE MEMORY OF ISABEL SOUTHEY.—*Mrs. Southey.*

'T is ever thus,—'t is ever thus, when Hope hath built a bower
Like that of Eden, wreathed about with every thornless flower,
To dwell therein securely, the self-deceiver's trust,
A whirlwind from the desert comes, and "all is in the dust."

'Tis ever thus,—'t is ever thus, that, when the poor heart clings
With all its finest tendrils, with all its flexile rings,

That goodly thing it cleaveth to, so fondly and so fast,
Is struck to earth by lightning, or shattered by the blast.

'T is ever thus, — 't is ever thus, with beams of mortal bliss,
With looks too bright and beautiful for such a world as this;
One moment round about us their angel lightnings play,
Then down the veil of darkness drops, and all hath passed away.

'T is ever thus, — 't is ever thus, with sounds too sweet for earth, —
Seraphic sounds, that float away (borne heavenward) in their birth;
The golden shell is broken, the silver chord is mute,
The sweet bells all are silent, and hushed the lovely lute.

'T is ever thus, — 't is ever thus, with all that 's best below,
The dearest, noblest, loveliest, are always first to go;
The bird that sings the sweetest, the pine that crowns the rock,
The glory of the garden, the flower of the flock.

'T is ever thus, — 't is ever thus, with creatures heavenly fair,
Too finely framed to 'bide the brunt more earthly creatures bear;
A little while they dwell with us, blest ministers of love,
Then spread the wings we had not seen, and seek their home above.

EMPLOYMENT. — *George Herbert.*

If, as a flower doth spread and die,
Thou wouldst extend me to some good,
Before I were by frost's extremity
Nipt in the bud, —

The sweetness and the praise were thine;
But the extension and the room,
Which in thy garland I should fill, were mine
At thy great doom.

For as thou dost impart thy grace,
The greater shall our glory be.
The measure of our joys is in this place,
The stuff with thee.

Let me not languish, then, and spend
A life as barren to thy praise
As is the dust, to which that life doth tend,
But with delays.

All things are busy; only I
Neither bring honey with the bees,
Nor flowers to make that, nor the husbandry
To water these.

I am no link of thy great chain,
But all my company is as a weed.
Lord, place me in thy concert, give one strain
To my poor reed.

THE ISLES OF GREECE. — *Byron.*

The isles of Greece! the isles of Greece
  Where burning Sappho loved and sung, —
Where grew the arts of war and peace, —
  Where Delos rose and Phœbus sprung!
Eternal summer gilds them yet,
But all, except their sun, is set.

The Scian and the Teian Muse,
  The hero's harp, the lover's lute,
Have found the fame your shores refuse;
  Their place of birth alone is mute
To sounds which echo farther west
Than your sires' "Islands of the Blest."

The mountains look on Marathon, —
  And Marathon looks on the sea;
And musing there an hour alone,
  I dreamed that Greece might still be free;
For, standing on the Persians' grave,
I could not deem myself a slave.

A king sat on the rocky brow
  Which looks o'er sea-born Salamis;
And ships, by thousands, lay below,
  And men in nations; — all were his!
He counted them at break of day, —
And when the sun set, where were they?

And where are they? and where art thou,
  My country? On thy voiceless shore
The heroic lay is tuneless now, —
  The heroic bosom beats no more!

And must thy lyre, so long divine,
Degenerate into hands like mine?

'T is something, in the dearth of fame,
Though linked among a fettered race,
To feel at least a patriot's shame,
Even as I sing, suffuse my face;
For what is left the poet here?
For Greeks a blush, — for Greece a tear.

Must *we* but weep o'er days more blest?
Must *we* but blush? — Our fathers bled.
Earth! render back from out thy breast
A remnant of our Spartan dead!
Of the three hundred grant but three,
To make a new Thermopylæ.

What, silent still? and silent all?
Ah! no; — the voices of the dead
Sound like a distant torrent's fall,
And answer, "Let one living head,
But one, arise, — we come, we come!"
'T is but the living who are dumb.

In vain, — in vain; strike other chords;
Fill high the cup with Samian wine!
Leave battles to the Turkish hordes,
And shed the blood of Scio's vine!
Hark! rising to the ignoble call,
How answers each bold bacchanal!

You have the Pyrrhic dance as yet, —
Where is the Pyrrhic phalanx gone?
Of two such lessons, why forget
The nobler and the manlier one?

You have the letters Cadmus gave, —
Think ye he meant them for a slave?

Fill high the bowl with Samian wine!
  We will not think of themes like these!
It made Anacreon's song divine:
  He served — but served Polycrates —
A tyrant; but our masters then
Were still, at least, our countrymen.

The tyrant of the Chersonese
  Was freedom's best and bravest friend;
That tyrant was Miltiades!
  O, that the present hour would lend
Another despot of the kind!
Such chains as his were sure to bind.

Fill high the bowl with Samian wine!
  On Suli's rock, and Parga's shore,
Exists the remnant of a line
  Such as the Doric mothers bore;
And there, perhaps, some seed is sown,
The Heracleidan blood might own.

Trust not for freedom to the Franks, —
  They have a king who buys and sells.
In native swords and native ranks
  The only hope of courage dwells;
But Turkish force and Latin fraud
Would break your shield, however broad.

Fill high the bowl with Samian wine!
  Our virgins dance beneath the shade, —
I see their glorious black eyes shine;
  But, gazing on each glowing maid,
My own the burning tear-drop laves,
To think such breasts must suckle slaves.

Place me on Sunium's marbled steep, —
  Where nothing, save the waves and I,
May hear our mutual murmurs sweep ;
  There, swan-like, let me sing and die.
A land of slaves shall ne'er be mine, —
Dash down yon cup of Samian wine !

EXPOSTULATION AND REPLY. — *Wordsworth.*

" Why, William, on that old gray stone,
  Thus for the length of half a day,
Why, William, sit you thus alone,
  And dream your time away ?

" Where are your books ? — that light bequeathed
  To beings else forlorn and blind !
Up ! up ! and drink the spirit breathed
  From dead men to their kind.

" You look round on your mother earth,
  As if she for no purpose bore you ;
As if you were her first-born birth,
  And none had lived before you ! "

One morning thus, by Esthwaite lake,
  When life was sweet, I knew not why,
To me my good friend Matthew spake,
  And thus I made reply : —

" The eye, — it cannot choose but see ;
  We cannot bid the ear be still ;
Our bodies feel, where'er they be,
  Against or with our will.

"Nor less I deem that there are Powers
Which of themselves our minds impress;
That we can feel this mind of ours
In a wise passiveness.

"Think you, 'mid all this mighty sum
Of things for ever speaking,
That nothing of itself will come,
But we must still be seeking?

"Then ask not wherefore, here, alone,
Conversing as I may,
I sit upon this old gray stone,
And dream my time away."

THE TABLES TURNED. — *Wordsworth.*

AN EVENING SCENE ON THE SAME SUBJECT.

Up! up! my friend, and quit your books;
Or surely you 'll grow double:
Up! up! my friend, and clear your looks;
Why all this toil and trouble?

The sun, above the mountain's head,
A freshening lustre mellow
Through all the long green fields has spread,
His first sweet evening yellow.

Books! 'tis a dull and endless strife:
Come, hear the woodland linnet,
How sweet his music! on my life,
There 's more of wisdom in it.

And hark! how blithe the throstle sings!
He, too, is no mean preacher:
Come forth into the light of things,
Let Nature be your teacher.

She has a world of ready wealth,
Our minds and hearts to bless, —
Spontaneous wisdom breathed by health
Truth breathed by cheerfulness.

One impulse from a vernal wood
May teach you more of man,
Of moral evil and of good,
Than all the sages can.

Sweet is the lore which Nature brings;
Our meddling intellect
Misshapes the beauteous forms of things;
We murder to dissect.

Enough of Science and of Art;
Close up these barren leaves;
Come forth, and bring with you a heart
That watches and receives.

MANHOOD. — *C. A. Dana.*

Dear, noble soul, wisely thy lot thou bearest;
For, like a god toiling in earthly slavery,
Fronting thy sad fate with a joyous bravery,
Each darker day a sunnier smile thou wearest.
No grief can touch thy sweet and spiritual smile:
No pain is keen enough that it has power
Over thy childlike love, that all the while
Upon the cold earth builds its heavenly bower, —

And thus with thee bright angels make their dwelling,
Bringing thee stores of strength when no man knoweth;
The ocean-stream from God's heart ever swelling,
That forth through each least thing in Nature goeth,
In thee, O truest hero, deeper floweth; —
With joy I bathe, and many souls beside
Feel a new life in the celestial tide.

THE CLOUD. — *Shelley*

I BRING fresh showers for the thirsting flowers,
From the seas and the streams;
I bear light shades for the leaves, when laid
In their noonday dreams.
From my wings are shaken the dews that waken
The sweet buds every one,
When rocked to rest on their mother's breast,
As she dances about the sun.
I wield the flail of the lashing hail,
And whiten the green plains under,
And then again I dissolve in rain,
And laugh as I pass in thunder.

I sift the snow on the mountains below,
And their great pines groan aghast;
And all the night 't is my pillow white,
While I sleep in the arms of the blast.
Sublime on the towers of my skyey bowers,
Lightning my pilot sits;
In a cavern under is fettered the thunder, —
It struggles and howls at fits;

Over earth and ocean, with gentle motion,
This pilot is guiding me,
Lured by the love of the genii that move
In the depths of the purple sea;
Over the rills, and the crags, and the hills,
Over the lakes and the plains,
Wherever he dream, under mountain or stream,
The spirit he loves remains;
And I all the while bask in heaven's blue smile,
Whilst he is dissolving in rains.

The sanguine sunrise, with his meteor eyes,
And his burning plumes outspread,
Leaps on the back of my sailing rack,
When the morning star shines dead.
As on the jag of a mountain crag,
Which an earthquake rocks and swings,
An eagle alit one moment may sit
In the light of its golden wings.
And when sunset may breathe, from the lit sea beneath,
Its ardors of rest and of love,
And the crimson pall of eve may fall
From the depth of heaven above,
With wings folded I rest, on mine airy nest,
As still as a brooding dove.

That orbed maiden, with white fire laden,
Whom mortals call the moon,
Glides glimmering o'er my fleece-like floor,
By the midnight breezes strewn;
And wherever the beat of her unseen feet,
Which only the angels hear,
May have broken the woof of my tent's thin roof,
The stars peep behind her and peer;
And I laugh to see them whirl and flee,
Like a swarm of golden bees,

When I widen the rent in my wind-built tent,
Till the calm rivers, lakes, and seas,
Like strips of the sky fallen through me on high,
Are each paved with the moon and these.

I bind the sun's throne with a burning zone,
And the moon's with a girdle of pearl;
The volcanoes are dim, and the stars reel and swim,
When the whirlwinds my banner unfurl.
From cape to cape, with a bridge-like shape,
Over a torrent sea,
Sunbeam-proof, I hang like a roof,—
The mountains its columns be.
The triumphal arch through which I march
With hurricane, fire, and snow,
When the powers of air are chained to my chair,
Is the million-colored bow;
The sphere-fire above its soft colors wove,
While the moist earth was laughing below.

I am the daughter of earth and water,
And the nursling of the sky;
I pass through the pores of the ocean and shores;
I change, but I cannot die.
For after the rain, when with never a stain
The pavilion of heaven is bare,
And the winds and sunbeams, with their convex gleams,
Build up the blue dome of air,
I silently laugh at my own cenotaph,
And out of the caverns of rain,
Like a child from the womb, like a ghost from the tomb,
I arise and unbuild it again.

BREAK, BREAK, BREAK. — *Tennyson*

Break, break, break,
On thy cold, gray stones, O Sea,
And I would that my tongue could utter
The thoughts that arise in me.

O, well for the fisherman's boy
That he shouts with his sister at play!
O, well for the sailor lad
That he sings in his boat on the bay!

And the stately ships go on
To the haven under the hill;
But, O, for the touch of a vanished hand,
And the sound of a voice that is still!

Break, break, break,
At the foot of thy crags, O Sea,
But the tender grace of a day that is dead
Will never come back to me.

MAN WAS MADE TO MOURN. — *Burns.*

A DIRGE.

When chill November's surly blast
Made fields and forests bare,
One evening, as I wandered forth
Along the banks of Ayr,

I spied a man whose aged step
  Seemed weary, worn with care ;
His face was furrowed o'er with years,
  And hoary was his hair.

" Young stranger, whither wanderest thou ? "
  Began the reverend sage ;
" Does thirst of wealth thy step constrain,
  Or youthful pleasure's rage ?
Or haply, prest with cares and woes,
  Too soon thou hast began
To wander forth, with me, to mourn
  The miseries of man.

" The sun that overhangs yon moors,
  Outspreading far and wide,
Where hundreds labor to support
  A haughty lordling's pride, —
I 've seen yon weary winter-sun
  Twice forty times return,
And every time has added proofs
  That man was made to mourn.

" O man ! while in thy early years,
  How prodigal of time !
Misspending all thy precious hours,
  Thy glorious youthful prime !
Alternate follies take the sway ;
  Licentious passions burn ;
Which tenfold force gives Nature's law,
  That man was made to mourn.

" Look not alone on youthful prime,
  Or manhood's active might ;
Man then is useful to his kind,
  Supported is his right :

But see him on the edge of life,
  With cares and sorrows worn;
Then age and want — O ill-matched pair! —
  Show man was made to mourn.

"A few seem favorites of fate,
  In pleasure's lap carest;
Yet, think not all the rich and great
  Are likewise truly blest.
But, O, what crowds in every land,
  All wretched and forlorn!
Through weary life this lesson learn, —
  That man was made to mourn.

"Many and sharp the numerous ills
  Inwoven with our frame!
More pointed still, we make ourselves
  Regret, remorse, and shame!
And man, whose heaven-erected face
  The smiles of love adorn,
Man's inhumanity to man
  Makes countless thousands mourn!

"See yonder poor o'erlabored wight,
  So abject, mean, and vile,
Who begs a brother of the earth
  To give him leave to toil;
And see his lordly fellow-worm
  The poor petition spurn,
Unmindful though a weeping wife
  And helpless offspring mourn.

"If I 'm designed yon lordling's slave, —
  By Nature's law designed, —
Why was an independent wish
  E'er planted in my mind?

If not, why am I subject to
His cruelty or scorn?
Or why has man the will and power
To make his fellow mourn?

"Yet, let not this too much, my son,
Disturb thy youthful breast;
This partial view of human kind
Is surely not the best!
The poor, oppressèd, honest man
Had never, sure, been born,
Had there not been some recompense
To comfort those that mourn!

"O Death! the poor man's dearest friend,—
The kindest and the best!
Welcome the hour my aged limbs
Are laid with thee at rest!
The great, the wealthy, fear thy blow,
From pomp and pleasure torn!
But, O, a blest relief to those
That weary-laden mourn!"

THE MARIGOLD. — *George Wither.*

When with a serious musing I behold
The grateful and obsequious marigold,
How duly, every morning, she displays
Her open breast, when Titan spreads his rays;
How she observes him in his daily walk,
Still bending towards him her small, slender stalk;
How, when he down declines, she droops and mourns,
Bedewed as 't were with tears, till he returns;

And how she veils her flowers when he is gone,
As if she scornèd to be lookèd on
By an inferior eye, or did contemn
To wait upon a meaner light than him: —
When I thus meditate, methinks the flowers
Have spirits far more generous than ours,
And give us fair examples, to despise
The servile fawnings and idolatries
Wherewith we court these earthly things below
Which merit not the service we bestow.
But, O my God! though grovelling I appear
Upon the ground, and have a rooting here,
Which hauls me downward, yet in my desire
To that which is above me I aspire,
And all my best affections I profess
To Him that is the Sun of Righteousness.
O, keep the morning of his incarnation,
The burning noontide of his bitter passion,
The night of his descending, and the height
Of his ascension, ever in my sight;
That, imitating him in what I may,
I never follow an inferior way!

SONNET. — *W. E. Channing.*

Hearts of eternity, — hearts of the deep!
Proclaim from land to sea your mighty fate;
How that for you no living comes too late;
How ye cannot in Theban labyrinth creep;
How ye great harvests from small surface reap; —
Shout, excellent band, in grand, primeval strain,
Like midnight winds that foam along the main,
And do all things rather than pause and weep.

A human heart knows naught of littleness,
Suspects no man, compares with no one's ways,
Hath in one hour most glorious length of days,
A recompense, a joy, a loveliness;
Like eaglet keen, shoots into azure far,
And, always dwelling nigh, is the remotest star.

LIFE. — *Henry King.*

Like to the falling of a star,
Or as the flights of eagles are,
Or like the fresh spring's gaudy hue,
Or silver drops of morning dew,
Or like a wind that chafes the flood,
Or bubbles which on water stood, —
Even such is man, whose borrowed light
Is straight called in, and paid to-night.
The wind blows out; the bubble dies;
The spring entombed in autumn lies;
The dew dries up; the star is shot;
The flight is past; and man forgot.

SIN. — *Herbert.*

Lord, with what care hast thou begirt us round!
Parents first season us; then schoolmasters
Deliver us to laws; they send us bound
To rules of reason, holy messengers —

Pulpits and Sundays, sorrow dogging sin;
Afflictions sorted; anguish of all sizes;
Fine nets and stratagems to catch us in;
Bibles laid open; millions of surprises;

Blessings beforehand; ties of gratefulness;
  The sound of glory ringing in our ears;
Without, our shame; within, our consciences;
  Angels and grace; eternal hopes and fears; —

Yet all these fences, and their whole array,
One cunning bosom-sin blows quite away.

SONNET. — *Henry Alford.*

Out, palsied soul, that dost but tremble ever
In sight of the bright sunshine; — mine be joy,
And the full heart, and the eye that faileth never
In the glad morning! — I am yet a boy; —
I have not wandered from the crystal river
That flowed by me in childhood: my employ
Hath been to take the gift, and praise the Giver;
To love the flowers thy heedless steps destroy.
I wonder if the bliss that flows to me
In youth shall be exhaled and scorched up dry
By the noonday glare of life: I must not lie
For ever in the shade of childhood's tree:
But I must venture forth, and make advance
Along the toilèd path of human circumstance.

LABOR. — *R. M. Milnes.*

Heart of the people! working men!
Marrow and nerve of human powers;
Who on your sturdy backs sustain,
Through streaming time, this world of ours:

Hold by that title, which proclaims
That ye are undismayed and strong,
Accomplishing whatever aims
May to the sons of earth belong.

Yet not on you alone depend
These offices, or burdens fall;
Labor, for some or other end,
Is lord and master of us all.
The high-born youth from downy bed
Must meet the morn with horse and hound,
While Industry for daily bread
Pursues afresh his wonted round.

With all his pomp of pleasure, he
Is but your working comrade now,
And shouts and winds his horn as ye
Might whistle by the loom or plough;
In vain for him has wealth the use
Of warm repose and careless joy, —
When, as ye labor to produce,
He strives, as active to destroy.

But who is this with wasted frame,
Sad sign of vigor overwrought?
What toil can this new victim claim?
Pleasure, for Pleasure's sake besought.
How men would mock her flaunting shows,
Her golden promise, if they knew
What weary work she is to those
Who have no better work to do!

And he who still and silent sits
In closèd room or shady nook,
And seems to nurse his idle wits
With folded arms or open book:

To things now working in *that* mind
Your children's children well may owe
Blessings that hope has ne'er defined,
Till from his busy thoughts they flow.

Thus all must work, with head or hand,
For self or others, good or ill;
Life is ordained to bear, like land,
Some fruit, be fallow as it will;
Evil has force itself to sow,
Where we deny the healthy seed;
And all our choice is this, — to grow
Pasture and grain, or noisome weed.

Then in content possess your hearts,
Unenvious of each other's lot, —
For those which seem the easiest parts
Have travail which ye reckon not:
And he is bravest, happiest, best,
Who, from the task within his span,
Earns for himself his evening rest,
And an increase of good for man.

ALMS-GIVING. — *R. M. Milnes.*

When Poverty, with mien of shame,
The sense of pity seeks to touch, —
Or, bolder, makes the simple claim,
That I have nothing, you have much, —
Believe not either man or book
That bids you close the opening hand,
And with reproving speech and look
Your first and free intent withstand.

It may be, that the tale you hear,
Of pressing wants and losses borne
Is heaped or colored for your ear,
And tatters for the purpose worn ;
But surely Poverty has not
A sadder need than this, — to wear
A mask still meaner than her lot,
Compassion's scanty food to share.

It may be that you err, to give
What will but tempt to further spoil
Those who in low content would live
On theft of others' time and toil:
Yet sickness *may* have broke or bent
The active frame or vigorous will;
Or hard occasion may prevent
Their exercise of humble skill.

It may be that the suppliant's life
Has lain on many an evil way
Of foul delight and brutal strife,
And lawless deeds that shun the day ;
But how can any gauge of yours
The depth of that temptation try ?
What man resists, what man endures,
Is open to one only eye.

Why not believe the homely letter,
That all you give will God restore ?
The poor man *may* deserve it better,
And surely, surely, wants it more :
Let but the rich man do his part,
And, whatsoe'er the issue be
To those wno ask, his answering heart
Will gain and grow in sympathy.

Suppose that each from nature got
Bare quittance of his labor's worth,
That yearly-teeming flocks were not,
Nor manifold-producing earth;
No wilding growths of fruit and flower,
Cultured to beautiful and good,
No creatures for the arm of power
To take and tame from waste and wood!

That all men to their mortal rest
Passed shadow-like, and left behind
No free result, no clear bequest,
Won by their work of hand or mind!
That every separate life begun,
A present to the past unbound,
A lonely, independent one,
Sprung from the cold mechanic ground!

What would the record of the past,
The vision of the future be?
Nature unchanged from first to last,
And base the best humanity:
For in these gifts lies all the space
Between our England's noblest men,
And the most vile Australian race
Outprowling from their bushy den.

Then freely, as from age to age
Descending generations bear
The accumulated heritage
Of friendly and parental care,—
Freely as Nature tends her wealth
Of air and fire, of sea and land,
Of childhood's happiness and health,—
So freely open you your hand!

Between you and your best intent
Necessity her brazen bar
Will often interpose, as sent
Your pure benevolence to mar:
Still every gentle word has sway
To teach the pauper's desperate mood,
That misery shall not take away
Franchise of human brotherhood.

And if this lesson comes too late,
Woe to the rich and poor and all!
The maddened outcast of the gate
Plunders and murders in the hall:
Justice can crush and hold in awe,
While Hope in social order reigns;
But if the myriads break the law,
They break it as a slave his chains!

THE PATIENCE OF THE POOR.—*R. M. Milnes.*

When leisurely the man of ease
His morning's daily course begins,
And round him in bright circle sees
The comforts Independence wins,
He seems unto himself to hold
An uncontested natural right
In life a volume to unfold
Of simple, ever-new delight.

And if, before the evening close,
The hours their rainbow wings let fall,
And sorrow shakes his bland repose,
And too continuous pleasures pall,

He murmurs, as if Nature broke
Some promise plighted at his birth,
In bending him beneath the yoke
Borne by the common sons of earth.

They starve beside his plenteous board,
They halt behind his easy wheels,
But sympathy in vain affords
The sense of ills he never feels.
He knows he is the same as they,
A feeble, piteous, mortal thing,
And still expects that every day
Increase and change of bliss should bring.

Therefore, when he is called to know
The deep realities of pain,
He shrinks as from a viewless blow,
He writhes as in a magic chain:
Untaught that trial, toil, and care
Are the great charter of his kind,
It seems disgrace for him to share
Weakness of flesh and human mind.

Not so the People's honest child,
The field-flower of the open sky,
Ready to live while winds are wild,
Nor, when they soften, loth to die:
To him there never came the thought
That this, his life, was meant to be
A pleasure-house, where peace, unbought
Should minister to pride or glee.

You oft may hear him murmur loud
Against the uneven lots of Fate,
You oft may see him inly bowed
Beneath affliction's weight on weight;—

But rarely turns he on his grief
A face of petulant surprise,
Or scorns whate'er benign relief
The hand of God or man supplies.

Behold him on his rustic bed,
The unluxurious couch of need,
Striving to raise his aching head
And sinking powerless as a reed:
So sick in both, he hardly knows
Which is his heart's or body's sore;
For, the more keen his anguish grows,
His wife and children pine the more.

No search for him of dainty food,
But coarsest sustenance of life, —
No rest by artful quiet wooed,
But household cries and wants and strife;
Affection can at best employ
Her utmost of unhandy care, —
Her prayers and tears are weak to buy
The costly drug, the purer air.

Pity herself, at such a sight,
Might lose her gentleness of mien,
And clothe her form in angry might,
And as a wild despair be seen,
Did she not hail the lesson taught
By this unconscious suffering boor
To the high sons of lore and thought, —
The sacred Patience of the Poor.

This great endurance of each ill,
As a plain fact, whose right or wrong
They question not, confiding still
That it shall last not overlong;

Willing, from first to last, to take
The mysteries of our life, as given, —
Leaving the time-worn soul to slake
Its thirst in an undoubted heaven.

DELIGHT IN GOD ONLY. — *Francis Quarles.*

I LOVE (and have some cause to love) the Earth:
She is my Maker's creature; therefore good:
She is my mother, for she gave me birth:
She is my tender nurse; she gives me food:
  But what 's a creature, Lord, compared with Thee?
  Or what 's my mother or my nurse to me?

I love the Air: her dainty sweets refresh
My drooping soul, and to new sweets invite me,
Her shrill-mouthed choir sustain me with their flesh,
And with their polyphonian notes delight me:
  But what 's the air or all the sweets that she
  Can bless my soul withal, compared to Thee?

I love the Sea: she is my fellow-creature,
My careful purveyor; she provides me store:
She walls me round; she makes my diet greater;
She wafts my treasure from a foreign shore:
  But, Lord of oceans, when compared with Thee,
  What is the ocean or her wealth to me?

To heaven's high city I direct my journey,
Whose spangled suburbs entertain mine eye;
Mine eye, by contemplation's great attorney,
Transcends the crystal pavement of the sky:
  But what is heaven, great God, compared to Thee?
  Without Thy presence, heaven 's no heaven to me.

The highest honors that the world can boast
Are subjects far too low for my desire;
The highest beams of glory are, at most,
But dying sparkles of Thy living fire:
  The loudest flames that earth can kindle be
  But nightly glowworms, if compared to Thee.

Without Thy presence, wealth is bags of cares;
Wisdom, but folly; joy, disquiet, — sadness;
Friendship is treason, and delights are snares;
Pleasures but pain, and mirth but pleasing madness:
  Without Thee, Lord, things be not what they be,
  Nor have they being when compared with Thee.

In having all things, and not Thee, what have I?
Not having Thee, what have my labors got?
Let me enjoy but Thee, what farther crave I?
And having Thee alone, what have I not?
  I wish nor sea nor land; nor would I be
  Possessed of heaven, heaven unpossessed of Thee

HYMN OF APOLLO. — *Shelley.*

The sleepless Hours who watch me as I lie,
  Curtained with star-inwoven tapestries,
From the broad moonlight of the sky,
  Fanning the busy dreams from my dim eyes, —
Waken me, when their Mother, the gray Dawn,
Tells them that dreams, and that the moon is gone.

Then I arise, and, climbing heaven's blue dome,
  I walk over the mountains and the waves,
Leaving my robe upon the ocean foam;
  My footsteps pave the clouds with fire; the caves

Are filled with my bright presence; and the air
Leaves the green earth to my embraces bare.

The sunbeams are my shafts, with which I kill
  Deceit, that loves the night and fears the day;
All men who do or even imagine ill
  Fly me, and from the glory of my ray
Good minds and open actions take new might,
Until diminished by the reign of night.

I feed the clouds, the rainbows, and the flowers
  With their ethereal colors; the moon's globe,
And the pure stars in their eternal bowers,
  Are cinctured with my power as with a robe;
Whatever lamps on earth or heaven may shine
Are portions of one power, which is mine.

I stand at noon upon the peak of heaven,
  Then with unwilling steps I wander down
Into the clouds of the Atlantic even;
  For grief that I depart, they weep and frown:
What look is more delightful than the smile
With which I soothe them from the western isle?

I am the eye with which the Universe
  Beholds itself, and knows itself divine;
All harmony of instrument or verse,
  All prophecy, all medicine, are mine,
All light of art or nature; — to my song
Victory and praise in their own right belong.

A GENIAL MOMENT OFT HAS GIVEN. — *Trench.*

A GENIAL moment oft has given
What years of toil and pain,
Of long industrious toil, have striven
To win, and all in vain.

Yet count not, when thine end is won,
That labor merely lost;
Nor say it had been wiser done
To spare the painful cost.

When heaped upon the altar lie
All things to feed the fire, —
One spark alighting from on high, —
The flames at once aspire.

But those sweet gums and fragrant woods
Its rich materials rare,
By tedious quest o'er lands and floods
Had first been gathered there.

A DEWDROP FALLING. — *Trench.*

A DEWDROP, falling on the wild sea wave,
Exclaimed in fear, — "I perish in this grave!"
But, in a shell received, that drop of dew
Unto a pearl of marvellous beauty grew;
And, happy now, the grace did magnify
Which thrust it forth, as it had feared, to die; —

Until again, "I perish quite," it said,
Torn by rude diver from its ocean bed;
O unbelieving! — so it came to gleam
Chief jewel in a monarch's diadem.

THE SEED MUST DIE. — *Trench.*

The seed must die, before the corn appears
Out of the ground, in blade and fruitful ears.
Low must those ears by sickle's edge be lain,
Ere thou canst treasure up the golden grain.
The grain is crushed before the bread is made,
And the bread broke ere life to man conveyed.
O, be content to die, to be laid low,
And to be crushed, and to be broken so;
If thou upon God's table may'st be bread,
Life-giving food for souls an hungerèd!

THE PRIORESS'S TALE. — *Chaucer.*

There was in Asia, in a great citỳ,
  Amongès Christian folk a Jewèry,
Sustainèd by a lord of that countrỳ,
  For foul usure and lucre of villainy,
  Hateful to Christ and to his company;
And through the street men mighten ride and wend,
For it was free, and open at either end.

A little school of Christian folk there stood
  Down at the further end, in which there were
Children a heape comen of Christian blood,

That learnèd in that schoolè year by year
  Such manner doctrine as men usèd there;
This is to say, to singen and to read,
As smallè children do in their childhede.

Among these children was a widow's son,
  A little clergion,[1] seven years of age,
That day by day to schoolè was his won[2];
  And eke alsò, whereas he saw the imàge
  Of Christès mother, had he in usàge,
As him was taught, to kneel adown, and say,
Ave Maria, as he go'th by the way.

Thus hath this widow her little son ytaught
  Our blissful Lady, Christès mother dear,
To worship aye, and he forgot it nought;
  For sely[3] childè will alway soon lere;[4]
  But aye when I remember on this mattère,
Saint Nicholas stant[5] ever in my presènce,
For he so young to Christ did reverence.

This little child his little book learnìng,
  As he sat in the school at his primère,
He *Alma Redemptoris* heardè sing,
  As children learnèd their antiphonere;[6]
  And as he durst, he drew him near and near
And hearkened aye the wordès and the note,
Till he the firstè verse could all by rote.

Nought wist[7] he what this Latin was to say,
  For he so young and tender was of age;
But on a day his fellow 'gan to pray

---

[1] Young clerk. [2] Custom. [3] Simple. [4] Learn
[5] Standeth. [6] Chanting alternate verses of the Psalms.
[7] Knew.

T' expounden him this song in his languàge,
Or tell him why this song was in usàge;
This pray'd he him to construe and declare,
Full often time upon his kneès bare.

His fellow, which that elder was than he,
Answered him thus: "This song, I have heard say,
Was makèd of our blissful Lady free,[1]
Her to salue,[2] and eke her for to pray
To be our help and succour when we dey.[3]
I can no more expound in this mattère:
I learnè song; I can[4] but small grammère."

"And is this song makèd in reverence
Of Christès mother?" said this innocent:
"Now certès I will do my diligence
To conn[5] it all ere Christèmas be went,
Though that I for my primer shall be shent,[6]
And shall be beaten thriès in an hour,
I will it conn our Lady for t' honòur."

His fellow taught him homeward privily
From day to day till he could it by rote,
And then he sang it well and boldèly
From word to word according with the note:
Twiès a day it passèd through his throat,
To schoolward and homeward when he went;
On Christès mother set was his intent.

As I have said, throughout the Jewèry
This little child, as he came to and fro,
Full merrily then would he sing and cry,

---

[1] Bountiful. [2] Praise. [3] Die.
[4] Know. [5] Learn.
[6] Punished, — the strict meaning is *ruined*.

O Alma Redemptoris! ever mo.
The sweetness hath his heartè piercèd so
Of Christès mother, that to her to pray
He cannot stint[1] of singing by the way.

Our firstè foe, the serpent Sathanas,
That hath in Jewès heart his waspès nest,
Up swelled and said: "O Ebraike people, alas!
Is this to you a thing that is honèst,
That such a boy shall walken as him lest
In your despite, and sing of such sentènce,
Which is against our lawès reverence?"

From thennèsforth the Jewès have conspired
This innocent out of this world to chase:
A homicidè thereto have they hired,
That in an alley had a private place,
And as the child 'gan forth by for to pace,
This cursed Jew him hent[2] and held him fast,
And cut his throat, and in a pit him cast.

I say that in a wardrope[3] they him threw,
Where as these Jewès casten their offàle.
O cursèd folk! of Herodès all-new,[4]
What may your evil intente you avail?
Murder will out, certain it will not fail;
And namely there the honòur of God shall spread
The blood out crieth on your cursèd deed.

This poorè widow waiteth all that night
After her little child, and he came nought;
For which, as soon as it was dayès light,
With facè pale of dread and busy thought,
She hath at school and ellèswhere him sought,

---

[1] Cease. [2] Caught.
[3] Drain, common sewer. [4] Fresh-revived.

Till finally she 'gan so far espy[1]
That he last seen was in the Jewèry.

With mother's pity in her breast enclosed,
She go'th, as she were half out of her mind,
To every placè where she hath supposed
By likelihood her little child to find;
And ever on Christès mother meek and kind
She cried, and at the lastè thus she wrought,
Among the cursed Jewès she him sought.

She feyneth[2] and she prayèth piteously
To every Jew that dwelt in thilkè place
To tell her if her child went ought forth by;
They saiden, Nay; but Jesu of his grace
Gave in her thought, within a little space,
That in that place after her son she cried,
There[3] he was casten in a pit beside.

O great God, that performest thy laud
By mouth of innocents, lo here thy might!
This gem of chastity, this emeraud,
And eke of martyrdom the ruby bright,
There he with throat ycarven[4] lay upright,
He *Alma Redemptoris* 'gan to sing
So loud, that all the placè 'gan to ring.

The Christian folk that through the streetè went
In comen for to wonder upon this thing,
And hastily they for the provost sent:
He came anon withouten tarrying,
And herieth[5] Christ, that is of heaven king,
And eke his mother, honour of mankind,
And after that the Jewès let he bind.

---

[1] Discover. [2] Asketh. [3] Where.
[4] Cut. [5] Praiseth.

This child with piteous lamentatiòn
Was taken up, singing his song alway,
And with honòur and great processiòn
They carrien him unto the next abbèy;
His mother swooning by the bière lay:
Unnethes might[1] the people that was there
This newè Rachel bringen from his bier.

With torment and with shameful death each one
This provost doth these Jewès for to starve[2]
That of this murder wist,[3] and that anon:
He n' oldè[4] no such cursedness observe;[5]
Evil shall he have that evil will deserve;
Therefore with wildè horse he did them draw,
And after that he hung them by the law.

Upon his bier aye li'th this innocent
Before the altar while the massè last,
And after that, th' abbot with his convent
Have sped them for to bury him full fast;
And when they holy water on him cast,
Yet spake this child, when sprent[6] with th' holy water,
And sang, *O Alma Redemptoris Mater!*

This abbot, which that was a holy man,
As monkès be, or elles ought to be,
This youngè child to conjure he began,
And said: "O dearè child! I halsè[7] thee,
In virtue of the holy Trinity,
Tell me what is thy causè for to sing,
Since that thy throat is cut, to my seeming."

Scarcely were the people able. [2] Die.
Knew. [4] Would not. [5] Attend to
[6] Sprinkled. [7] Implore.

"My throat is cut unto my neckè bone,"
  Saidè this childe, "and as by way of kind[1]
I should have died, yea longè time agone;
  But Jesu Christ, as ye in bookès find,
  Will that his glory last and be in mind,
And for the worship of his mother dear,
Yet may I sing *O Alma* loud and clear.

"This well[2] of mercy, Christès mother sweet,
  I lovèd alway, as after my conning[3];
And when that I my lifè would forlete[4]
  To me she came, and bade me for to sing
  This anthem verily in my dying,
As ye have heard; and when that I had sung,
Me thought she laid a grain upon my tongue.

"Wherefore I sing, and sing I must certàin,
  In honour of that blissful maiden free,
Till from my tongue off taken is the grain.
  And after that thus saidè she to me:
  'My little child, then will I fetchen thee,
When that the grain is from thy tongue ytake:
Be not aghast, I will thee not forsake.'"

This holy monk, this abbot him mean I,
  His tongue out caught, and took away the grain,
And he gave up the ghost full softily.
  And when this abbot had this wonder see
  His saltè tearès trill'd adown as rain,
And groff he fell all plat upon the ground,[5]
And still he lay as he had been ybound.

---

[1] In the course of nature. Spring. [3] Ability.
[4] Forsake. [5] Flat on the groung.

The convent lay eke on the pavèment
Weeping and herying[1] Christès mother dear,
And after that they risen, and forth been went,
And took away this martyr from his bier,
And in a tomb of marble stonès clear
Enclosen they his little body sweet:
There he is now God lene[2] us for to meet.

CHARACTER OF THE HAPPY WARRIOR.—*Wordsworth.*

Who is the happy warrior? Who is he
That every man in arms should wish to be?—
It is the generous spirit, who, when brought
Among the tasks of real life, hath wrought
Upon the plan that pleased his childish thought:
Whose high endeavours are an inward light
That makes the path before him always bright:
Who, with a natural instinct to discern
What knowledge can perform, is diligent to learn,
Abides by this resolve, and stops not there,
But makes his moral being his prime care:
Who, doomed to go in company with Pain,
And Fear, and Bloodshed, miserable train!
Turns his necessity to glorious gain;
In face of these doth exercise a power
Which is our human nature's highest dower;
Controls them and subdues, transmutes, bereaves
Of their bad influence, and their good receives:
By objects which might force the soul to abate
Her feeling, rendered more compassionate;

---

[1] Praising. [2] Grant.

Is placable, — because occasions rise
So often that demand such sacrifice;
More skilful in self-knowledge, even more pure,
As tempted more; more able to endure,
As more exposed to suffering and distress;
Thence, also, more alive to tenderness. —
'T is he whose law is reason; who depends
Upon that law as on the best of friends;
Whence, in a state where men are tempted still
To evil for a guard against worse ill,
And what in quality or act is best
Doth seldom on a right foundation rest,
He labors good on good to fix, and owes
To virtue every triumph that he knows:
Who, if he rise to station of command,
Rises by open means; and there will stand
On honorable terms, or else retire,
And in himself possess his own desire:
Who comprehends his trust, and to the same
Keeps faithful with a singleness of aim;
And therefore does not stoop, nor lie in wait
For wealth, or honors, or for worldly state;
Whom they must follow; on whose head must fall,
Like showers of manna, if they come at all:
Whose powers shed round him in the common strife,
Or mild concerns of ordinary life,
A constant influence, a peculiar grace;
But who, if he be called upon to face
Some awful moment to which Heaven has joined
Great issues, good or bad for human kind,
Is happy as a lover, and attired
With sudden brightness, like a man inspired;
And, through the heat of conflict, keeps the law
In calmness made, and sees what he foresaw;
Or, if an unexpected call succeed,
Come when it will, is equal to the need:

He who, though thus endued, as with a sense
And faculty for storm and turbulence,
Is yet a soul whose master-bias leans
To homefelt pleasures and to gentle scenes;
Sweet images! which, wheresoe'er he be,
Are at his heart; and such fidelity
It is his darling passion to approve;
More brave for this, that he hath much to love:
'T is, finally, the man, who, lifted high,
Conspicuous object in a nation's eye,
Or left unthought of in obscurity,—
Who, with a toward or untoward lot,
Prosperous or adverse, to his wish or not,—
Plays, in the many games of life, that one
Where what he most doth value must be won:
Whom neither shape of danger can dismay,
Nor thought of tender happiness betray:
Who, not content that former worth stand fast,
Looks forward, persevering to the last,
From well to better, daily self-surpassed:
Who, whether praise of him must walk the earth
For ever, and to noble deeds give birth,
Or he must fall and sleep without his fame,
And leave a dead, unprofitable name,—
Finds comfort in himself and in his cause;
And, while the mortal mist is gathering, draws
His breath in confidence of Heaven's applause:—
This is the happy warrior; this is he
Whom every man in arms should wish to be.

COMPENSATION.— *Trench.*

Wouldst thou from each man's coronal select
The choicest leaves with which his brows are decked;

That, all into one chaplet for thy head
Entwined, thou may'st be proudly garlanded?

Look round thee, — is not every thing content,
Having a share, not all the ornament?

The sweetest nightingale is dusky-brown;
While golden-feathered birds no music own.

The ruby long outlasts the scented rose;
But then the ruby no such fragrance knows

From Egypt Moses did the people lead;
To plant in Canaan must be Joshua's deed.

David might lay all rich materials by;
His son first raised the goodly fane on high.

But once and but to One it did compete,
All rays of glory round his head should meet.

SONNET. — *Trench.*

Ulysses, sailing by the Sirens' isle,
Sealed first his comrades' ears, then bade them fast
Bind him with many a fetter to the mast,
Lest those sweet voices should their souls beguile,
And to their ruin flatter them, the while
Their homeward bark was sailing swiftly past:
And thus the peril they behind them cast,
Though chased by those weird voices many a mile.
But yet a nobler cunning Orpheus used;
No fetter he put on, nor stopped his ear,
But ever, as he passed, sang high and clear
The blisses of the gods, their holy joys,
And with diviner melody confused
And marred earth's sweetest music to a noise.

HYMN BEFORE SUNRISE, IN THE VALE OF CHAMOUNI. — *Coleridge.*

Besides the rivers Arve and Arveiron, which have their sources in the foot of Mont Blanc, five conspicuous torrents rush down its sides; and within a few paces of the Glaciers, the Gentiana Major grows in immense numbers, with its "flowers of loveliest blue."

HAST thou a charm to stay the morning-star
In his steep course? so long he seems to pause
On thy bald awful head, O sovran Blanc!
The Arve and Arveiron at thy base
Rave ceaselessly; but thou, most awful form,
Risest from forth thy silent sea of pines,
How silently! Around thee and above
Deep is the air and dark, substantial, black,
An ebon mass: methinks thou piercest it,
As with a wedge! But when I look again,
It is thine own calm home, thy crystal shrine,
Thy habitation from eternity!
O dread and silent mount! I gazed upon thee,
Till thou, still present to the bodily sense,
Didst vanish from my thought: entranced in prayer
I worshipped the Invisible alone.

Yet, like some sweet, beguiling melody,
So sweet, we know not we are listening to it,
Thou, the meanwhile, wast blending with my thought
Yea, with my life and life's own secret joy:
Till the dilating soul, enrapt, transfused,
Into the mignty vision passing, — there,
As in her natural form, swelled vast to heaven!

Awake, my soul! not only passive praise
Thou owest, — not alone these swelling tears,
Mute thanks, and secret ecstasy! Awake,

Voice of sweet song! Awake, my heart, awake!
Green vales and icy cliffs, all join my hymn!

Thou first and chief, sole sovran of the vale!
O, struggling with the darkness all the night,
And visited all night by troops of stars,
Or when they climb the sky or when they sink:
Companion of the morning-star at dawn,
Thyself earth's rosy star, and of the dawn
Co-herald: wake, O, wake, and utter praise!
Who sank thy sunless pillars deep in earth?
Who filled thy countenance with rosy light?
Who made thee parent of perpetual streams?

And you, ye five wild torrents fiercely glad!
Who called you forth from night and utter death,
From dark and icy caverns called you forth,
Down those precipitous, black, jagged rocks,
For ever shattered and the same for ever?
Who gave you your invulnerable life,
Your strength, your speed, your fury, and your joy,
Unceasing thunder and eternal foam?
And who commanded (and the silence came),
Here let the billows stiffen, and have rest?

Ye ice-falls! ye that from the mountain's brow
Adown enormous ravines slope amain,—
Torrents, methinks, that heard a mighty voice,
And stopped at once amid their maddest plunge!
Motionless torrents! silent cataracts!
Who made you glorious as the gates of heaven
Beneath the keen full moon? Who bade the sun
Clothe you with rainbows? Who, with living flowers
Of loveliest blue, spread garlands at your feet?—
God! let the torrents, like a shout of nations,
Answer; and let the ice-plains echo, God!
God! sing, ye meadow-streams with gladsome voice!

Ye pine-groves, with your soft and soul-like sounds!
And they, too, have a voice, yon piles of snow,
And in their perilous fall shall thunder, God!

Ye living flowers that skirt the eternal frost!
Ye wild goats sporting round the eagle's nest!
Ye eagles, playmates of the mountain-storm!
Ye lightnings, the dread arrows of the clouds!
Ye signs and wonders of the elements!
Utter forth God, and fill the hills with praise!

Thou, too, hoar mount, with thy sky-pointing peaks!
Oft from whose feet the avalanche, unheard,
Shoots downward, glittering through the pure serene,
Into the depths of clouds that veil thy breast, —
Thou, too, again, stupendous mountain! thou
That as I raise my head, awhile bowed low
In adoration, upward from thy base
Slow travelling with dim eyes suffused with tears,
Solemnly seemest, like a vapory cloud,
To rise before me, — rise, O, ever rise,
Rise like a cloud of incense, from the earth!
Thou kingly spirit throned among the hills,
Thou dread ambassador from earth to heaven,
Great hierarch! tell thou the silent sky,
And tell the stars, and tell yon rising sun,
Earth, with her thousand voices, praises God.

THE PRAISE OF MEN. — *Trench.*

"Cum laudaris, teipsum contemne."
Augustine.

WHEN men exalt thee with their flatteries,
Be thou provoked thine own self to despise,
And, for an help to this, the meanest thing
Which thou hast ever done to memory bring.

Think, too, that now thou dost in peril fall
Of doing a yet meaner thing than all,
If, being what thou art in thine own sight,
Thou canst this praise appropriate as thy right

COUPLETS. — *Trench.*

To halls of heavenly truth admission wouldst thou win?
Oft Knowledge stands without, while Love may enter in.

Lovingly to each other sun and moon give place,
Else were the mighty heaven for them too narrow space.

Despise not little sins; for mountain-high may stand
The pilèd heap made up of smallest grains of sand.

Despise not little sins; the gallant ship may sink,
Though only drop by drop the watery tide it drink.

God many a spiritual house has reared, but never one
Where lowliness was not laid first, the corner-stone.

Rear highly as thou wilt thy branches in the air,
But that thy roots shall strike as deep in earth have care.

Sin, not till it is left, will duly sinful seem;
A man must waken first, ere he can tell his dream.

When thou art fain to trace a map of thine own heart,
As undiscovered land set down the largest part.

Wouldst thou do harm, and yet unharmed thyself abide?
None ever struck another, save through his own side

God's dealings still are love,— his chastenings are alone
Love now compelled to take an altered, louder tone.

From our ill-ordered hearts we oft are fain to roam,
As men go forth who find unquietness at home.

Why furnish with such care thy lodging of a night,
And leave the while thy home in such a naked plight?

When thou hast thanked thy God for every blessing sent,
What time will then remain for murmurs or lament?

Envy detects the spots in the clear orb of light,
And Love the little stars in the gloomiest, saddest night.

Thou canst not choose but serve,— man's lot is servitude,—
But thou hast this much choice, a bad lord or a good.

Before the eyes of men let duly shine thy light,
But ever let thy life's best part be out of sight.

Wouldst thou go forth to bless, be sure of thine own ground,
Fix well thy centre first, then draw thy circles round.

Sin may be clasped so close we cannot see its face,
Nor seen nor loathed until held from us a small space.

If humble, next of thy humility beware,
And lest thou shouldst grow proud of such a grace have care.

How fearful is his case whom now God does not chide
When sinning worst, to whom even chastening is denied!

God often would enrich, but finds not where to place
His treasure, nor in hand nor heart a vacant space.

O, leave to God at sight of sin *incensed* to be!
Sinner if thou art *grieved*, that is enough for thee.

Set not thy heart on things given only with intent
To be alleviations of thy banishment.

Ill fares the child of heaven, who will not entertain
On earth the stranger's grief, the exile's sense of pain.

Mark how there still has run, enwoven from above,
Through thy life's darkest woof, the golden thread of love.

Things earthly we must know ere love them: 't is alone
Things heavenly that must be first loved and after known.

The sinews of Love's arm use makes more firm and strong,
Which, being left unused, will disappear ere long.

Wouldst thou abolish quite strongholds of self and sin?
Fear can but make the breach for Love to enter in.

When God afflicts thee, think he hews a rugged stone,
Which must be shaped, or else aside as useless thrown.

Evil, like a rolling stone upon a mountain-top,
A child may first set off, a giant cannot stop.

He knew, who healed our wounds, we quickly should
be fain
Our old hurts to forget, — so let the scars remain.

When will the din of earth grate harshly on our ears?
When we have once heard plain the music of the
spheres.

Why win we not at once what we in prayer require?
That we may learn great things as greatly to desire.

The tasks, the joys of earth, the same in heaven will
be;
Only the little brook has widened to a sea.

Who hunt this world's delight too late their hunting
rue,
When it a lion proves, the hunter to pursue.

INTIMATIONS OF IMMORTALITY FROM RECOLLECTIONS OF EARLY CHILDHOOD. — *Wordsworth.*

I.

There was a time when meadow, grove, and stream,
The earth, and every common sight,
To me did seem
Apparelled in celestial light,
The glory and the freshness of a dream.
It is not now as it hath been of yore; —
Turn wheresoe'er I may,
By night or day,
The things which I have seen I now can see no more.

II.

The rainbow comes and goes,
And lovely is the rose;
The moon doth with delight
Look round her when the heavens are bare;
Waters on a starry night
Are beautiful and fair;
The sunshine is a glorious birth;
But yet I know, where'er I go,
That there hath passed away a glory from the earth

III.

Now while the birds thus sing a joyous song,
And while the young lambs bound,
As to the tabour's sound,
To me alone there came a thought of grief:
A timely utterance gave that thought relief,
And I again am strong:
The cataracts blow their trumpets from the steep,
No more shall grief of mine the season wrong;
I hear the echoes through the mountains throng,
The winds come to me from the fields of sleep,
And all the earth is gay;
Land and sea
Give themselves up to jollity,
And with the heart of May
Doth every beast keep holiday;—
Thou child of joy,
Shout round me, let me hear thy shouts, thou happy
Shepherd boy'

IV.

Ye blessed creatures, I have heard the call
Ye to each other make; I see
The heavens laugh with you in your jubilee;
My heart is at your festival,

My head hath its coronal,
The fulness of your bliss I feel, — I feel it all.
O evil day! if I were sullen,
While the earth herself is adorning
This sweet May-morning,
And the children are culling
On every side,
In a thousand valleys far and wide,
Fresh flowers; while the sun shines warm
And the babe leaps up on his mother's arm: —
I hear, I hear, with joy I hear! —
But there 's a tree, of many one,
A single field which I have looked upon,
Both of them speak of something that is gone:
The pansy at my feet
Doth the same tale repeat:
Whither is fled the visionary gleam?
Where is it now, the glory and the dream?

V.

Our birth is but a sleep and a forgetting:
The soul that rises with us, our life's star,
Hath had elsewhere its setting,
And cometh from afar:
Not in entire forgetfulness,
And not in utter nakedness,
But trailing clouds of glory do we come
From God, who is our home:
Heaven lies about us in our infancy!
Shades of the prison-house begin to close
Upon the growing boy;
But he beholds the light, and whence it flows, —
He sees it in his joy;
The youth, who daily farther from the east
Must travel, still is Nature's priest,

And by the vision splendid
Is on his way attended;
At length the man perceives it die away,
And fade into the light of common day.

VI.

Earth fills her lap with pleasures of her own;
Yearnings she hath in her own natural kind,
And, even with something of a mother's mind,
And no unworthy aim,
The homely nurse doth all she can
To make her foster-child, her inmate man,
Forget the glories he hath known,
And that imperial palace whence he came.

VII.

Behold the child among his new-born blisses,
A six years' darling of a pigmy size!
See, where 'mid work of his own hand he lies,
Fretted by sallies of his mother's kisses,
With light upon him from his father's eyes!
See, at his feet, some little plan or chart,
Some fragment from his dream of human life,
Shaped by himself with newly-learnèd art;
A wedding or a festival,
A mourning or a funeral!
And this hath now his heart,
And unto this he frames his song:
Then will he fit his tongue
To dialogues of business, love, or strife;
But it will not be long,
Ere this be thrown aside,
And with new joy and pride
The little actor cons another part;

Filling from time to time his "humorous stage"
With all the persons, down to palsied age,
That life brings with her in her equipage;
As if his whole vocation
Were endless imitation.

VII.

Thou whose exterior semblance doth belie
Thy soul's immensity!
Thou best philosopher, who yet dost keep
Thy heritage! thou eye among the blind,
That, deaf, and silent, read'st the eternal deep,
Haunted for ever by the Eternal Mind, —
Mighty prophet! seer blest!
On whom those truths do rest,
Which we are toiling all our lives to find,
In darkness lost, the darkness of the grave;
Thou, over whom thy immortality
Broods like the day, a master o'er a slave,
A presence which is not to be put by!
Thou little child, yet glorious in the might
Of heaven-born freedom on thy being's height,
Why with such earnest pains dost thou provoke
The years to bring the inevitable yoke,
Thus blindly with thy blessedness at strife?
Full soon thy soul shall have her earthly freight,
And custom lie upon thee with a weight
Heavy as frost, and deep almost as life!

IX.

O, joy! that in our embers
Is something that doth live, —
That nature yet remembers
What was so fugitive!

The thought of our past years in me doth breed
Perpetual benediction : not indeed
For that which is most worthy to be blest ;
Delight and liberty, the simple creed
Of childhood whether busy or at rest,
With new-fledged hope still fluttering in his breast : —
Not for these I raise
The song of thanks and praise ;
But for those obstinate questionings
Of sense and outward things,
Fallings from us, vanishings ;
Blank misgivings of a creature
Moving about in worlds not realized ;
High instincts before which our mortal nature
Did tremble like a guilty thing surprised :
But for those first affections,
Those shadowy recollections,
Which, be they what they may,
Are yet the fountain light of all our day,
Are yet a master light of all our seeing ;
Uphold us, cherish, and have power to make
Our noisy years seem moments in the being
Of the eternal silence : truths that wake,
To perish never ;
Which neither listlessness, nor mad endeavour,
Nor man, nor boy,
Nor all that is at enmity with joy,
Can utterly abolish or destroy !
Hence, in a season of calm weather,
Though inland far we be,
Our souls have sight of that immortal sea,
Which brought us hither,
Can in a moment travel thither,
And see the children sport upon the shore,
And hear the mighty waters rolling evermore.

X.

Then sing, ye birds, sing, sing a joyous song!
And let the young lambs bound,
As to the tabour's sound!
We in thought will join your throng,
Ye that pipe and ye that play,
Ye that through your hearts to-day
Feel the gladness of the May!
What though the radiance which was once so bright
Be now for ever taken from my sight,
Though nothing can bring back the hour
Of splendor in the grass, of glory in the flower;
We will grieve not, rather find
Strength in what remains behind,
In the primal sympathy
Which having been must ever be,
In the soothing thoughts that spring
Out of human suffering,
In the faith that looks through death,
In years that bring the philosophic mind.

XI.

And, O ye fountains, meadows, hills, and groves,
Forebode not any severing of our loves!
Yet in my heart of hearts I feel your might;
I only have relinquished one delight
To live beneath your more habitual sway.
I love the brooks which down their channels fret,
Even more than when I tripped lightly as they;
The innocent brightness of a new-born day
Is lovely yet;
The clouds that gather round the setting sun
Do take a sober coloring from an eye
That hath kept watch o'er man's mortality;
Another race hath been, and other palms are won.

Thanks to the human heart by which we live,
Thanks to its tenderness, its joys and fears,
To me the meanest flower that blows can give
Thoughts that do often lie too deep for tears.

SONNET. — *Wordsworth.*

THE world is too much with us; late and soon,
Getting and spending, we lay waste our powers;
Little we see in nature that is ours;
We have given our hearts away, a sordid boon!
This sea that bares her bosom to the moon;
The winds that will be howling at all hours,
And are up-gathered now like sleeping flowers;
For this, for every thing, we are out of tune;
It moves us not. — Great God! I 'd rather be
A pagan, suckled in a creed outworn;
So might I, standing on this pleasant lea,
Have glimpses that would make me less forlorn
Have sight of Proteus coming from the sea;
Or hear old Triton blow his wreathed horn.

MESSIAH. — *Pope.*

A SACRED ECLOGUE.

YE Nymphs of Solyma! begin the song:
To heavenly themes sublimer strains belong.
The mossy fountains, and the sylvan shades,
The dreams of Pindus and the Aonian maids,
Delight no more. — O thou my voice inspire,
Who touched Isaiah's hallowed lips with fire!

Rapt into future times, the bard begun:
A virgin shall conceive, a virgin bear a son !
From Jesse's root behold a branch arise,
Whose sacred flower with fragrance fills the skies;
The ethereal spirit o'er its leaves shall move,
And on its top descends the mystic dove.
Ye heavens, from high the dewy nectar pour,
And in soft silence shed the kindly shower!
The sick and weak the healing plant shall aid,
From storms a shelter, and from heat a shade.
All crimes shall cease, and ancient fraud shall fail;
Returning Justice lift aloft her scale ;
Peace o'er the world her olive wand extend,
And white-robed Innocence from heaven descend.
Swift fly the years, and rise the expected morn!
O, spring to light, auspicious babe, be born!
See, Nature hastes her earliest wreaths to bring,
With all the incense of the breathing spring!
See lofty Lebanon his head advance !
See nodding forests on the mountains dance!
See spicy clouds from lowly Saron rise,
And Carmel's flowery top perfume the skies !
Hark ! a glad voice the lonely desert cheers :
Prepare the way ! a God, a God appears !
A God, a God ! the vocal hills reply,
The rocks proclaim the approaching Deity.
Lo, earth receives him from the bending skies!
Sink down, ye mountains, and ye valleys, rise!
With heads declined, ye cedars, homage pay!
Be smooth, ye rocks ! ye rapid floods, give way!
The Saviour comes, by ancient bards foretold :
Hear him, ye deaf, and all ye blind, behold!
He from thick films shall purge the visual ray,
And on tne sightless eyeball pour the day:
'T is he the obstructed paths of sound shall clear,
And bid new music charm the unfolding ear:

The dumb shall sing, the lame his crutch forego,
And leap exulting, like the bounding roe.
No sigh, no murmur, the wide world shall hear;
From every face he wipes off every tear.
In adamantine chains shall Death be bound,
And Hell's grim tyrant feel the eternal wound.
As the good shepherd tends his fleecy care,
Seeks freshest pasture and the purest air,
Explores the lost, the wandering sheep directs,
By day o'ersees them and by night protects,
The tender lambs he raises in his arms,
Feeds from his hand, and in his bosom warms
Thus shall mankind his guardian care engage,
The promised father of the future age.
No more shall nation against nation rise,
Nor ardent warriors meet, with hateful eyes,
Nor fields with gleaming steel be covered o'er,
The brazen trumpets kindle rage no more;
But useless lances into scythes shall bend,
And the broad falchion in a ploughshare end.
Then palaces shall rise; the joyful son
Shall finish what his short-lived sire begun;
Their vines a shadow to their race shall yield,
And the same hand that sowed shall reap the field.
The swain in barren deserts, with surprise,
Sees lilies spring, and sudden verdure rise;
And starts, amid the thirsty wilds to hear
New falls of water murmuring in his ear.
On rifted rocks, the dragon's late abodes,
The green reed trembles, and the bulrush nods.
Waste sandy valleys, once perplexed with thorn,
The spiry fir and shapely box adorn:
To leafless shrubs the flowering palms succeed,
And odorous myrtle to the noisome weed.
The lambs with wolves shall graze the verdan mead
And boys in flowery bands the tiger lead;

The steer and lion at one crib shall meet,
And harmless serpents lick the pilgrim's feet
The smiling infant in his hand shall take
The crested basilisk and speckled snake,
Pleased, the green lustre of the scales survey,
And with their forky tongue shall innocently play.
Rise, crowned with light, imperial Salem, rise!
Exalt thy towery head, and lift thy eyes!
See a long race thy spacious courts adorn;
See future sons and daughters, yet unborn,
In crowding ranks on every side arise,
Demanding life, impatient for the skies!
See barbarous nations at thy gates attend,
Walk in thy light, and in thy temple bend;
See thy bright altars thronged with prostrate kings,
And heaped with products of Sabæan springs!
For thee Idume's spicy forests blow,
And seeds of gold in Ophir's mountains glow.
See heaven its sparkling portals wide display,
And break upon thee in a flood of day!
No more the rising sun shall gild the morn,
Nor evening Cynthia fill her silver horn;
But lost, dissolved, in thy superior rays,
One tide of glory, one unclouded blaze,
O'erflow thy courts: the Light himself shall shine
Revealed, and God's eternal day be thine!
The seas shall waste, the skies in smoke decay,
Rocks fall to dust, and mountains melt away;
But fixed his word, his saving power remains;
Thy realm for ever lasts, thy own MESSIAH reigns!

LADY CLARA VERE DE VERE. — *Tennyson.*

Lady Clara Vere de Vere,
 Of me you shall not win renown;
You thought to break a country heart
 For pastime, ere you went to town.
At me you smiled, but unbeguiled
 I saw the snare, and I retired:
The daughter of a hundred earls,—
 You are not one to be desired.

Lady Clara Vere de Vere,
 I know you proud to bear your name;
Your pride is yet no mate to mine,
 Too proud to care from whence I came.
Nor would I break, for your sweet sake,
 A heart that doats on truer charms;
A simple maiden in her flower
 Is worth a hundred coats-of-arms.

Lady Clara Vere de Vere,
 Some meeker pupil you must find;
For were you queen of all that is,
 I could not stoop to such a mind.
You sought to prove how I could love,
 And my disdain is my reply;
The lion on your old stone gates
 Is not more cold to you than I.

Lady Clara Vere de Vere,
 You put strange memories in my head:
Not thrice your branching limes have blown,
 Since I beheld young Lawrence dead.

O, your sweet eyes, your low replies!
  A great enchantress you may be;
But there was that across his throat
  Which you had hardly cared to see.

Lady Clara Vere de Vere,
  When thus he met his mother's view,
She had the passions of her kind,
  She spake some certain truths of you
Indeed, I heard one bitter word
  That scarce is fit for you to hear.
Her manners had not that repose
  Which stamps the caste of Vere de Vere.

Lady Clara Vere de Vere,
  There stands a spectre in your hall:
The guilt of blood is at your door;
  You changed a wholesome heart to gall.
You held your course without remorse,
  To make him trust his modest worth,
And, last, you fixed a vacant stare,
  And slew him with your noble birth.

Trust me, Clara Vere de Vere,
  From yon blue heavens above us bent,
The gardener Adam and his wife
  Smile at the claims of long descent.
Howe'er it be, it seems to me,
  'T is only noble to be good;
Kind hearts are more than coronets,
  And simple faith than Norman blood.

I know you, Clara Vere de Vere,
  You pine among your halls and towers;
The languid light of your proud eyes
  Is wearied of the rolling hours.

In glowing health, with boundless wealth,
But sickening of a vague disease
You know so ill to deal with time,
You needs must play such pranks as these.

Clara, Clara Vere de Vere,
If time be heavy on your hands,
Are there no beggars at your gate,
Nor any poor about your lands?
O, teach the orphan-boy to read,
Or teach the orphan-girl to sew,
Pray Heaven for a human heart,
And let the foolish yeoman go.

TRIAL BEFORE REWARD. — *Francis Quarles.*

WHAT joyful harvester did e'er obtain
The sweet fruition of his hopeful gain,
Till he in hardy labors first had passed
The summer's heat and stormy winter's blast?
A sable night returns a shining morrow,
And days of joy ensue sad nights of sorrow;
The way to bliss lies not on beds of down,
And he that had no cross deserves no crown.
There 's but one heaven, one place of perfect ease;
In man it lies to take it where he please,
Above, or here below: and few men do
Enjoy the one, and taste the other too:
Sweating and constant labor win the goal
Of rest; afflictions clarify the soul,
And, like hard masters, give more hard directions,
Tutoring the nonage of uncurbed affections.
Wisdom, the antidote of sad despair,
Makes sharp afflictions seem not as they are,

Through patient sufferance; and doth apprehend,
Not as they seeming are, but as they end.
To bear affliction with a bended brow,
Or stubborn heart, is but to disallow
The speedy means to health; salve heals no sore,
If misapplied, but makes the grief the more.
Who sends affliction sends an end, and he
Best knows what 's best for him, what 's best for me:
'T is not for me to carve me where I like;
Him pleases when he list to stroke or strike.
I 'll neither wish nor yet avoid temptation,
But still expect it, and make preparation:
If he thinks best my faith shall not be tried,
Lord, keep me spotless from presumptuous pride!
If otherwise, with his trial give me care
By thankful patience to prevent despair;
Fit me to bear whate'er thou shalt assign;
I kiss the rod, because the rod is thine!
  Howe'er, let me not boast, nor yet repine;
  With trial, or without, Lord, make me thine!

THE BARD. — *Gray.*

The following ode is founded on a tradition current in Wales, that Edward the First, when he completed the conquest of that country, ordered all the bards that fell into his hands to be put to death.

"Ruin seize thee, ruthless king!
Confusion on thy banners wait!
Though fanned by conquest's crimson wing,
They mock the air with idle state.
Helm nor hauberk's twisted mail,
Nor e'en thy virtues, tyrant, shall avail

To save thy secret soul from nightly fears,
From Cambria's curse, from Cambria's tears!
Such were the sounds that o'er the crested pride
Of the first Edward scattered wild dismay,
As down the steep of Snowdon's shaggy side
He wound with toilsome march his long array.
Stout Gloster stood aghast in speechless trance:
"To arms!" cried Mortimer, and couched his quivering lance.

On a rock whose haughty brow
Frowns o'er old Conway's foaming flood,
Robed in the sable garb of woe,
With haggard eyes the poet stood
(Loose his beard, and hoary hair
Streamed like a meteor to the troubled air),
And with a master's hand, and prophet's fire,
Struck the deep sorrows of his lyre.
"Hark, how each giant oak, and desert cave,
Sighs to the torrent's awful voice beneath!
O'er thee, O king, their hundred arms they wave,
Revenge on thee in hoarser murmurs breathe;
Vocal no more, since Cambria's fatal day,
To highborn Hoel's harp, or soft Llewellyn's lay.
Cold is Cadwallo's tongue,
That hushed the stormy main;
Brave Urien sleeps upon his craggy bed;
Mountains, ye mourn in vain
Modred, whose magic song
Made huge Plinlimmon bow his cloud-topped head!
On dreary Arvon's shore they lie,
Smeared with gore, and ghastly pale:
Far, far aloof the affrighted ravens sail;
The famished eagle screams and passes by.
Dear lost companions of my tuneful art,
Dear as the light that visits these sad eyes,

Dear as the ruddy drops that warm my heart,
Ye died amidst your dying country's cries! —
No more I weep. They do not sleep.
On yonder cliffs, a grisly band,
I see them sit! they linger yet,
Avengers of their native land:
With me in dreadful harmony they join,
And weave with bloody hands the tissue of thy lire!"

"Weave the warp, and weave the woof,
The winding-sheet of Edward's race;
Give ample room, and verge enough
The characters of hell to trace!
Mark the year, and mark the night,
When Severn shall reëcho with affright
The shrieks of death through Berkeley's roofs tha ring, —
Shrieks of an agonizing king![1]
She-wolf of France,[2] with unrelenting fangs,
That tear'st the bowels of thy mangled mate,
From thee be born who o'er thy country hangs
The scourge of Heaven! What terrors round him wait!
Amazement in his van, with flight combined;
And sorrow's faded form, and solitude behind![3]

"Mighty victor, mighty lord,
Low on his funeral couch he lies!
No pitying heart, no eye afford
A tear to grace his obsequies![4]

---

1 Edward the Second, cruelly butchered in Berkeley castle.
2 Isabel of France, queen of Edward the Second.
3 Triumphs of Edward the Third in France.
4 Death of that king, abandoned by his children, and even robbed in his last moments by his courtiers.

Is the sable warrior[1] fled?
Thy son is gone. He rests among the dead.
The swarm, that in the noontide beam were borne,
Gone to salute the rising morn.
Fair laughs the morn, and soft the zephyr blows,
While proudly riding o'er the azure realm
In gallant trim the gilded vessel goes;
Youth on the prow, and Pleasure at the helm;[2]
Regardless of the sleeping whirlwind's sway,
That, hushed in grim repose, expects his evening prey.

"Fill high the sparkling bowl,
The rich repast prepare;
Reft of a crown, he yet may share the feast:
Close by the regal chair
Fell thirst and famine scowl
A baleful smile upon their baffled guest.[3]
Heard ye the din of battle bray,
Lance to lance, and horse to horse?
Long years of havoc urge their destined course,
And through the kindred squadrons mow their way.[4]
Ye towers of Julius, London's lasting shame,
With many a foul and midnight murder fed,[5]

---

[1] Edward, the Black Prince, dead some time before his father.

[2] Magnificence of Richard the Second's reign.

[3] Richard the Second, as we are told by all the older writers, was starved to death.

[4] Ruinous civil wars of York and Lancaster.

[5] Henry the Sixth, George, Duke of Clarence, Edward the Fifth, Richard, Duke of York, &c. believed to be murdered secretly in the Tower of London. The oldest part of that structure is attributed to Julius Cæsar.

Revere his consort's [1] faith, his father's [2] fame,
And spare the meek usurper's holy head! [3]
Above, below, the rose of snow
Twined with her blushing foe [4] we spread:
The bristled boar [5] in infant gore
Wallows beneath the thorny shade.
Now, brothers, bending o'er the accursed loom,
Stamp we our vengeance deep, and ratify his doom!

"Edward, lo! to sudden fate
(Weave we the woof. The thread is spun.)
Half of thy heart we consecrate! [6]
(The web is wove. The work is done.)"
"Stay, O, stay! nor thus forlorn
Leave me unblessed, unpitied, here to mourn!
In yon bright track that fires the western skies,
They melt, they vanish from my eyes!
But, O, what solemn scenes on Snowdon's height
Descending slow their glittering skirts unroll?
Visions of glory, spare my aching sight!
Ye unborn ages, crowd not on my soul!
No more our long-lost Arthur we bewail.[7]
All hail, ye genuine kings! Britannia's issue, hail! [8]

---

[1] Margaret of Anjou, a woman of heroic spirit, who struggled hard to save her husband and her crown.

[2] Henry the Fifth.

[3] Henry the Sixth, very near being canonized. The line of Lancaster had no right of inheritance to the crown.

[4] The white and red roses, devices of York and Lancaster.

[5] The silver boar was the badge of Richard the Third; whence he was usually known in his own time by the name of the Boar.

[6] Eleanor of Castile died a few years after the conquest of Wales.

[7] It was the common belief of the Welsh nation that king Arthur was still alive in Fairy-land, and would return again to reign over Britain.

[8] Both Medin and Taliessin had prophesied that the Welsh should regain the sovereignty of this island; which seemed to be accomplished in the House of Tudor.

"Girt with many a baron bold,
Sublime their stony fronts they rear;
And gorgeous dames, and statesmen old,
In bearded majesty appear.
In the midst a form divine![1]
Her eye proclaims her of the Briton line;
Her lion-port, her awe-commanding face,
Attempered sweet to virgin grace.
What strings symphonious tremble in the air!
What strains of vocal transport round her play!
Hear from the grave, great Taliessin,[2] hear!
They breathe a soul to animate thy clay;
Bright rapture calls, and soaring, as she sings,
Waves in the eye of heaven her many-colored wings.

"The verse adorn again,
Fierce war, and faithful love,
And truth severe, by fairy fiction dressed.
In buskined measures[3] move
Pale grief, and pleasing pain,
With honor, tyrant of the throbbing breast.
A voice,[4] as of the cherub-choir,
Gales from blooming Eden bear;
And distant warblings[5] lessen on my ear,
That lost in long futurity expire.
Fond, impious man, think'st thou yon sanguine cloud
Raised by thy breath, has quenched the orb of day?
To-morrow he repairs the golden flood,
And warms the nations with redoubled ray.

---

[1] Queen Elizabeth.

[2] Taliessin, chief of the bards, flourished in the sixth century. His works are still preserved, and his memory held in high veneration among his countrymen.

[3] Shakspeare.

[4] Milton.

[5] The succession of poets after Milton's time.

Enough for me: with joy I see
The different doom our fates assign.
Be thine despair, and sceptred care·
To triumph and to die are mine."
He spoke, and headlong from the mountain's height
Deep in the roaring tide he plunged to endless night.

SLEEP. — *Miss Barrett.*

Of all the thoughts of God that are
Borne inward unto souls afar,
Along the Psalmist's music deep, —
Now tell me if that any is
For gift or grace surpassing this, —
"He giveth his belovèd sleep"?

What would we give to our beloved?
The hero's heart, to be unmoved, —
The poet's star-tuned harp to sweep, —
The senate's shout to patriot vows, —
The monarch's crown, to light the brows?
"He giveth his belovèd sleep!"

What do we give to our beloved?
A little faith, all undisproved, —
A little dust to overweep, —
And bitter memories, to make
The whole earth blasted for our sake!
"He giveth his belovèd sleep!"

"Sleep soft, beloved!" we sometimes say,
But have no tune to charm away

Sad dreams, that through the eyelids creep
But never doleful dream again
Shall break the happy slumber, when
"He giveth his belovèd sleep!"

O earth, so full of dreary noises!
O men, with wailing in your voices!
O delvèd gold, the wailer's heap!
O strife, O curse, that o'er it fall!
God makes a silence through you all,
And "giveth his belovèd sleep!"

His dews drop mutely on the hill,
His cloud above it saileth still;
Though on its slope men toil and reap,
More softly than the dew is shed,
Or cloud is floated overhead,
"He giveth his belovèd sleep."

Yea, men may wonder, while they scan
A living, thinking, feeling man
In such a rest his heart to keep;
But angels say, — and through the word
I ween their blessed smile is heard, —
"He giveth his belovèd sleep!"

For me, my heart, that erst did go
Most like a tired child at a show,
That sees through tears the juggler's leap,
Would now its weary vision close, —
Would, childlike, on his love repose,
'Who giveth his belovèd sleep!"

And friends! — dear friends! — when it shall be
That his low breath is gone from me,

And round my bier ye come to weep,
Let one, most loving of you all,
Say, "Not a tear must o'er her fall,—
'He giveth his belovèd sleep!'"

PROVIDENCE.—*Herbert.*

O SACRED Providence, who, from end to end,
Strongly and sweetly movest! shall I write,
And not of thee, through whom my fingers bend
To hold my quill? Shall they not do thee right?

Of all the creatures, both in sea and land,
Only to man thou hast made known thy ways,
And put the pen alone into his hand,
And made him secretary of thy praise.

Beasts fain would sing; birds ditty to their notes·
Trees would be tuning on their native lute
To thy renown: but all their hands and throats
Are brought to man, while they are lame and mute.

Man is the world's high priest; he doth present
The sacrifice for all; while they below
Unto the service mutter an assent,—
Such as springs use that fall, and winds that blow.

Tempests are calm to thee; they know thy hand,
And hold it fast, as children do their father's,
Which cry and follow. Thou hast made poor sand
Check the proud sea, even when it swells and gathers

How finely dost thou times and seasons spin,
And make a twist checkered with night and day!
Which, as it lengthens, winds, and winds us in,
As bowls go on, but turning all the way.

Each creature hath a wisdom for his good:
The pigeons feed their tender offspring, crying,
When they are callow; but withdraw their food,
When they are fledged, that need may teach 'em
flying.

Bees work for man, and yet they never bruise
Their master's flower, but leave it, having done,
As fair as ever, and as fit to use:
So both the flower doth stay, and honey run.

Who hath the virtue to express the rare
And curious virtues both of herbs and stones?
Is there an herb for that? O, that thy care
Would show a root that gives expressions!

E'en poisons praise thee. Should a thing be lost?
Should creatures want, for want of heed, their due?
Since where are poisons, antidotes are most;
The help stands close, and keeps the fear in view.

The sea, which seems to stop the traveller,
Is by a ship the speedier passage made;
The winds, who think they rule the mariner,
Are ruled by him, and taught to serve his trade.

And as thy house is full, so I adore
Thy curious art in marshalling thy goods.
The hills with health abound; the vales, with store;
The south, with marble; north, with furs and woods

All countries have enough to serve their need:
If they seek fine things, thou dost make them run
For their offence; and then dost turn their speed
To be commerce and trade from sun to sun.

Sometimes thou dost divide thy gifts to man,
Sometimes unite. The Indian nut alone
Is clothing, meat and trencher, drink and can,
Boat, cable, sail and needle, all in one.

But who hath praise enough? Nay, who hath any?
None can express thy works, but he that knows them
And none can know thy works, which are so many
And so complete, but only he that owns them.

All things that are, though they have several ways,
Yet in their being join with one advice
To honor thee; and so I give thee praise
In all my other hymns, but in this twice.

Each thing that is, although in use and name
It go for one, hath many ways in store
To honor thee: and so each hymn thy fame
Extolleth many ways; yet this, one more.

ARETHUSA. — *Shelley.*

Arethusa arose
From her couch of snows,
In the Acroceraunian mountains, —
From cloud and from crag,
With many a jag,
Shepherding her bright fountains.

She leapt down the rocks
With her rainbow locks
Streaming among the streams; —
Her steps paved with green
The downward ravine,
Which slopes to the western gleams:
And gliding and springing
She went, ever singing
In murmurs as soft as sleep;
The Earth seemed to love her,
And Heaven smiled above her,
As she lingered towards the deep.
Then Alpheus bold,
On his glacier cold,
With his trident the mountains strook
And opened a chasm
In the rocks; — with the spasm
All Erymanthus shook.
And the black south wind
It concealed behind
The urns of the silent snow,
And earthquake and thunder
Did rend in sunder
The bars of the springs below:
The beard and the hair
Of the river-god were
Seen through the torrent's sweep,
As he followed the light
Of the fleet nymph's flight
To the brink of the Dorian deep.

"O, save me! O, guide me,
And bid the deep hide me;
For he grasps me now by the hair!"
The loud Ocean heard,
To its blue depth stirred,
And divided at her prayer;

And under the water
The Earth's white daughter
Fled like a sunny beam;
Behind her descended
Her billows unblended
With the brackish Dorian stream.
Like a gloomy stain
On the emerald main,
Alpheus rushed behind, —
As an eagle pursuing
A dove to its ruin
Down the streams of the cloudy wind.

Under the bowers
Where the Ocean Powers
Sit on their pearlèd thrones, —
Through the coral woods
Of the weltering floods,
Over heaps of unvalued stones, —
Through the dim beams
Which amid the streams
Weave a net-work of colored light,
And under the caves
Where the shadowy waves
Are as green as the forest's night: —
Outspeeding the shark,
And the sword-fish dark,
Under the ocean-foam,
And up through the rifts
Of the mountain clifts
They passed to their Dorian home.
And now from their fountains
In Enna's mountains,
Down one vale where the morning basks,
Like friends once parted,
Grown single-hearted,
They ply their watery tasks.

At sunrise they leap
From their cradles steep
In the cave of the shelving hill;
At noontidè they flow
Through the woods below,
And the meadows of Asphodel
And at night they sleep
In the rocking deep
Beneath the Ortygian shore;—
Like spirits that lie
In the azure sky,
When they love, but live no more.

THE COTTER'S SATURDAY NIGHT.—*Burns.*

INSCRIBED TO ROBERT AIKEN, ESQ.

My loved, my honored, much respected friend!
No mercenary bard his homage pays;
With honest pride I scorn each selfish end:
My dearest meed, a friend's esteem and praise:
To you I sing, in simple Scottish lays,
The lowly train in life's sequestered scene;
The native feelings strong, the guileless ways;
What Aiken in a cottage would have been;
Ah! tho' his worth unknown, far happier there, I ween!

November chill blaws loud wi' angry sugh;
The shortening winter-day is near a close;
The miry beasts retreating frae the pleugh,
The blackening trains o' craws to their repose:

The toil-worn cotter frae his labor goes, —
This night his weekly moil is at an end, —
Collects his spades, his mattocks, and his hoes,
Hoping the morn in ease and rest to spend,
And weary o'er the moor his course does homeward bend.

At length his lonely cot appears in view,
Beneath the shelter of an aged tree;
Th' expectant wee-things, toddlin', stacher thro'
To meet their dad, wi' flichterin' noise and glee.
His wee bit ingle, blinkin' bonnily,
His clean hearth-stane, his thriftie wifie's smile,
The lisping infant prattling on his knee,
Does all his weary, karking care beguile,
An' makes him quite forget his labor an' his toil.

Belyve, the elder bairns come drapping in,
At service out, among the farmers roun';
Some ca' the pleugh, some herd, some tentie rin
A cannie errand to a neebor town:
Their eldest hope, their Jenny, woman grown,
In youthfu' bloom, love sparkling in her e'e,
Comes hame, perhaps, to show a braw new gown,
Or deposit her sair-won penny-fee,
To help her parents dear, if they in hardship be.

With joy unfeigned, brothers and sisters meet,
An' each for other's welfare kindly spiers:
The social hours, swift-winged, unnoticed fleet;
Each tells the unco's that he sees or hears;
The parents, partial, eye their hopeful years;
Anticipation forward points the view.
The mother, wi' her needle an' her shears,
Gars auld claes look amaist as weel 's the new;
The father mixes a' wi' admonition due.

Their master's an' their mistress's command
  The younkers a' are warnèd to obey;
And mind their labors wi' an eydent hand,
  An' ne'er, tho' out o' sight, to jauk or play:
"And, O, be sure to fear the Lord alway!
  And mind your duty, duly, morn and night!
Lest in temptation's path ye gang astray,
  Implore his counsel and assisting might:
They never sought in vain, that sought the Lord aright!"

But, hark! a rap comes gently to the door;
  Jenny, wha kens the meaning o' the same,
Tells how a neebor lad cam o'er the moor,
  To do some errands, and convoy her hame.
The wily mother sees the conscious flame
  Sparkle in Jenny's e'e, and flush her cheek;
With heart-struck, anxious care inquires his name,
  While Jenny hafflins is afraid to speak;
Weel pleased the mother hears, it 's nae wild, worthless rake.

Wi' kindly welcome Jenny brings him ben;
  A strappan youth; he takes the mother's eye;
Blythe Jenny sees the visit 's no ill-ta'en;
  The father cracks of horses, pleughs, and kye.
The youngster's artless heart o'erflows with joy,
  But blate and laithfu', scarce can weel behave;
The mother, wi' a woman's wiles, can spy
  What makes the youth sae bashfu' and sae grave;
Weel pleased to think her bairn 's respected like the lave.

O happy love, where love like this is found!
  O heart-felt raptures! bliss beyond compare!
I 've pacèd much this weary, mortal round,
  And sage experience bids me this declare:

"If Heaven a draught of heavenly pleasure spare
  One cordial, in this melancholy vale,
'T is when a youthful, loving, modest pair,
  In other's arms breathe out the tender tale,
Beneath the milk-white thorn that scents the evening gale."

Is there, in human form, that bears a heart,—
  A wretch! a villain! lost to love and truth!—
That can, with studied, sly, ensnaring art,
  Betray sweet Jenny's unsuspecting youth?
Curse on his perjured arts! dissembling smooth!
  Are honor, virtue, conscience, all exiled?
Is there no pity, no relenting ruth,
  Points to the parents fondling o'er their child,—
Then paints the ruined maid, and their distraction wild?

But now the supper crowns their simple board,
  The halesome parritch, chief of Scotia's food;
The soup their only hawkie does afford,
  That 'yont the hallan snugly chows her cood:
The dame brings forth, in complimental mood,
  To grace the lad, her weel-hained kebbuck fell,
An' aft he 's pressed, an' aft he ca's it guid;
  The frugal wifie garrulous will tell,
How was a towmond auld, sin' lint was i' the bell.

The cheerfu' supper done, wi' serious face,
  They round the ingle form a circle wide;
The sire turns o'er, with patriarchal grace,
  The big ha'-Bible, ance his father's pride;
His bonnet reverently is laid aside,
  His lyart haffets wearing thin an' bare;
Those strains that once did sweet in Zion glide,
  He wales a portion with judicious care;
And "Let us worship God!" he says, with solemn air.

They chant their artless notes in simple guise
They tune their hearts, by far the noblest aim;
Perhaps "Dundee's" wild-warbling measures rise
Or plaintive "Martyrs," worthy of the name;
Or noble "Elgin" beats the heavenward flame,
The sweetest far of Scotia's holy lays:
Compared with these, Italian trills are tame;
The tickled ear no heart-felt raptures raise;
Nae unison hae they with our Creator's praise.

The priest-like father reads the sacred page,—
How Abram was the friend of God on high;
Or Moses bade eternal warfare wage
With Amalek's ungracious progeny;
Or how the royal bard did groaning lie
Beneath the stroke of Heaven's avenging ire;
Or Job's pathetic plaint and wailing cry;
Or rapt Isaiah's wild, seraphic fire;
Or other holy seers that tune the sacred lyre.

Perhaps the Christian volume is the theme,—
How guiltless blood for guilty man was shed;
How He, who bore in heaven the second name,
Had not on earth whereon to lay his head;
How his first followers and servants sped,
The precepts sage they wrote to many a land;
How he who lone in Patmos banishèd
Saw in the sun a mighty angel stand,
And heard great Babylon's doom pronounced by Heaven's command.

Then kneeling down, to heaven's eternal King,
The saint, the father, and the husband prays:
Hope "springs exulting on triumphant wing,"
That thus they all shall meet in future days;

There ever bask in uncreated rays
No more to sigh, or shed the bitter tear,
Together hymning their Creator's praise,
In such society, yet still more dear,
While circling time moves round in an eternal sphere.

Compared with this, how poor religion's pride,
In all the pomp of method and of art,
When men display to congregations wide
Devotion's every grace except the heart!
The Power, incensed, the pageant will desert,
The pompous strain, the sacerdotal stole;
But haply, in some cottage far apart,
May hear, well pleased, the language of the soul,
And in his book of life the inmates poor enroll.

Then homeward all take off their several way;
The youngling cottagers retire to rest;
The parent-pair their secret homage pay,
And proffer up to Heaven the warm request,
That He, who stills the raven's clamorous nest,
And decks the lily fair in flowery pride,
Would, in the way his wisdom sees the best,
For them and for their little ones provide;
But chiefly in their hearts with grace divine preside.

From scenes like these old Scotia's grandeur springs,
That makes her loved at home, revered abroad:
Princes and lords are but the breath of kings,
"An honest man 's the noblest work of God";
And certes, in fair virtue's heavenly road,
The cottage leaves the palace far behind;
What is a lordling's pomp? a cumbrous load,
Disguising oft the wretch of human kind,
Studied in arts of hell, in wickedness refined!

O Scotia! my dear, my native soil!
For whom my warmest wish to Heaven is sent
Long may thy hardy sons of rustic toil
Be blest with health, and peace, and sweet content!
And, O, may Heaven their simple lives prevent
From luxury's contagion, weak and vile!
Then, howe'er crowns and coronets be rent,
A virtuous populace may rise the while,
And stand a wall of fire around their much-loved isle.

O Thou, who poured the patriotic tide
That streamed through Wallace's undaunted heart;
Who dared to nobly stem tyrannic pride,
Or nobly die, the second glorious part,
(The patriot's God, peculiarly thou art,
His friend, inspirer, guardian, and reward!)
O, never, never, Scotia's realm desert,
But still the patriot, and the patriot bard,
In bright succession raise, her ornament and guard!

DISDAIN RETURNED. — *Carew.*

He that loves a rosie cheek,
Or a coral lip admires,
Or from star-like eyes doth seek
Fuel to maintain his fires;
As old Time makes these decay,
So his flames must waste away.

But a smooth and steadfast mind,
Gentle thoughts and calm desires,
Hearts with equal love combined,
Kindle never-dying fires.
Where these are not, I despise
Lovely cheeks, or lips, or eyes.

LAKE, WITH LAWNY BANKS THAT SLOPE

"Lake, with lawny banks that slope
  To the water's edge,
Softly rustles the wind thro'
  Thy long grass and sedge.

"Thou hadst been a gem of earth
  Couched amid these hills,
But some evil water-sprite
  Troubles the pure rills

"Whence thy hidden life is drawn.
  Why thus fretteth he,
Who should be thy good genie,
  Thy tranquillity ?"

Lightly by a ruffling wind
  Were the waters pressed,
And a liquid, swaying voice
  Issued from their breast.

Be it genie, be it fate,
  I know not, — but know
That the waves from yonder stream
  Ever turbid flow.

Earth may smile like Eden round,
   Heaven may open blue,
Child of sullied parentage
   Gives not back their hue.

"Stream, that feed'st the lake, there beams
   On thee a living sun;
Rapid, dark, thou rushest by;
   Wouldst thou doom outrun?"

Hoarsely thus the hurrying wave
   Answered, foaming on,
"Suns may beam, or skies may lower,
   I may stay for none.

"I am fed by those that draw
   From depths hid from me
Their mysterious energies,
   And I am not free.

"Peaceful mission is not mine;
   Springs that give me life
Burst from this strange earth, as if
   Born with inward strife."

"Turbid lake, thou must flow on,
   There is no redress,
And the river fed by thee
   Know unworthiness."

Ignorant, I grieved to see
   Nothing could be pure,
All must be as all had been,
   While it should endure.

I came again, — a river,
  Princely, calm, and clear,
Flowed from out the troubled lake,
  Like pure love from fear.

Heaven and earth were showed therein,
  The dark source defiled
To the ocean's large embrace
  Sent a noble child.

DEEP, DEEP WITHIN THE OCEAN'S BREAST.

Deep, deep within the ocean's breast
  A coral isle was shrined,
Round which light, water-swayèd nymphs
  Float with white arms entwined.

The centre of this little isle
  Was fixed a stony tree;
An outer growth encircled this,
  Like foliage, quiveringly.

In rigid pride the coral stone
  Surveyed its firm estate,
And said, with gratulating tone,
  "I floated, too, of late.

"But now no chance or change can come
  To me; mature in form,
I take my place with things of fate:
  I cool no more nor warm.

"Yes, I have been the sport of waves,
And like this mass around
I toiled and felt, — nor knew the rest,
Blest Neptune! which I 've found.

"Come, all of ye Sea-Nymphs, admire
My beautiful repose!" —
Out gushed the voice of one Sea-Nymph, —
"Give *me* the form which grows.

'I better please myself to watch
Life than a handsome death,
And, born of a quick element,
Like something which has breath.

"So, I 'll just feast my eyes awhile
On what goes on round you,
And never tire of watching this
Till it grows stony too."

How in the ocean's deepest depth
Is human life repeated!
By coral beds, who 've done with change,
How hardly youth is greeted!

ISABEL. — *Tennyson.*

Eyes not down-dropped nor over-bright, but fed
With the clear-pointed flame of chastity, —
Clear, without heat, undying, tended by
Pure vestal thoughts in the translucent fane

Of her still spirit, — locks not wide dispread,
Madonna-wise on either side her head, —
Sweet lips, whereon perpetually did reign
The summer calm of golden charity,
Were fixèd shadows of thy fixèd mood,
Reverèd Isabel, the crown and head,
The stately flower of female fortitude,
Of perfect wifehood and pure lowlihead.

The intuitive decision of a bright
And thorough-edgèd intellect, to part
Error from crime, — a prudence to withhold,
The laws of marriage charactered in gold
Upon the blanchèd tablets of her heart, —
A love still burning upward, giving light
To read those laws, — an accent very low
In blandishment, but a most silver flow
Of subtle-pacèd counsel in distress,
Right to the heart and brain, though undescried,
Winning its way with extreme gentleness
Thro' all the outworks of suspicious pride, —
A courage to endure and to obey, —
A hate of gossip parlance, and of sway,
Crowned Isabel, thro' all her placid life,
The queen of marriage, a most perfect wife.

The mellowed reflex of a winter moon, —
A clear stream flowing with a muddy one,
Till in its onward current it absorbs
With swifter movement and in purer light
The vexed eddies of its wayward brother, —
A leaning and upbearing parasite,
Clothing the stem, which else had fallen quite,
With clustered flower-bells and ambrosial orbs
Of rich fruit-bunches leaning on each other,
Shadow forth thee: — the world hath not another

(Though all her fairest forms are types of thee,
And thou of God in thy great charity)
Of such a finished, chastened purity.

SUNDAY. — *Herbert.*

O DAY most calm, most bright!
The fruit of this, the next world's bud;
The endorsement of supreme delight,
Writ by a friend, and with his blood;
The couch of time; care's balm and bay: —
The week were dark but for thy light;
Thy torch doth show the way.

The other days and thou
Make up one man; whose face *thou* art,
Knocking at heaven with thy brow:
The working days are the back-part;
The burden of the week lies there,
Making the whole to stoop and bow,
Till thy release appear.

Man had straight forward gone
To endless death. But thou dost pull
And turn us round, to look on one,
Whom, if we were not very dull,
We could not choose but look on still;
Since there is no place so alone
The which he doth not fill.

Sundays the pillars are
On which heaven's palace archèd lies:

The other days fill up the spare
And hollow room with vanities.
They are the fruitful beds and borders
In God's rich garden; that is bare
    Which parts their ranks and orders.

HYMN OF PAN. — *Shelley.*

From the forests and highlands
  We come, we come;
From the river-girt islands,
  Where loud waves are dumb,
    Listening to my sweet pipings.
The wind in the reeds and rushes,
  The bees on the bells of thyme,
The birds on the myrtle-bushes,
  The cicale above in the lime,
And the lizards below in the grass,
Were as silent as ever old Tmolus was,
    Listening to my sweet pipings.

Liquid Peneus was flowing,
  And all dark Tempe lay
In Pelion's shadow, outgrowing
  The light of the dying day,
    Speeded by my sweet pipings.
The Sileni, and Sylvans, and Fauns,
  And the Nymphs of the woods and waves,
To the edge of the moist river-lawns,
  And the brink of the dewy caves,
And all that did then attend and follow,
Were silent with love, as you now, Apollo,
    With envy of my sweet pipings

I sang of the dancing stars,
  I sang of the dædal earth,
And of heaven, and the giant wars,
  And love, and death, and birth;
    And then I changed my pipings,—
Singing how down the vale of Menalus
  I pursued a maiden and clasped a reed:
Gods and men, we are all deluded thus!
  It breaks in our bosom, and then we bleed:
All wept, as I think both ye now would,
If envy or age had not frozen your blood,
    At the sorrow of my sweet pipings.

L'ALLEGRO.—*Milton.*

HENCE, loathed Melancholy,
  Of Cerberus and blackest Midnight born!
In Stygian cave forlorn,
  'Mongst horrid shapes, and shrieks, and sights unholy,
Find out some uncouth cell,
  Where brooding Darkness spreads his jealous wings,
And the night raven sings;
  There, under ebon shades, and low-browed rocks,
As ragged as thy locks,
  In dark Cimmerian desert ever dwell.
    But come, thou Goddess, fair and free,
    In heaven ycleped Euphrosyne,
    And by men, heart-easing Mirth!
    Whom lovely Venus at a birth
    With two sister Graces more,
    To ivy-crownèd Bacchus bore;
    Or whether (as some sages sing)
    The frolic wind that breathes the spring,

Zephyr with Aurora playing,
As he met her once a Maying;
There, on beds of violets blue,
And fresh-blown roses washed in dew,
Filled her with thee, a daughter fair,
So buxom, blithe, and debonair.
  Haste, then, Nymph, and bring with thee
Jest, and youthful Jollity,
Quips, and Cranks, and wanton Wiles,
Nods, and Becks, and wreathed Smiles,
Such as hang on Hebe's cheek,
And love to live in dimple sleek;
Sport that wrinkled love derides,
And Laughter holding both his sides!
Come, and trip it as you go,
On the light, fantastic toe;
And in thy right hand lead with thee
The mountain Nymph, sweet Liberty;
And if I give thee honor due,
Mirth, admit me of thy crew,
To live with her, and live with thee,
In unreprovèd pleasures free;
To hear the lark begin his flight,
And, singing, startle the dull night,
From his watch-tower in the skies,
Till the dappled dawn doth rise;
Then to come, in spite of sorrow,
And at my window bid good morrow,
Through the sweet-brier, or the vine,
Or the twisted eglantine:
While the cock, with lively din,
Scatters the rear of darkness thin,
And to the stack, or the barn-door,
Stoutly struts his dames before.
Oft listening how the hounds and horn
Cheerly rouse the slumbering morn,

From the side of some hoar hill,
Through the high wood echoing shrill.
Some time walking, not unseen,
By hedge-row elms, on hillocks green,
Right against the eastern gate,
Where the great sun begins his state,
Robed in flames and amber light,
The clouds in thousand liveries dight;
While the ploughman near at hand
Whistles o'er the furrowed land,
And the milkmaid singeth blithe,
And the mower whets his scythe,
And every shepherd tells his tale
Under the hawthorn in the dale.
Straight mine eye hath caught new pleasures,
Whilst the landscape round it measures:
Russet lawns, and fallows gray,
Where the nibbling flocks do stray;
Mountains, on whose barren breast
The laboring clouds do often rest;
Meadows trim, with daisies pied,
Shallow brooks, and rivers wide.
Towers and battlements it sees
Bosomed high in tufted trees,
Where perhaps some beauty lies,
The cynosure of neighbouring eyes.
Hard by, a cottage chimney smokes,
From betwixt two aged oaks,
Where Corydon and Thyrsis, met,
Are at their savory dinner set,
Of herbs, and other country messes,
Which the neat-handed Phillis dresses;
And then in haste her bower she leaves,
With Thestylis to bind the sheaves;
Or, if the earlier season lead,
To the tanned haycock in the mead,

Sometimes with secure delight
The upland hamlets will invite,
When the merry bells ring round,
And the jocund rebecks sound
To many a youth and many a maid,
Dancing in the checkered shade ;
And young and old come forth to play,
On a sunshine holiday,
Till the livelong daylight fail;
Then to the spicy nut-brown ale,
With stories told of many a feat,
How fairy Mab the junkets eat;
She was pinched, and pulled, she said,
And he by friars' lanthorn led
Tells how the drudging goblin sweat,
To earn his cream-bowl duly set,
When in one night, ere glimpse of morn
His shadowy flail hath threshed the corn,
That ten day-laborers could not end ;
Then lies him down the lubber fiend,
And, stretched out all the chimney's length,
Basks at the fire his hairy strength,
And crop-full out of doors he flings,
Ere the first cock his matin rings.
Thus done the tales, to bed they creep,
By whispering winds soon lulled asleep.
Towered cities please us then,
And the busy hum of men,
Where throngs of knights and barons bold
In weeds of peace high triumphs hold,
With store of ladies, whose bright eyes
Rain influence, and judge the prize
Of wit or arms, while both contend
To win her grace whom all commend.
There let Hymen oft appear
In saffron robe, with taper clear,

And pomp, and feast, and revelry,
With mask, and antique pageantry,
Such sights as youthful poets dream
On summer eves by haunted stream.
Then to the well trod stage anon,
If Jonson's learned sock be on,
Or sweetest Shakspeare, Fancy's child,
Warble his native wood-notes wild.
  And ever against eating cares,
Lap me in soft Lydian airs,
Married to immortal verse;
Such as the meeting soul may pierce,
In notes, with many a winding bout
Of linkèd sweetness long drawn out,
With wanton heed and giddy cunning,
The melting voice through mazes running,
Untwisting all the chains that tie
The hidden soul of harmony;
That Orpheus' self may heave his head
From golden slumber on a bed
Of heaped Elysian flowers, and hear
Such strains as would have won the ear
Of Pluto to have set quite free
His half-regained Eurydice.
  These delights if thou canst give,
Mirth, with thee I mean to live.

IL PENSEROSO. — *Milton.*

HENCE, vain, deluding joys,
  The brood of folly, without father bred!
How little you bestead,
  Or fill the fixèd mind with all your toys!

Dwell in some idle brain,
And fancies fond with gaudy shapes possess,
As thick and numberless
As the gay motes that people the sunbeams,
Or likest hovering dreams,
The fickle pensioners of Morpheus' train.
But hail, thou Goddess, sage and holy!
Hail, divinest Melancholy!
Whose saintly visage is too bright
To hit the sense of human sight,
And therefore to our weaker view
O'erlaid with black, staid wisdom's hue;
Black, but such as in esteem
Prince Memnon's sister might beseem,
Or that starred Ethiop queen that strove
To set her beauty's praise above
The Sea-Nymphs, and their powers offended:
Yet thou art higher far descended;
Thee bright-haired Vesta, long of yore,
To solitary Saturn bore;
His daughter she (in Saturn's reign
Such mixture was not held a stain):
Oft in glimmering bowers and glades
He met her, and in secret shades
Of woody Ida's inmost grove,
While yet there was no fear of Jove.
Come, pensive nun, devout and pure,
Sober, steadfast, and demure,
All in a robe of darkest grain,
Flowing with majestic train,
And sable stole of Cyprus lawn
Over thy decent shoulders drawn.
Come, but keep thy wonted state,
With even step, and musing gait,
And looks commercing with the skies,
Thy rapt soul sitting in thine eyes:

There held in holy passion still,
Forget thyself to marble, till
With a sad, leaden, downward cast
Thou fix them on the earth as fast;
And join with thee calm Peace and Quiet.
Spare Fast, that oft with gods doth diet,
And hears the Muses in a ring
Aye round about Jove's altar sing;
And add to these retired Leisure,
That in trim gardens takes his pleasure;
But first and chiefest, with thee bring
Him that yon soars on golden wing,
Guiding the fiery-wheeled throne,
The cherub Contemplation;
And the mute Silence hist along,
'Less Philomel will deign a song,
In her sweetest, saddest plight,
Smoothing the rugged brow of night,
While Cynthia checks her dragon yoke,
Gently o'er the accustomed oak.
Sweet bird, that shunn'st the noise of folly,
Most musical, most melancholy!
Thee, chauntress, oft the woods among
I woo, to hear thy even-song;
And, missing thee, I walk unseen
On the dry smooth-shaven green,
To behold the wandering moon,
Riding near her highest noon,
Like one that had been led astray
Through the heaven's wide, pathless way;
And oft, as if her head she bowed,
Stooping through a fleecy cloud.
Oft, on a plat of rising ground,
I hear the far-off curfew sound
Over some wide-watered shore,
Swinging slow with sullen roar;

Or, if the air will not permit,
Some still, removèd place will fit,
Where glowing embers through the room
Teach light to counterfeit a gloom;
Far from all resort of mirth,
Save the cricket on the hearth,
Or the bellman's drowsy charm,
To bless the doors from nightly harm;
Or let my lamp at midnight hour
Be seen in some high, lonely tower,
Where I may oft outwatch the Bear,
With thrice-great Hermes, or unsphere
The spirit of Plato, to unfold
What worlds or what vast regions hold
The immortal mind that hath forsook
Her mansion in this fleshly nook:
And of those Demons that are found
In fire, air, flood, or under ground,
Whose power hath a true consent
With planet, or with element.
Sometime let gorgeous Tragedy
In sceptred pall come sweeping by,
Presenting Thebes, or Pelops' line,
Or the tale of Troy divine,
Or what (though rare) of later age
Ennobled hath the buskined stage.
But, O sad Virgin, that thy power
Might raise Musæus from his bower;
Or bid the soul of Orpheus sing
Such notes as, warbled to the string,
Drew iron tears down Pluto's cheek,
And made Hell grant what love did seek;
Or call up him that left half told
The story of Cambuscan bold,
Of Camball, and of Algarsife,
And who had Canacè to wife,

That owned the virtuous ring and glass,
And of the wondrous horse of brass,
On which the Tartar king did ride;
And if aught else great bards beside
In sage and solemn tunes have sung,
Of turneys and of trophies hung,
Of forests, and enchantments drear,
Where more is meant than meets the ear!
Thus, Night, oft see me in thy pale career,
Till civil-suited Morn appear,
Not tricked and frounced as she was wont
With the Attic boy to hunt,
But kerchiefed in a comely cloud,
While rocking winds are piping loud,
Or ushered with a shower still,
When the gust hath blown his fill,
Ending on the rustling leaves,
With minute drops from off the eaves.
And when the sun begins to fling
His flaring beams, me, Goddess, bring
To archèd walks of twilight groves,
And shadows brown, that Sylvan loves,
Of pine, or monumental oak,
Where the rude axe, with heavèd stroke,
Was never heard the Nymphs to daunt,
Or fright them from their hallowed haunt:
There, in close covert, by some brook,
Where no profaner eye may look,
Hide me from day's garish eye,
While the bee with honeyed thigh,
That at her flowery work doth sing,
And the waters murmuring
With such consort as they keep,
Entice the dewy-feathered sleep;
And let some strange, mysterious dream
Wave at his wings in aëry stream

Of lively portraiture displayed,
Softly on my eyelids laid ;
And as I wake, sweet music breathe
Above, about, or underneath,
Sent by some spirit to mortals good,
Or the unseen Genius of the wood.
But let my due feet never fail
To walk the studious cloisters pale,
And love the high embowèd roof,
With antic pillars massy proof,
And storied windows richly dight,
Casting a dim, religious light:
There let the pealing organ blow,
To the full-voiced choir below,
In service high, and anthems clear,
As may with sweetness, through mine ear,
Dissolve me into ecstasies,
And bring all heaven before mine eyes.
And may at last my weary age
Find out the peaceful hermitage,
The hairy gown and mossy cell,
Where I may sit and rightly spell
Of every star that heaven doth show,
And every herb that sips the dew ;
Till old experience do attain
To something like prophetic strain.
These pleasures, Melancholy, give,
And I with thee will choose to live.

WHY THUS LONGING ? — *Miss Winslow.*

Why thus longing, thus for ever sighing
  For the far-off, unattained, and dim ;
While the beautiful, all round thee lying,
  Offers up its low, perpetual hymn ?

Wouldst thou listen to its gentle teaching,
  All thy restless yearnings it would still ;
Leaf, and flower, and laden bee are preaching,
  Thine own sphere, though humble, first to fill.

Poor indeed thou must be, if around thee
  Thou no ray of light and joy canst throw ;
If no silken cord of love hath bound thee
  To some little world through weal and woe ;

If no dear eyes thy fond love can brighten, —
  No fond voices answer to thine own ;
If no brother's sorrow thou canst lighten
  By daily sympathy and gentle tone.

Not by deeds that win the crowd's applauses.
  Not by works that give thee world-renown,
Not by martyrdom, or vaunted crosses,
  Canst thou win and wear the immortal crown.

Daily struggling, though unloved and lonely,
  Every day a rich reward will give ;
Thou wilt find, by hearty striving only,
  And truly loving, thou canst truly live.

Dost thou revel in the rosy morning,
  When all nature hails the Lord of light,
And his smile, the mountain-tops adorning,
  Robes yon fragrant fields in radiance bright?

Other hands may grasp the field and forest,
  Proud proprietors in pomp may shine;
But with fervent love if thou adorest,
  Thou art wealthier, — all the world is thine!

Yet if through earth's wide domains thou rovest,
  Sighing that they are not thine alone, —
Not those fair fields, but thyself, thou lovest,
  And their beauty and thy wealth is gone.

Nature wears the colors of the spirit,
  Sweetly to her worshipper she sings, —
All the glow, the grace, she doth inherit,
  Round her trusting child she fondly flings.

VANITY. — *Herbert.*

  The fleet astronomer can bore
And thread the spheres with his quick-piercing mind.
He views their stations; walks from door to door;
  Surveys, as if he had designed
To make a purchase there. He sees their dances;
  And knoweth, long before,
Both their full-eyed aspects and secret glances.

  The nimble diver with his side
Cuts through the working waves, that he may fetch
His dearly earnèd pearl, which God did hide
  On purpose from the venturous wretch,

That he might save his life, — and also her's
      Who, with excessive pride,
Her own destruction and his danger wears.

      The subtle chymic can divest
And strip the creature naked, till he find
The callow principles within their nest.
      There he imparts to them his mind,
Admitted to their bed-chamber, before
      They appear trim and dressed
To ordinary suitors at the door.

      What hath not man sought out and found,
But his dear God? who yet his glorious law
Embosoms in us, mellowing the ground
      With showers and frosts, with love and awe;
So that we need not say, "Where 's this command?'
      Poor man! thou searchest round
To find out death, but missest life at hand.

THE CLOUD. — *Leigh Hunt.*

A FRAGMENT.

As I stood thus, a neighbouring wood of elms
Was moved, and stirred, and whispered loftily,
Much like a pomp of warriors with plumed helms,
When some great general, whom they long to see,
Is heard behind them, coming in swift dignity;
And then there fled by me a rush of air,
That stirred up all the other foliage there,
Filling the solitude with panting tongues;
At which the pines woke up into their songs,

Shaking their choral locks; and on the place
There fell a shade, as on an awe-struck face;
And overhead, like a portentous rim
Pulled over the wide world, to make all dim,
A grave, gigantic cloud came hugely uplifting him.

It passed with its slow shadow; and I saw
Where it went down beyond me on a plain,
Sloping its dusky ladders of thick rain;
And on the mist it made, and blinding awe,
The sun, reissuing in the opposite sky,
Struck the all-colored arch of his great eye,
And the disburdened country laughed again,
The leaves were amber; the sunshine
Scored on the ground its conquering line;
And the quick birds, for scorn of the great cloud,
Like children after fear, were merry and loud.

THE DRYADS. — *Leigh Hunt.*

These are the tawny Dryads, who love nooks
In the dry depth of oaks;
Or feel the air in groves, or pull green dresses
For their glad heads in rooty wildernesses;
Or on the gold turf, o'er the dark lines
Which the sun makes when he declines,
Bend their linked dances in and out the pines.
They tend all forests old, and meeting trees,
Wood, copse, or queach, or slippery dell o'erhung
With firs, and with their dusty apples strewn;
And let the visiting beams the boughs among,
And bless the trunks from clingings of disease
And wasted hearts that to the night-wind groan.

They screen the cuckoo when he sings; and teach
The mother blackbird how to lead astray
The informed spirit of the foolish boy
From thick to thick, from hedge to bay or beach,
When he would steal the huddled nest away
Of yellow bills upgaping for their food,
And spoil the song of the free solitude.
And they, at sound of the brute, insolent horn,
Hurry the deer out of the dewy morn;
And take into their sudden laps with joy
The startled hare that did but peep abroad;
And from the trodden road
Help the bruised hedgehog. And at rest, they love
The back-turned pheasant, hanging from the tree
His sunny drapery;
And handy squirrel, nibbling hastily;
And fragrant hiving bee,
So happy that he will not move, not he,
Without a song; and hidden, loving dove,
With his deep breath; and bird of wakeful glen,
Whose louder song is like the voice of life,
Triumphant o'er death's image, but whose deep,
Low, lovelier note is like a gentle wife,
A poor, a pensive, yet a happy one,
Stealing, when daylight's common tasks are done,
An hour for mother's work, and singing low
While her tired husband and her children sleep.

MAN. — *Herbert.*

My God, I heard this day,
That none doth build a stately habitation,
But he that means to dwell therein.
What house more stately hath there been,
Or can be, than is Man? to whose creation
All things are in decay.

For Man is every thing,
And more. He is a tree, yet bears no fruit;
A beast, yet is, or should be, more.
Reason and speech we only bring.
Parrots may thank us, if they are not mute;
They go upon the score.

Man is all symmetry,
Full of proportions, one limb to another,
And all to all the world besides.
Each part may call the farthest brother:
For head with foot hath private amity;
And both with moons and tides.

Nothing hath got so far,
But Man hath caught and kept it, as his prey.
His eyes dismount the highest star;
He is, in little, all the sphere.
Herbs gladly cure our flesh, because that they
Find their acquaintance there.

For us the winds do blow,
The earth doth rest, heaven move, and fountains flow.

Nothing we see but means our good,
As our delight, or as our treasure;
The whole is either our cupboard of food,
Or cabinet of pleasure.

The stars have us to bed;
Night draws the curtain, which the sun withdraws
Music and light attend our head.
All things unto our flesh are kind,
In their descent and being; to our mind,
In their ascent and cause.

Each thing is full of duty:
Waters united are our navigation;
Distinguished, our habitation;
Below, our drink; above, our meat;
Both are our cleanliness. Hath one such beauty?
Then how all things are neat!

More servants wait on Man
Than he 'll take notice of. In every path
He treads down that which doth befriend him
When sickness makes him pale and wan.
O, mighty love! Man is one world, and hath
Another to attend him.

Since, then, my God, thou hast
So brave a palace built, O, dwell in it,
That it may dwell with thee at last!
Till then, afford us so much wit,
That, as the world serves us, we may serve thee;
And both thy servants be.

TO A SKYLARK. — *Shelley.*

Hail to thee, blithe spirit!
Bird thou never wert,
That from heaven, or near it,
Pourest thy full heart
In profuse strains of unpremeditated art.

Higher still and higher
From the earth thou springest
Like a cloud of fire;
The blue deep thou wingest,
And singing still dost soar, and soaring ever singest.

In the golden lightning
Of the sunken sun,
O'er which clouds are brightening,
Thou dost float and run;
Like an unbodied joy whose race is just begun.

The pale purple even
Melts around thy flight;
Like a star of heaven,
In the broad daylight
Thou art unseen, but yet I hear thy shrill delight.

Keen as are the arrows
Of that silver sphere
Whose intense lamp narrows
In the white dawn clear,
Until we hardly see, we feel that it is there.

All the earth and air
  With thy voice is loud,
As, when night is bare,
  From one lonely cloud
The moon rains out her beams, and heaven is overflowed.

What thou art we know not;
  What is most like thee?
From rainbow clouds there flow not
  Drops so bright to see,
As from thy presence showers a rain of melody.

Like a poet hidden
  In the light of thought,
Singing hymns unbidden,
  Till the world is wrought
To sympathy with hopes and fears it heeded not:

Like a highborn maiden
  In a palace tower,
Soothing her love-laden
  Soul in secret hour
With music sweet as love, which overflows her bower;

Like a glowworm golden
  In a dell of dew,
Scattering unbeholden
  Its aerial hue
Among the flowers and grass which screen it from the view;

Like a rose embowered
  In its own green leaves,
By warm winds deflowered,
  Till the scent it gives
Makes faint with too much sweet those heavy-winged thieves.

Sound of vernal showers
  On the twinkling grass,
Rain-awakened flowers,
  All that ever was
Joyous, and clear, and fresh, thy music doth surpass

Teach us, sprite or bird,
  What sweet thoughts are thine;
I have never heard
  Praise of love or wine
That panted forth a flood of rapture so divine.

Chorus hymeneal,
  Or triumphant chant,
Matched with thine, would be all
  But an empty vaunt, —
A thing wherein we feel there is some hidden want.

What objects are the fountains
  Of thy happy strain?
What fields, or waves, or mountains?
  What shapes of sky or plain?
What love of thine own kind? What ignorance of pain?

With thy clear, keen joyance
  Languor cannot be:
Shadow of annoyance
  Never came near thee:
Thou lovest; but ne'er knew love's sad satiety.

Waking or asleep,
  Thou of death must deem
Things more true and deep
  Than we mortals dream,
Or how could thy notes flow in such a crystal stream;

We look before and after,
And pine for what is not:
Our sincerest laughter
With some pain is fraught;
Our sweetest songs are those that tell of saddest thought.

Yet if we could scorn
Hate, and pride, and fear;
If we were things born
Not to shed a tear,
I know not how thy joy we ever should come near.

Better than all measures
Of delightful sound,
Better than all treasures
That in books are found,
Thy skill to poet were, thou scorner of the ground!

Teach me half the gladness
That thy brain must know,
Such harmonious madness
From my lips would flow,
The world should listen then, as I am listening now

THE PRISONER OF CHILLON.—*Byron.*

A FABLE.

SONNET ON CHILLON.

Eternal spirit of the chainless mind!
Brightest in dungeons, Liberty, thou art!
For there thy habitation is the heart,—

The heart which love of thee alone can bind;
And when thy sons to fetters are consigned,—
To fetters, and the damp vault's dayless gloom,
Their country conquers with their martyrdom,
And Freedom's fame finds wings on every wind.
Chillon! thy prison is a holy place,
And thy sad floor an altar,—for 't was trod,
Until his very steps have left a trace
Worn, as if thy cold pavement were a sod,
By Bonnivard!—May none those marks efface:
For they appeal from tyranny to God.

I.

My hair is gray, but not with years;
Nor grew it white
In a single night,
As men's have grown from sudden fears:
My limbs are bowed, though not with toil,
But rusted with a vile repose;
For they have been a dungeon's spoil,
And mine has been the fate of those
To whom the goodly earth and air
Are banned and barred, forbidden fare:
But this was for my father's faith
I suffered chains and courted death;
That father perished at the stake
For tenets he would not forsake;
And for the same his lineal race
In darkness found a dwelling-place;
We were seven, who now are one,—
Six in youth, and one in age,
Finished as they had begun,
Proud of Persecution's rage;
One in fire, and two in field,
Their belief with blood have sealed,

Dying as their father died,
For the God their foes denied;
Three were in a dungeon cast,
Of whom this wreck is left the last.

II.

There are seven pillars of Gothic mould
In Chillon's dungeons deep and old,
There are seven columns, massy and grey,
Dim with a dull imprisoned ray,
A sunbeam which hath lost its way,
And through the crevice and the cleft
Of the thick wall is fallen and left,
Creeping o'er the floor so damp,
Like a marsh's meteor lamp:
And in each pillar there is a ring,
   And in each ring there is a chain;
That iron is a cankering thing,
   For in these limbs its teeth remain,
With marks that will not wear away,
Till I have done with this new day,
Which now is painful to these eyes,
Which have not seen the sun so rise
For years, — I cannot count them o'er,
I lost their long and heavy score
When my last brother drooped and died,
And I lay living by his side.

III.

They chained us each to a column stone,
And we were three, — yet each alone:
We could not move a single pace,
We could not see each other's face,
But with that pale and livid light
That made us strangers in our sight.

And thus together, yet apart,
Fettered in hand, but pined in heart,
'T was still some solace, in the dearth
Of the pure elements of earth,
To hearken to each other's speech,
And each turn comforter to each
With some new hope, or legend old,
Or song heroically bold;
But even these at length grew cold
Our voices took a dreary tone,
An echo of the dungeon-stone,
A grating sound, — not full and free,
As they of yore were wont to be;
It might be fancy, — but to me
They never sounded like our own.

IV.

I was the eldest of the three,
And, to uphold and cheer the rest,
I ought to do, and did, my best, —
And each did well in his degree.
The youngest, whom my father loved
Because our mother's brow was given
To him, with eyes as blue as heaven, —
For him my soul was sorely moved;
And truly might it be distressed
To see such bird in such a nest;
For he was beautiful as day, —
(When day was beautiful to me
As to young eagles, being free,) —
A polar day, which will not see
A sunset till its summer 's gone,
Its sleepless summer of long light,
The snow-clad offspring of the sun:
And thus he was as pure and bright,
And in his natural spirit gay,

With tears for naught but others' ills,
And then they flowed like mountain rills,
Unless he could assuage the woe
Which he abhorred to view below.

V.

The other was as pure of mind,
But formed to combat with his kind;
Strong in his frame, and of a mood
Which 'gainst the world in war had stood
And perished in the foremost rank
  With joy:—but not in chains to pine;
His spirit withered with their clank,
  I saw it silently decline,—
  And so perchance in sooth did mine;
But yet I forced it on to cheer
Those relics of a home so dear.
He was a hunter of the hills,
  Had followed there the deer and wolf;
  To him this dungeon was a gulf,
And fettered feet the worst of ills.

VI.

  Lake Leman lies by Chillon's walls,—
A thousand feet in depth below,
Its massy waters meet and flow;
Thus much the fathom-line was sent
From Chillon's snow-white battlement,
  Which round about the wave enthralls:
A double dungeon wall and wave
Have made,—and like a living grave.
Below the surface of the lake
The dark vault lies wherein we lay,—
We heard it ripple night and day;

  Sounding o'er our heads it knocked;
And I have felt the winter's spray
Wash through the bars, when winds were high
And wanton in the happy sky;
  And then the very rock hath rocked,
  And I have felt it shake, unshocked,
Because I could have smiled to see
The death that would have set me free.

VII.

I said my nearer brother pined,
I said his mighty heart declined,
He loathed and put away his food;
It was not that 't was coarse and rude,
For we were used to hunter's fare,
And for the like had little care:
The milk drawn from the mountain goat
Was changed for water from the moat;
Our bread was such as captives' tears
Have moistened many a thousand years,
Since man first pent his fellow-men
Like brutes within an iron den:
But what were these to us or him?
These wasted not his heart or limb;
My brother's soul was of that mould
Which in a palace had grown cold,
Had his free breathing been denied
The range of the steep mountain's side:
But why delay the truth? — he died.
I saw, and could not hold his head,
Nor reach his dying hand, — nor dead;
Though hard I strove, but strove in vain,
To rend and gnash my bonds in twain.
He died, — and they unlocked his chain,
And scooped for him a shallow grave
Even from the cold earth of our cave.

I begged them, as a boon, to lay
His corse in dust whereon the day
Might shine, — it was a foolish thought,
But then within my brain it wrought,
That even in death his freeborn breast
In such a dungeon could not rest.
I might have spared my idle prayer, —
They coldly laughed, — and laid him there,
The flat and turfless earth above
The being we so much did love;
His empty chain above it leant,
Such murder's fitting monument!

VIII.

But he, the favorite and the flower,
Most cherished since his natal hour,
His mother's image in fair face,
The infant love of all his race,
His martyred father's dearest thought,
My latest care, for whom I sought
To hoard my life, that his might be
Less wretched now, and one day free;
He, too, who yet had held untired
A spirit natural or inspired, —
He, too, was struck, and day by day
Was withered on the stalk away.
O God! it is a fearful thing
To see the human soul take wing
In any shape, in any mood: —
I 've seen it rushing forth in blood,
I 've seen it on the breaking ocean
Strive with a swoln convulsive motion,
I 've seen the sick and ghastly bed
Of sin delirious with its dread:
But these were horrors; — this was woe
Unmixed with such, — but sure and slow.

He faded, and so calm and meek,
So softly worn, so sweetly weak,
So tearless, yet so tender, — kind,
And grieved for those he left behind;
With all the while a cheek whose bloom
Was as a mockery of the tomb,
Whose tints as gently sunk away
As a departing rainbow's ray, —
An eye of most transparent light,
That almost made the dungeon bright.
And not a word of murmur, not
A groan o'er his untimely lot, —
A little talk of better days,
A little hope my own to raise;
For I was sunk in silence, — lost
In this last loss, of all the most.
And then the sighs he would suppress,
Of fainting nature's feebleness,
More slowly drawn, grew less and less:
I listened, but I could not hear, —
I called, for I was wild with fear;
I knew 't was hopeless, but my dread
Would not be thus admonishèd;
I called, and thought I heard a sound, —
I burst my chain with one strong bound,
And rushed to him: — I found him not, —
I only stirred in this black spot,
I only lived, *I* only drew
The accursèd breath of dungeon-dew;
The last, the sole, the dearest link
Between me and the eternal brink,
Which bound me to my failing race,
Was broken in this fatal place.
One on the earth, and one beneath, —
My brothers, — both had ceased to breathe
I took that hand which lay so still,
Alas! my own was full as chill;

I had not strength to stir or strive,
But felt that I was still alive,—
A frantic feeling, when we know
That what we love shall ne'er be so.
I know not why
I could not die;
I had no earthly hope,— but faith,
And that forbade a selfish death.

IX.

What next befell me then and there
I know not well,— I never knew;
First came the loss of light, and air,
And then of darkness too:
I had no thought, no feeling,— none;
Among the stones I stood a stone,
And was, scarce conscious what I wist,
As shrubless crags within the mist:
For all was blank, and bleak, and gray,
It was not night, it was not day,
It was not even the dungeon-light,
So hateful to my heavy sight,
But vacancy absorbing space,
And fixedness — without a place;
There were no stars,— no earth,— no time,—
No check,— no change,— no good,— no crime,—
But silence, and a stirless breath
Which neither was of life nor death;
A sea of stagnant idleness,
Blind, boundless, mute, and motionless.

X.

A light broke in upon my brain,—
It was the carol of a bird;
It ceased, and then it came again,—
The sweetest song ear ever heard;

And mine was thankful till my eyes,
Ran over with the glad surprise,
And they that moment could not see
I was the mate of misery.
But then by dull degrees came back
My senses to their wonted track:
I saw the dungeon walls and floor
Close slowly round me as before;
I saw the glimmer of the sun
Creeping as it before had done, —
But through the crevice where it came
That bird was perched, as fond and tame,
  And tamer than upon the tree;
A lovely bird, with azure wings,
And song that said a thousand things,
  And seemed to say them all for me!
I never saw its like before,
I ne'er shall see its likeness more:
It seemed like me to want a mate,
But was not half so desolate,
And it was come to love me when
None lived to love me so again,
And cheering from my dungeon's brink
Had brought me back to feel and think.
I know not if it late were free,
  Or broke its cage to perch on mine,
But knowing well captivity,
  Sweet bird! I could not wish for thine,
Or if it were, in wingèd guise,
A visitant from paradise;
For—Heaven forgive that thought! the while
Which made me both to weep and smile —
. sometimes deemed that it might be
My brother's soul come down to me.
But then at last away it flew,
And then 't was mortal well I knew;

For he would never thus have flown,
And left me twice so doubly lone,—
Lone as the corse within its shroud,
Lone as a solitary cloud,
  A single cloud on a sunny day
While all the rest of heaven is clear,
A frown upon the atmosphere,
That hath no business to appear
  When skies are blue and earth is gay.

XI.

A kind of change came in my fate,—
My keepers grew compassionate:
I know not what had made them so,
They were inured to sights of woe,
But so it was:—my broken chain
With links unfastened did remain,
And it was liberty to stride
Along my cell from side to side,
And up and down, and then athwart,
And tread it over every part,
And round the pillars one by one,
Returning where my walk begun,—
Avoiding only, as I trod,
My brothers' graves without a sod;
For if I thought with heedless tread
My step profaned their lowly bed,
My breath came gaspingly and thick,
And my crushed heart fell blind and sick.

XII.

I made a footing in the wall,—
  It was not therefrom to escape;
For I had buried one and all
  Who loved me in a human shape,

And the whole earth would henceforth be
A wider prison unto me:
No child, no sire, no kin had I,
No partner in my misery;
I thought of this, and I was glad,
For thought of them had made me mad
But I was curious to ascend
To my barred windows, and to bend
Once more upon the mountains high
The quiet of a loving eye.

XIII.

I saw them, — and they were the same,
They were not changed like me in frame;
I saw their thousand years of snow
On high, — their wide long lake below,
And the blue Rhone in fullest flow;
I heard the torrents leap and gush
O'er channelled rock and broken bush;
I saw the white-walled distant town,
And whiter sails go skimming down;
And then there was a little isle,
Which in my very face did smile,
    The only one in view;
A small green isle, — it seemed no more, —
Scarce broader than my dungeon floor;
But in it there were three tall trees,
And o'er it blew the mountain breeze,
And by it there were waters flowing,
And on it there were young flowers growing
    Of gentle breath and hue.
The fish swam by the castle wall,
And they seemed joyous each and all;
The eagle rode the rising blast, —
Methought he never flew so fast

As then to me he seemed to fly,
And then new tears came in my eye,
And I felt troubled, — and would fain
I had not left my recent chain ·
And when I did descend again,
The darkness of my dim abode
Fell on me as a heavy load;
It was as is a new-dug grave
Closing o'er one we sought to save,
And yet my glance, too much oppressed,
Had almost need of such a rest.

XIV.

It might be months, or years, or days, —
  I kept no count, I took no note,
I had no hope my eyes to raise,
  And clear them of their dreary mote;
At last men came to set me free, —
  I asked not why, and recked not where,
It was at length the same to me
Fettered or fetterless to be,
  I learned to love despair.
And thus when they appeared at last,
And all my bonds aside were cast,
These heavy walls to me had grown
A hermitage, — and all my own!
And half I felt as they were come
To tear me from a second home:
With spiders I had friendship made,
And watched them in their sullen trade,
Had seen the mice by moonlight play,
And why should I feel less than they?
We were all inmates of one place,
And I, the monarch of each race,
Had power to kill, — yet, strange to tell,
In quiet we had learned to dwell;

My very chains and I grew friends,
So much a long communion tends
To make us what we are: — even I
Regained my freedom with a sigh.

SONNET. — *J. Blanco White.*

Mysterious night! when our first parent knew
Thee, from report divine, and heard thy name,
Did he not tremble for this lovely frame,
This glorious canopy of light and blue?
Yet 'neath a curtain of translucent dew,
Bathed in the rays of the great setting flame,
Hesperus with the host of heaven came,
And, lo! creation widened in man's view.
Who could have thought such darkness lay concealed
Within thy beams, O sun? or who could find,
Whilst fly, and leaf, and insect stood revealed,
That to such countless orbs thou mad'st us blind?
Why do we, then, shun death with anxious strife?
If light can thus deceive, wherefore not life

THE ANCIENT MARINER. — *Coleridge.*

PART I.

It is an ancient mariner,
And he stoppeth one of three.
"By thy long gray beard and glittering eye,
Now wherefore stopp'st thou me?

An ancient mariner meeteth three gallants bidden to a wedding-feast and detaineth one.

"The bridegroom's doors are opened wide,
And I am next of kin;
The guests are met, the feast is set:
May'st hear the merry din."

He holds him with his skinny hand,
"There was a ship," quoth he.
"Hold off! unhand me, graybeard loon!
Eftsoons his hand dropt he.

The wedding-guest is spell-bound by the eye of the old sea-faring man, and constrained to hear his tale.

He holds him with his glittering eye,—
The wedding-guest stood still,
And listens like a three-years' child:
The mariner hath his will.

The wedding-guest sat on a stone:
He cannot choose but hear;
And thus spake on that ancient man,
The bright-eyed mariner.

The ship was cheered, the harbour cleared,
Merrily did we drop
Below the kirk, below the hill,
Below the lighthouse top.

The mariner tells how the ship sailed southward, with a good wind and fair weather, till it reached the line.

The sun came up upon the left,
Out of the sea came he;
And he shone bright, and on the right
Went down into the sea.

Higher and higher every day,
Till over the mast at noon——
The wedding-guest here beat his breast,
For he heard the loud bassoon.

The wedding-guest heareth the bridal mu-

The bride hath paced into the hall,
Red as a rose is she;

Nodding their heads, before her goes
The merry minstrelsy.

sic; but the mariner continueth his tale.

The wedding-guest he beat his breast,
Yet he cannot choose but hear;
And thus spake on that ancient man,
The bright-eyed mariner.

And now the storm-blast came, and he
Was tyrannous and strong;
He struck with his o'ertaking wings,
And chased us south along.

The ship drawn by a storm toward the south pole.

With sloping masts and dipping prow,
As who pursued with yell and blow
Still treads the shadow of his foe
And forward bends his head,
The ship drove fast, loud roared the blast,
And southward aye we fled.

And now there came both mist and snow,
And it grew wondrous cold;
And ice, mast-high, came floating by,
As green as emerald.

And through the drifts the snowy clifts
Did send a dismal sheen;
Nor shapes of men nor beasts we ken:
The ice was all between.

The land of ice and of fearful sounds, where no living thing was to be seen.

The ice was here, the ice was there,
The ice was all around:
It cracked and growled, and roared and howled,
Like noises in a swound.

At length did cross an albatross,
Thorough the fog it came:

Till a great sea-bird, called the albatross,

came through the snow-fog, and was received with great joy and hospitality.

As if it had been a Christian soul,
We hailed it in God's name.

It ate the food it ne'er had eat,
And round and round it flew.
The ice did split with a thunder-fit;
The helmsman steered us through.

And, lo! the albatross proveth a bird of good omen, and followeth the ship as it returned northward through fog and floating ice.

And a good south wind sprung up behind
The albatross did follow,
And every day, for food or play,
Came to the mariner's hollo.

In mist or cloud, on mast or shroud,
It perched for vespers nine;
Whiles all the night, through fog-smoke white
Glimmered the white moonshine.

The ancient mariner inhospitably killeth the pious bird of good omen.

"God save thee, ancient mariner,
From the fiends that plague thee thus! —
Why look'st thou so?" — With my crossbow
I shot the albatross.

PART II.

THE sun now rose upon the right:
Out of the sea came he,
Still hid in mist, and on the left
Went down into the sea.

And the good south wind still blew behind
But no sweet bird did follow,
Nor any day, for food or play,
Came to the mariner's hollo.

His shipmates cry out against the ancient

And I had done a hellish thing,
And it would work 'em woe;

For all averred, I had killed the bird
That made the breeze to blow:
Ah, wretch! said they, the bird to slay
That made the breeze to blow!

mariner for killing the bird of good luck.

Nor dim nor red, like God's own head,
The glorious sun uprist;
Then all averred, I had killed the bird
That brought the fog and mist:
'T was right, said they, such birds to slay,
That bring the fog and mist.

But when the fog cleared off, they justify the same, and thus make themselves accomplices in the crime.

The fair breeze blew, the white foam flew,
The furrow followed free;
We were the first that ever burst
Into that silent sea.

The fair breeze continues; the ship enters the Pacific Ocean, and sails northward even till it reaches the line

Down dropt the breeze, the sails dropt down,
'T was sad as sad could be;
And we did speak only to break
The silence of the sea!

The ship hath been suddenly becalmed.

All in a hot and copper sky,
The bloody sun at noon
Right up above the mast did stand,
No bigger than the moon.

Day after day, day after day,
We stuck, nor breath nor motion;
As idle as a painted ship
Upon a painted ocean.

Water, water, everywhere,
And all the boards did shrink;
Water, water, everywhere,
Nor any drop to drink.

And the albatross begins to be avenged.

The very deep did rot: O Christ!
That ever this should be!
Yea, slimy things did crawl with legs
Upon the slimy sea.

About, about, in reel and rout,
The death-fires danced at night;
The water, like a witch's oils,
Burnt green, and blue, and white.

A spirit had followed them, one of the invisible inhabitants of this planet, neither departed souls nor angels; concerning whom the learned Jew, Josephus, and the Platonic Constantinopolitan Michael Psellus, may be consulted. They are very numerous, and there is no climate or element without one or more.

And some in dreams assurèd were
Of the spirit that plagued us so;
Nine fathom deep he had followed us
From the land of mist and snow.

And every tongue, through utter drought,
Was withered at the root;
We could not speak, no more than if
We had been choked with soot.

The shipmates, in their sore distress, would fain throw the whole guilt on the ancient mariner; in sign whereof, they hang the dead sea-bird round his neck.

Ah! well-a-day! what evil looks
Had I from old and young!
Instead of the cross, the albatross
About my neck was hung.

PART III.

THERE passed a weary time. Each throat
Was parched, and glazed each eye.
A weary time! a weary time!
How glazed each weary eye,
When, looking westward, I beheld
A something in the sky.

The ancient mariner beholdeth a sign in the element afar off.

At first it seemed a little speck,
And then it seemed a mist;
It moved, and moved, and took at last
A certain shape, I wist.

A speck, a mist, a shape I wist,
And still it neared and neared:
As if it dodged a water-sprite,
It plunged, and tacked, and veered.

With throats unslaked, with black lips baked,
We could not laugh nor wail;
Through utter drought all dumb we stood;
I bit my arm, I sucked the blood,
And cried, A sail! a sail!

At its nearer approach, it seemeth him to be a ship, and at a dear ransom he freeth his speech from the bonds of thirst.

With throats unslaked, with black lips baked,
Agape they heard me call;
Gramercy! they for joy did grin,
And all at once their breath drew in,
As they were drinking all.

A flash of joy.

See! see! I cried, she tacks no more!
Hither, to work us weal,
Without a breeze, without a tide,
She steadies with upright keel!

And horror follows; fo can it be a ship that comes onward without wind or tide?

The western wave was all a-flame,
The day was wellnigh done,
Almost upon the western wave
Rested the broad bright sun;
When that strange shape drove suddenly
Betwixt us and the sun.

And straight the sun was flecked with bars,
(Heaven's mother send us grace!)

It seemeth him but the skeleton of a ship.

As if through a dungeon-grate he peered
With broad and burning face.

Alas! thought I, and my heart beat loud,
How fast she nears and nears!
Are those her sails that glance in the sun
Like restless gossameres?

And its ribs are seen as bars on the face of the setting sun. The spectre woman and her death-mate, and no other, on board the skeleton ship.

Are those her ribs through which the sun
Did peer, as through a grate?
And is that woman all her crew?
Is that a Death? and are there two?
Is Death that woman's mate?

Like vessel, like crew.

Her lips were red, her looks were free,
Her locks were yellow as gold;
Her skin was as white as leprosy,
The Nightmare Life-in-Death was she,
Who thicks man's blood with cold.

Death and Life-in-Death have diced for the ship's crew; and she (the latter) winneth the ancient mariner.

The naked hulk alongside came,
And the twain were casting dice;
"The game is done! I 've won, I 've won!"
Quoth she, and whistles thrice.

No twilight within the courts of the sun.

The sun's rim dips; the stars rush out;
At one stride comes the dark;
With far-heard whisper, o'er the sea
Off shot the spectre-bark.

At the rising of the moon,

We listened and looked sideways up!
Fear at my heart, as at a cup,
My life-blood seemed to sip!
The stars were dim, and thick the night;
The steersman's face by his lamp gleamed whit

From the sails the dew did drip ;—
Till clomb above the eastern bar
The hornèd moon, with one bright star
Within the nether tip.

One after one, by the star-dogged moon,
Too quick for groan or sigh,
Each turned his face, with a ghastly pang,
And cursed me with his eye.

One after another,

Four times fifty living men
(And I heard nor sigh nor groan),
With heavy thump, a lifeless lump,
They dropped down one by one.

His ship-mates drop down dead ;

The souls did from their bodies fly, —
They fled to bliss or woe !
And every soul it passed me by,
Like the whizz of my crossbow !

But Life-in Death begins her work on the ancient mariner.

PART IV.

" I FEAR thee, ancient mariner!
I fear thy skinny hand !
And thou art long, and lank, and brown,
As is the ribbed sea-sand ! *

The wedding-guest feareth that a spirit is talking to him ;

" I feàr thee and thy glittering eye,
And thy skinny hand, so brown." —

* For the last two lines of this stanza, I am indebted to Mr. Wordsworth. It was on a delightful walk from Nether Stowey to Dulverton, with him and his sister, in the autumn of 1797, that this poem was planned, and in part composed

But the ancient mariner assureth him of his bodily life, and proceedeth to relate his horrible penance.

Fear not, fear not, thou wedding-guest!
This body dropt not down.

Alone, alone, all, all alone,
Alone on a wide, wide sea!
And never a saint took pity on
My soul in agony.

He despiseth the creatures of the calm;

The many men, so beautiful!
And they all dead did lie!
And a thousand thousand slimy things
Lived on: and so did I.

And envieth that they should live, and so many lie dead.

I looked upon the rotting sea,
And drew my eyes away;
I looked upon the rotting deck,
And there the dead men lay.

I looked to heaven and tried to pray;
But or ever a prayer had gusht,
A wicked whisper came and made
My heart as dry as dust.

I closed my lids, and kept them close,
And the balls like pulses beat;
For the sky and the sea, and the sea and the sky
Lay like a load on my weary eye,
And the dead were at my feet.

But the curse liveth for him in the eye of the dead men.

The cold sweat melted from their limbs,
Nor rot nor reek did they;
The look with which they looked on me
Had never passed away.

An orphan's curse would drag to hell
A spirit from on high;

But, O, more horrible than that
Is the curse in a dead man's eye!
Seven days, seven nights, I saw that curse,
And yet I could not die.

The moving moon went up the sky,
And nowhere did abide;
Softly she was going up,
And a star or two beside.

In his loneliness and fixedness he yearneth towards the journeying moon, and the stars that still sojourn yet still move onward, and everywhere the blue sky belongs to them, and is their appointed rest, and their native country, and their own natural homes, which they enter unannounced, as lords that are certainly expected, and yet there is a silent joy at their arrival.

Her beams bemocked the sultry main,
Like April hoar-frost spread;
But where the ship's huge shadow lay,
The charmèd water burnt alway
A still and awful red.

By the light of the moon he beholdeth God's creatures of the great calm.

Beyond the shadow of the ship,
I watched the water-snakes;
They moved in tracks of shining white,
And when they reared, the elfish light
Fell off in hoary flakes.

Within the shadow of the ship
I watched their rich attire;
Blue, glossy green, and velvet black,
They coiled and swam; and every track
Was a flash of golden fire.

Their beauty and their happiness.

O happy living things! no tongue
Their beauty might declare:
A spring of love gushed from my heart,
And I blessed them unaware:
Sure, my kind saint took pity on me,
And I blessed them unaware.

He blesseth them in his heart.

The spell begins to break.

The selfsame moment I could pray ;
And from my neck so free
The albatross fell off, and sank
Like lead into the sea.

PART V.

O SLEEP ! it is a gentle thing,
Beloved from pole to pole !
To Mary Queen the praise be given !
She sent the gentle sleep from heaven,
That slid into my soul.

By grace of the Holy Mother, the ancient mariner is refreshed with rain.

The silly buckets on the deck,
That had so long remained,
I dreamt that they were filled with dew,
And when I woke it rained.

My lips were wet, my throat was cold,
My garments all were dank ;
Sure, I had drunken in my dreams,
And still my body drank.

I moved, and could not feel my limbs,
I was so light, — almost
I thought that I had died in sleep,
And was a blessed ghost.

He heareth sounds and seeth strange sights and commotions in the sky and the element.

And soon I heard a roaring wind ;
It did not come a-near ;
But with its sound it shook the sails,
That were so thin and sere.

The upper air burst into life,
And a hundred fire-flags sheen ;

To and fro they were hurried about,
And to and fro, and in and out,
The wan stars danced between.

And the coming wind did roar more loud,
And the sails did sigh like sedge ·
And the rain poured down from one black cloud,
The moon was at its edge.

The thick black cloud was cleft, and still
The moon was at its side ;
Like waters shot from some high crag,
The lightning fell with never a jag,
A river steep and wide.

The loud wind never reached the ship,
Yet now the ship moved on !
Beneath the lightning and the moon ·
The dead men gave a groan.

The bodies of the ship' crew are inspired, and the ship moves on.

They groaned, they stirred, they all uprose,
Nor spake, nor moved their eyes ;
It had been strange, even in a dream,
To have seen those dead men rise.

The helmsman steered, the ship moved on,
Yet never a breeze upblew ,
The mariners all 'gan work the ropes,
Where they were wont to do ;
They raised their limbs like lifeless tools :
We were a ghastly crew.

The body of my brother's son
Stood by me knee to knee :
The body and I pulled at one rope,
But he said naught to me.

"I fear thee, ancient mariner!"
Be calm, thou wedding-guest!
'T was not those souls that fled in pain
Which to their corses came again,
But a troop of spirits blest.

But not by the souls of the men, nor by demons of earth or middle air, but by a blessed troop of angelic spirits sent down by the invocation of the guardian saint.

For when it dawned, they dropped their arms,
And clustered round the mast;
Sweet sounds rose slowly through their mouths,
And from their bodies passed.

Around, around, flew each sweet sound,
Then darted to the sun;
Slowly the sounds came back again, —
Now mixed, now one by one.

Sometimes a-dropping from the sky
I heard the sky-lark sing;
Sometimes all little birds that are,
How they seemed to fill the sea and air
With their sweet jargoning!

And now 't was like all instruments,
Now like a lonely flute,
And now it is an angel's song,
That makes the heavens be mute.

It ceased; yet still the sails made on
A pleasant noise till noon,
A noise like of a hidden brook,
In the leafy month of June,
That to the sleeping woods all night
Singeth a quiet tune.

Till noon we quietly sailed on,
Yet never a breeze did breathe:
Slowly and smoothly went the ship,
Moved onward from beneath.

Under the keel nine fathom deep,
From the land of mist and snow,
The spirit slid; and it was he
That made the ship to go.
The sails at noon left off their tune,
And the ship stood still also.

The lonesome spirit from the south pole carries on the ship as far as the line, in obedience to the angelic troop, but still requireth vengeance.

The sun, right up above the mast,
Had fixed her to the ocean:
But in a minute she 'gan to stir
With a short, uneasy motion, —
Backwards and forwards half her length,
With a short, uneasy motion.

Then, like a pawing horse let go,
She made a sudden bound;
It flung the blood into my head,
And I fell down in a swound.

How long in that same fit I lay
I have not to declare;
But ere my living life returned,
I heard, and in my soul discerned,
Two voices in the air.

The polar spirit's fellow-demons the invisible inhabitants of the element, take part in his wrong, and two of them relate, one to the other, that penance long and heavy for the ancient mariner hath been accorded to the polar spirit, who returneth southward.

"Is it he?" quoth one, "Is this the man?
By him who died on cross,
With his cruel bow he laid full low
The harmless albatross.

"The spirit who bideth by himself
In the land of mist and snow,
He loved the bird that loved the man
Who shot him with his bow."

The other was a softer voice,
As soft as honey-dew:
Quoth he, "The man hath penance done,
And penance more will do."

PART VI.

FIRST VOICE.

But tell me, tell me! speak again,
Thy soft response renewing, —
What makes that ship drive on so fast?
What is the ocean doing?

SECOND VOICE.

Still as a slave before his lord,
The ocean hath no blast;
His great bright eye most silently
Up to the moon is cast, —

If he may know which way to go,
For she guides him smooth or grim.
See, brother, see! how graciously
She looketh down on him!

FIRST VOICE.

The mariner hath been cast into a trance; for the angelic power causeth the vessel to drive northward faster than human life could endure.

But why drives on that ship so fast,
Without or wave or wind?

SECOND VOICE.

The air is cut away before,
And closes from behind.

Fly, brother, fly! more high, more high!
Or we shall be belated!
For slow and slow that ship will go,
When the mariner's trance is abated.

The supernatural motion is retarded; the mariner awakes, and his penance begins anew.

I woke, and we were sailing on,
As in a gentle weather;
'T was night, calm night, the moon was high;
The dead men stood together.

All stood together on the deck,
For a charnel-dungeon fitter;
All fixed on me their stony eyes,
That in the moon did glitter.

The pang, the curse, with which they died,
Had never passed away;
I could not draw my eyes from theirs,
Nor turn them up to pray.

And now this spell was snapt; once more
I viewed the ocean green,
And looked far forth, yet little saw
Of what had else been seen; —

The curse is finally expiated;

Like one that on a lonesome road
Doth walk in fear and dread,
And, having once turned round, walks on,
And turns no more his head;
Because he knows a frightful fiend
Doth close behind him tread.

But soon there breathed a wind on me,
Nor sound nor motion made;
Its path was not upon the sea
In ripple or in shade.

It raised my hair, it fanned my cheek,
Like a meadow-gale of spring, —
It mingled strangely with my fears,
Yet it felt like a welcoming.

Swiftly, swiftly, flew the ship,
Yet she sailed softly too;
Sweetly, sweetly, blew the breeze, —
On me alone it blew.

And the ancient mariner beholdeth his native country.

O dream of joy! is this, indeed,
The lighthouse top I see?
Is this the hill? is this the kirk?
Is this mine own countree?

We drifted o'er the harbour-bar,
And I with sobs did pray, —
O, let me be awake, my God!
Or let me sleep alway.

The harbour-bay was clear as glass,
So smoothly it was strewn;
And on the bay the moonlight lay,
And the shadow of the moon.

The rock shone bright, the kirk no less,
That stands above the rock;
The moonlight steeped in silentness
The steady weathercock.

The angelic spirits leave the dead bodies,

And the bay was white with silent light,
Till, rising from the same,
Full many shapes, that shadows were,
In crimson colors came.

And appear in their own forms of light.

A little distance from the prow
Those crimson shadows were;
I turned my eyes upon the deck, —
O Christ! what saw I there!

Each corse lay flat, lifeless and flat,
And, by the holy rood!
A man all light, a seraph-man,
On every corse there stood.

This seraph-band each waved his hand;
It was a heavenly sight!

They stood as signals to the land,
Each one a lovely light;

This seraph-band each waved his hand,
No voice did they impart, —
No voice; but, O, the silence sank
Like music on my heart!

But soon I heard the dash of oars,
I heard the pilot's cheer;
My head was turned perforce away,
And I saw a boat appear.

The pilot and the pilot's boy,
I heard them coming fast;
Dear Lord in heaven, it was a joy
The dead men could not blast.

I saw a third, — I heard his voice;
It is the hermit good!
He singeth loud his godly hymns
That he makes in the wood.
He 'll shrieve my soul, he 'll wash away
The albatross's blood.

PART VII.

The hermit of the wood,

THIS hermit good lives in that wood
Which slopes down to the sea.
How loudly his sweet voice he rears!
He loves to talk with marineres
That come from a far countree.

He kneels at morn, and noon, and eve, —
He hath a cushion plump;

It is the moss that wholly hides
The rotted old oak-stump.

The skiff-boat neared: I heard them talk,
"Why, this is strange, I row!
Where are those lights so many and fair,
That signal made but now?"

Approacheth the ship with wonder.

"Strange, by my faith!" the hermit said,—
"And they answered not our cheer!
The planks look warped! and see those sails,
How thin they are and sere!
I never saw aught like to them,
Unless perchance it were

"Brown skeletons of leaves that lag
My forest-brook along;
When the ivy-tod is heavy with snow,
And the owlet whoops to the wolf below,
That eats the she-wolf's young."

"Dear Lord! it hath a fiendish look,"
The pilot made reply;
"I am a-feared."—"Push on, push on!"
Said the hermit cheerily.

The boat came closer to the ship,
But I nor spake nor stirred;
The boat came close beneath the ship,
And straight a sound was heard.

The ship suddenly sinketh.

Under the water it rumbled on,
Still louder and more dread;
It reached the ship, it split the bay;
The ship went down like lead.

Stunned by that loud and dreadful sound,
Which sky and ocean smote,
Like one that hath been seven days drowned,
My body lay afloat;
But, swift as dreams, myself I found
Within the pilot's boat.

The ancient mariner is saved in the pilot' boat.

Upon the whirl, where sank the ship,
The boat spun round and round;
And all was still, save that the hill
Was telling of the sound.

I moved my lips, — the pilot shrieked,
And fell down in a fit;
The holy hermit raised his eyes,
And prayed where he did sit.

I took the oars: the pilot's boy,
Who now doth crazy go,
Laughed loud and long, and all the while
His eyes went to and fro.
"Ha! ha!" quoth he, "full plain I see,
The Devil knows how to row."

And now, all in my own countree,
I stood on the firm land;
The hermit stepped forth from the boat,
And scarcely he could stand.

"O, shrieve me, shrieve me, holy man!"
The hermit crossed his brow.
"Say quick," quoth he, "I bid thee say
What manner of man art thou?"

The ancien mariner earnestly entreateth the hermit to shrieve him; and the penance of life falls on him:

Forthwith this frame of mine was wrenched
With a woful agony,

Which forced me to begin my tale;
And then it left me free.

And ever and anon, throughout his future life, an agony constraineth him to travel from land to land,

Since then, at an uncertain hour,
That agony returns:
And till my ghastly tale is told,
This heart within me burns.

I pass like night from land to land;
I have strange power of speech;
That moment that his face I see,
I know the man that must hear me:
To him my tale I teach.

What loud uproar bursts from that door!
The wedding-guests are there:
But in the garden bower the bride
And bridemaids singing are:
And hark the little vesper bell
Which biddeth me to prayer!

O wedding-guest! this soul hath been
Alone on a wide, wide sea;
So lonely 't was, that God himself
Scarce seemèd there to be.

O, sweeter than the marriage-feast,
'T is sweeter far to me
To walk together to the kirk
With a goodly company! —

To walk together to the kirk, —
And all together pray,
While each to his great Father bends,
Old men, and babes, and loving friends,
And youths and maidens gay!

Farewell, farewell! but this I tell
To thee, thou wedding-guest!
He prayeth well who loveth well
Both man, and bird, and beast.

And to teach, by his own example, love and reverence to all things that God made and loveth.

He prayeth best who loveth best
All things both great and small;
For the dear God who loveth us,
He made and loveth all.

The mariner, whose eye is bright,
Whose beard with age is hoar,
Is gone: and now the wedding-guest
Turned from the bridegroom's door.

He went like one that hath been stunned
And is of sense forlorn:
A sadder and a wiser man
He rose the morrow morn.

MIRABEAU. — *Sterling*.

Not oft has peopled Earth sent up
  So deep and wide a groan before,
As when the word astounded France, —
  "The life of Mirabeau is o'er!"
From its one heart a nation wailed;
  For well the startled sense divined
A greater power had fled away
  Than aught that now remained behind.

The scathed and haggard face of will,
  And look so strong with weaponed thought,
Had been to many million hearts
  The All between themselves and naught;

And so they stood aghast and pale,
  As if to see the azure sky
Come shattering down, and show beyond
  The black and bare Infinity.

For he, while all men trembling peered
  Upon the Future's empty space,
Had strength to bid above the void
  The oracle unveil its face ;
And when his voice could rule no more,
  A thicker weight of darkness fell,
And tombed in its sepulchral vault
  The wearied master of the spell.

A myriad hands like shadows weak,
  Or stiff and sharp as bestial claws,
Had sought to steer the fluctuant mass
  That bore his country's life and laws ;
The rudder felt his giant hand,
  And quailed beneath the living grasp
That now must drop the helm of Fate,
  Nor pleasure's cup can madly clasp.

France did not reck how fierce a storm
  Of rending passion, blind and grim,
Had ceased its audible uproar
  When death sank heavily on him ;
Nor heeded they the countless days
  Of toiling smoke and blasting flame,
That now by this one final hour
  Were summed for him as guilt and shame.

The wondrous life that flowed so long,
  A stream of all commixtures vile,
Had seemed for them in morning light
  With gold and crystal waves to smile.

It rolled with mighty breadth and sound
  A new creation through the land,
Then sudden vanished into earth,
  And left a barren waste of sand.

To them at first the world appeared
  Aground, and lying shipwrecked there,
And freedom's folded flag no more
  With dazzling sun-burst filled the air;
But 't is in after years for men
  A sadder and a greater thing,
To muse upon the inward heart
  Of him who lived the People's King.

O wasted strength! O light and calm
  And better hopes so vainly given!
Like rain upon the herbless sea
  Poured down by too benignant Heaven.
We see not stars unfixed by winds,
  Or lost in aimless thunder-peals;
But man's large soul, the star supreme,
  In guideless whirl how oft it reels!

The mountain hears the torrent dash,
  But rocks will not in billows run;
No eagle's talons rend away
  Those eyes that joyous drink the sun:
Yet man, by choice and purpose weak,
  Upon his own devoted head
Calls down the flash, as if its fires
  A crown of peaceful glory shed.

Alas!—Yet wherefore mourn? The law
  Is holier than a sage's prayer;
The godlike power bestowed on men
  Demands of them a godlike care;

And noblest gifts, if basely used,
  Will sternliest avenge the wrong,
And grind with slavish pangs the slave
  Whom once they made divinely strong

The lamp, that, 'mid the sacred cell,
  On heavenly forms its glory sheds,
Untended dies, and in the gloom
  A poisonous vapor glimmering spreads
It shines and flares, and reeling ghosts
  Enormous through the twilight swell,
Till o'er the withered world and heart
  Rings loud and slow the dooming knell.

No more I hear a nation's shout
  Around the hero's tread prevailing,
No more I hear above his tomb
  A nation's fierce, bewildered wailing;
I stand amid the silent night,
  And think of man and all his woe
With fear and pity, grief and awe,
  When I remember Mirabeau.

THE STRANGER AND HIS FRIEND.—*James Montgomery*

"Ye have done it unto me."—MATT. xxv. 40.

A POOR wayfaring man of grief
  Hath often crossed me on my way,
Who sued so humbly for relief,
  That I could never answer, "Nay:"
I had not power to ask his name,
Whither he went, or whence he came;
Yet was there something in his eye
That won my love, I knew not why.

Once, when my scanty meal was spread,
  He entered;—not a word he spake;—
Just perishing, for want of bread:
  I gave him all; he blessed it, brake,
And ate,—but gave me part again;
Mine was an angel's portion then,
For while I fed with eager haste,
That crust was manna to my taste.

I spied him where a fountain burst
  Clear from the rock; his strength was gone;
The heedless water mocked his thirst;
  He heard it, saw it hurrying on:
I ran to raise the sufferer up;
Thrice from the stream he drained my cup,
Dipt, and returned it running o'er;
I drank, and never thirsted more.

'T was night; the floods were out; it blew
  A winter hurricane aloof;
I heard his voice abroad, and flew
  To bid him welcome to my roof;

I warmed, I clothed, I cheered my guest,
Laid him on my own couch to rest;
Then made the hearth my bed, and seemed
In Eden's garden, while I dreamed.

Stript, wounded, beaten nigh to death,
I found him by the highway side;
I roused his pulse, brought back his breath,
Revived his spirit, and supplied
Wine, oil, refreshment; he was healed;
I had myself a wound concealed;
But from that hour forgot the smart,
And Peace bound up my broken heart.

In prison I saw him next, condemned
To meet a traitor's doom at morn;
The tide of lying tongues I stemmed,
And honored him 'midst shame and scorn:
My friendship's utmost zeal to try,
He asked, if I for him would die;
The flesh was weak, my blood ran chill,
But the free spirit cried, "I will."

Then in a moment to my view
The stranger darted from disguise;
The tokens in his hands I knew,
My Saviour stood before mine eyes;
He spake; and my poor name he named:
"Of me thou hast not been ashamed;
These deeds shall thy memorial be;
Fear not, thou didst them unto me."

LEGEND OF ST. JODOCUS. — *Translated from the German.*

In trial of his servant's truth,
One day came begging, as a youth
Of humble mien, in garments poor,
The Lord, to St. Jodocus' door.

"Give to him," St. Jodocus said;
"Open, good steward, thy store of bread."
"Here 's but one loaf, my master, see,
Left for our dog, and thee, and me."

"Yet give to him," the abbot cried,
"For us the Lord will still provide."
The sullen butler said no more,
But cut the loaf in pieces four.

"One for the abbot, one for me,
One for our dog, and one for thee,"
Unkindly to the youth he said,
And handed him his share of bread.

Again, in semblance yet more poor,
The Lord came to our abbot's door;
"Give, still," the good Jodocus said,
"Give him my little share of bread;
For us the good God still will care." —
And now he gives the abbot's share.

A hungered came the Lord again,
Nor asked he the third time in vain;
"Give now, O steward, thy little bit —
God will provide." — He yielded it.

More destitute and blind and lame,
The Lord yet for the fourth time came,

"Give," said Jodocus, "give again;
Doth not the dog's piece still remain?
For He who doth the ravens feed
Will not forget us in our need."

The steward gives, the beggar goes;
Then through the air a clear voice rose:
"Thou true disciple of thy Lord,
Great is thy faith, — take thy reward;
As thou believedst it should be,
So shall it happen unto thee."

The steward went to the open door —
Lo! onward toward the nearest shore
Four heavy-laden ships are borne,
With bread and fruit and wine and corn.

He to the strand runs joyfully,
And there no sailor can he see;
But to the shore a white wave rolled,
On which these words were traced in gold:

"Four ships are sent with large supply,
By Him who hears the raven's cry;
He sends them to the abbot good,
Who, this day, four times gave Him food.

"One, for the good man's self is sent;
Another for his dog is meant;
One for the steward is coming in;
One for the Sender's needy kin."

ELIZABETH AND THE ROSES.—*From the German.*

Know you not the stately dame?
From Wurtburg's castled height she came,
And in her basket brings she store
To satisfy the hungry poor.

The pages and the courtiers high
Marked the expense with grudging eye;
And e'en the Landgrave's kitchen folk
In murmurs their displeasure spoke.

Artfully told in Ludwig's ear,
The lady's charities appear
A weighty evil, as through her
His household's rights endangered were.

And he forbade, with cruel mind,
Such pleasure to his lady kind;
Asking, in scorn, if it were meet
A princess should a beggar greet.

Long to her lord's stern will she bowed,
Till upward to the castle loud
The starving shrieked in their despair;
No longer then would she forbear.

Her maid she beckoned stealthily
To find for her the hidden key;
Then filled her basket running o'er,
And glided from the gate once more.

One of the mischief-loving train
Of courtiers spied her, nor in vain;
Straight to the knight he made his way,
The gentle lady to betray.

Stern Ludwig o'er the drawbridge passed,
And down the steep rock rode he fast,
With anger pale, as 't were with death,
Woe! woe! to poor Elizabeth!

She hears her husband's clanging spurs,
Kindling with rage his eye meets hers;
Trembling, she knows not what to dread,
Her faint limbs move not, droops her head,

And underneath her apron's folds
Her timid hand the basket holds;
She reads no mercy in his eyes,
Heart-broken upon God she cries.

But Ludwig breaks her silent prayer, —
"Woman! what hast thou hidden there?"
And, curbing his wild rage no more,
The apron from the basket tore.

O miracle! therein are spread
Fairest of roses white and red;
Mercy in Ludwig's soul is born,
And fills the place of lordly scorn.

He cries, subdued his stubborn will,
"O purest, noblest, love me still!
Upon thy blessed errand hie,
Thy heart's kind impulse gratify."

And still she found her basket's store,
All veiled with roses, running o'er;
And safely through the valley trod,
She who had put her trust in God.

WEE WILLIE. — *Moir.*

Fare-thee-well, our last and fairest!
  Dear wee Willie, fare-thee-well!
God, who lent thee, hath recalled thee
  Back with him and his to dwell.
Fifteen moons their silver lustre
  Only o'er thy brow had shed,
When thy spirit joined the seraphs,
  And thy dust the dead.

Like a sunbeam, through our dwelling,
  Shone thy presence bright and calm;
Thou didst add a zest to pleasure;
  To our sorrows thou wert balm; —
Brighter beamed thine eyes than summer,
  And thy first attempt at speech
Thrilled our heart-strings with a rapture
  Music ne'er could reach.

As we gazed upon thee sleeping,
  With thy fine, fair locks outspread,
Thou didst seem a little angel,
  Who to earth from heaven had strayed;
And, entranced, we watched the vision,
  Half in hope, and half affright,
Lest what we deemed ours, and earthly,
  Should dissolve in light.

Snows o'ermantled hill and valley,
  Sullen clouds begrimed the sky,
When the first drear doubt oppressed us,
  That our child was doomed to die!
Through each long night-watch, the taper
  Showed the hectic of his cheek;
And each anxious dawn beheld him
  More worn out and weak.

Like the shot-star, in blue midnight,
  Like the rainbow, ray by ray,
Thou wert waning as we watched thee,
  Loveliest in thy last decay!
As a zephyr, so serenely
  Came and went thy last, low breath,
That we paused, and asked our spirits,
  Is it so? Can this be death?

Yet while thinking, oh! our lost ones,
  Of how dear ye were to us,
Why should dreams of doubt and darkness
  Haunt our troubled spirits thus?
Why across the cold, dim churchyard,
  Flit our visions of despair?
Seated on the tomb, Faith's angel
  Says, "Ye are not there!"

Where, then, are ye? With the Saviour
  Blest, forever blest, are ye,
'Mid the sinless little children,
  Who have heard his "Come to me!"
'Yond the shades of death's dark valley,
  Now ye lean upon his breast,
Where the wicked dare not enter,
  And the weary rest.

We are wicked — we are weary —
  For us pray, and for us plead;
God, who ever hears the sinless,
  May through you the sinful heed; —
Pray that, through the Mediator,
  All our faults may be forgiven;
Plead that ye be sent to greet us
  At the gates of heaven!

THE BOY AND THE ANGEL.—*Browning.*

Morning, evening, noon, and night,
"Praise God!" sang Theocrite.

Then to his poor trade he turned,
By which the daily meal was earned.

Hard he labored, long and well;
O'er his work the boy's curls fell:

But ever, at each period,
He stopped and sang, "Praise God."

Then back again his curls he threw,
And cheerful turned to work anew.

Said Blaise, the listening monk, "Well done!
I doubt not thou art heard, my son,

"As well as if thy voice to-day
Were praising God, the Pope's great way.

"This Easter Day, the Pope at Rome
Praises God from Peter's dome."

Said Theocrite, "Would God that I
"Might praise Him, that great way, and die!"

Night passed, day shone,
And Theocrite was gone.

With God a day endures alway,
A thousand years are but a day.

God said in heaven, "Nor day nor night
Now brings the voice of my delight."

Then Gabriel, like a rainbow's birth,
Spread his wings, and sank to earth;

Entered, in flesh, the empty cell,
Lived there, and played the craftsman well·

And morning, evening, noon, and night,
Praised God in place of Theocrite.

And from a boy to youth he grew —
The man put off the stripling's hue;

The man matured, and fell away
Into the season of decay;

And ever o'er the trade he bent,
And ever lived on earth content.

(He did God's will; to him, all one
If on the earth or in the sun.)

God said, "A praise is in mine ear;
There is no doubt in it, no fear;

"So sing old worlds, and so
New worlds that from my footstool go.

"Clearer loves sound other ways;
I miss my little human praise."

Then forth sprang Gabriel's wings, off fell
The flesh disguise, remained the cell.

'T was Easter Day; he flew to Rome,
And paused above Saint Peter's dome.

In the tiring-room, close by
The great outer gallery

With his holy vestments dight,
Stood the new pope, Theocrite:

And all his past career
Came back upon him clear,

Since when, a boy, he plied his trade,
Till on his life the sickness weighed;

And in his cell, when death drew near,
An angel in a dream brought cheer:

And, rising from the sickness drear,
He grew a priest, and now stood here.

To the East with praise he turned,
And on his sight the angel burned.

"I bore thee from thy craftsman's cell,
And set thee here; I did not well.

"Vainly I left my angel's sphere,
Vain was thy dream of many a year.

"Thy voice's praise seemed weak; it dropped
Creation's chorus stopped!

"Go back and praise again
The early way — while I remain.

"With that weak voice of our disdain,
Take up Creation's pausing strain.

"Back to the cell and poor employ;
Become the craftsman and the boy!"

Theocrite grew old at home;
A new pope dwelt in Peter's dome.

One vanished as the other died;
They sought God side by side.

THE CHIMNEY SWEEP.

Sweep ho! Sweep ho!
He trudges on through sleet and snow.

Tired and hungry both is he,
And he whistles vacantly.

Sooty black his rags and skin,
But the child is fair within.

Ice and cold are better far
Than his master's curses are.

Mother of this little one,
Could'st thou see thy little son!

Sweep ho! Sweep ho!
He trudges on through sleet and snow.

At the great man's door he knocks,
Which the servant maid unlocks.

Now let in with laugh and jeer,
In his eye there stands a tear.

He is young, but soon will know
How to bear both word and blow.

Sweep ho! Sweep ho!
In the chimney sleet and snow.

Gladly should his task be done,
Were 't the last beneath the sun.

Faithfully it now shall be,
But, soon spent, down droppeth he.

Gazes round, as in a dream,
Very strange, but true, things seem.

Led by a fantastic power
Which sets by the present hour,

Creeps he to a little bed,
Pillows there his aching head,

And, poor thing! he does not know
There he lay long years ago!

FROM EDWIN THE FAIR.—*Taylor.*

THE wind, when first he rose and went abroad
Through the waste region, felt himself at fault,
Wanting a voice; and suddenly to earth
Descended with a wafture and a swoop,
Where, wandering volatile from kind to kind,
He wooed the several trees to give him one.
First, he besought the ash; the voice she lent,
Fitfully, with a free and lashing change,
Flung here and there its sad uncertainties:
The aspen, next; a fluttered frivolous twitter
Was her sole tribute: from the willow came,
So long as dainty summer dressed her out,
A whispering sweetness, but her winter note
Was lisping, dry, and reedy: lastly, the pine
Did he solicit; and from her he drew
A voice so constant, soft, and lowly deep,
That there he rested, welcoming in her
A mild memorial of the ocean-cave
Where he was born.

A HOME SONNET.—*Hood.*

THE world is with me, and its many cares—
Its woes—its wants—the anxious hopes and fears
That wait on all terrestrial affairs—
The shades of former and of future years—
Foreboding fancies and prophetic tears,
Quelling a spirit that was once elate.
Heavens! what a wilderness the earth appears,
Where youth, and mirth, and health, are out of date

But no — a laugh of innocence and joy
Resounds, like music of that fairy race,
And, gladly turning from the world's annoy
I gaze upon a little radiant face,
And bless, internally, the merry boy
Who makes a *son*-shine in a shady place.

FROM HOURS WITH THE MUSES.--*J. C. Prince.*

SABBATH! thou art my Ararat of life,
Smiling above the deluge of my cares, —
My only refuge from the storms of strife,
When constant Hope her noblest aspect wears, —
When my torn mind its broken strength repairs,
And volant Fancy breathes a sweeter strain.
Calm season! when my thirsting spirit shares
A draught of joy unmixed with aught of pain,
Spending the quiet hours 'mid Nature's green domain

TO A FRIEND AFTER THE LOSS OF A CHILD.

WHEN on my ear your loss was knelled,
  And tender sympathy upburst,
A little spring from memory welled
  Which once had quenched my bitter thirst;

And I was fain to bear to you
  A portion of its mild relief,
That it might be as cooling dew
  To steal some fever from your grief

After our child's untroubled breath
  Up to the Father took its way,

And on our home the shade of death
  Like a long twilight haunting lay,

And friends came round with us to weep
  The little spirit's swift remove —
This story of the Alpine sheep
  Was told to us by one we love.

They, in the valley's sheltering care,
  Soon crop their meadow's tender prime,
And when the sod grows brown and bare,
  The shepherd strives to make them climb

To any shelves of pasture green
  That hang along the mountain side,
Where grass and flowers together lean,
  And down through mists the sunbeams glide.

But nought can lure the timid thing
  The steep and rugged path to try;
Though sweet the shepherd call and sing,
  And seared below the pastures lie —

Till in his arms their lambs he takes,
  Along the dizzy verge to go,
When, heedless of the rifts and breaks,
  They follow on o'er rock and snow.

And in those pastures lifted fair,
  More dewy soft than lowland mead,
The shepherd drops his tender care,
  And sheep and lambs together feed.

This parable, by nature breathed,
  Blew on me as the south wind free,
O'er frozen brooks that float unsheathed
  From icy thraldom to the sea.

A blissful vision through the night
   Would all my happy senses sway,
Of the good shepherd on the height,
   Or climbing up the starry way,

Holding our little lamb asleep—
   And like the burden of the sea
Sounded that voice along the deep,
   Saying, "Arise, and follow me!"